P9-AQP-018

The Year of the Woman

TRANSFORMING AMERICAN POLITICS
Lawrence C. Dodd, Series Editor

Dramatic changes in political institutions and behavior over the past three decades have underscored the dynamic nature of American politics, confronting political scientists with a new and pressing intellectual agenda. The pioneering work of early postwar scholars, while laying a firm empirical foundation for contemporary scholarship, failed to consider how American politics might change or to recognize the forces that would make fundamental change inevitable. In reassessing the static interpretations fostered by these classic studies, political scientists are now examining the underlying dynamics that generate transformational change.

Transforming American Politics brings together texts and monographs that address four closely related aspects of change. A first concern is documenting and explaining recent changes in American politics—in institutions, processes, behavior, and policymaking. A second is reinterpreting classic studies and theories to provide a more accurate perspective on postwar politics. The series looks at historical change to identify recurring patterns of political transformation within and across the distinctive eras of American politics. Last and perhaps most importantly, the series presents new theories and interpretations that explain the dynamic processes at work and thus clarify the direction of contemporary politics. All of the books focus on the central theme of transformation—transformation in both the conduct of American politics and in the way we study and understand its many aspects.

FORTHCOMING TITLES

The Year of the Woman

Myths and Realities

EDITED BY

Elizabeth Adell Cook, Sue Thomas, and Clyde Wilcox

Westview Press

BOULDER • SAN FRANCISCO • OXFORD

WITHDRAWN
SCCOC · LIBRARY
4601 Mid Rivers Mall Drive
St. Peters, MO 63376

For Chuck and Elaine

Transforming American Politics

All rights reserved. No part of this publication may be reproduced or transmitted in any form or by any means, electronic or mechanical, including photocopy, recording, or any information storage and retrieval system, without permission in writing from the publisher.

Copyright © 1994 by Westview Press, Inc.

Published in 1994 in the United States of America by Westview Press, Inc., 5500 Central Avenue, Boulder, Colorado 80301-2877, and in the United Kingdom by Westview Press, 36 Lonsdale Road, Summertown, Oxford OX2 7EW

A CIP catalog record for this book is available from the Library of Congress.
ISBN 0-8133-1970-6 — 0-8133-1971-4 (pbk.)

Printed and bound in the United States of America

The paper used in this publication meets the requirements
of the American National Standard for Permanence of Paper
for Printed Library Materials Z39.48-1984.

10   9   8   7   6   5   4   3   2   1

Contents

Tables and Figures

Figures

Acknowledgments

This book could not have been completed without the assistance of many people. Two, in particular, deserve our special thanks: John O'Donnell for his careful copyediting work and Donna Cutshaw for her assistance in preparing the camera-ready typescript. Additionally, Katherine Naff, Mary Bendyna, and Tom Brandt located information on female congressional candidates. Marni Ezra was instrumental in putting together the chapter on women's PACs. Peter Granda at the ICPSR at the University of Michigan supplied crucial exit poll data for the chapter authored by Elizabeth Cook, and Lou Kishton of the Georgetown University Academic Computing Center helped us access the data. We also wish to thank Jean R. Schroedel, Bruce Snyder, and Sandra Seymour for putting together a conference at the Claremont Graduate School that allowed the authors to meet together and discuss the implications of the "Year of the Woman." Finally, much appreciation goes to Jennifer Knerr, Eric Wright, and Cindy Hircshfeld at Westview Press for their help in manuscript preparation.

To all these people, we extend a heartfelt thanks.

Elizabeth Adell Cook
Sue Thomas
Clyde Wilcox

1

Why Was 1992 the "Year of the Woman"? Explaining Women's Gains in 1992

Clyde Wilcox

In many elections since the mid-1970s, journalists have written of a possible "Year of the Woman" in which record numbers of women would be elected to public office (Duerst-Lahti 1993). In 1990, when Republicans nominated a number of women to run for Senate seats, many anticipated the breakthrough election that would finally merit the label, but only incumbent Senator Nancy Kassebaum won.[1] In the months leading up to the 1992 general election, journalists again began to write of a coming "Year of the Woman." A record number of women had run for and won their parties' nominations for election to the House and Senate, and polls showed that several women candidates were running competitive Senate campaigns.

The 1992 elections proved markedly different from earlier ones. Four women won new Senate seats, and one woman incumbent easily won reelection, tripling women's representation in the upper chamber. Twenty-four new women were elected to the House, raising the number of women in that body from twenty-nine to forty-seven. Women continued to increase their numbers in state legislatures as well, to 20 percent of all seats.

After the election, the media proclaimed that 1992 had indeed been the Year of the Woman. A number of feminists and scholars objected to the label, however.[2] First, to declare a "year" of women might suggest that woman had gained political parity, although the 103rd Congress would still be overwhelmingly male. That Congress remains a male bastion was evident when Carol Moseley-Braun sought a congressional identification card, and was initially issued one labeled "spouse."[3] Women would need more than ten "Years of the Woman" to attain parity in the Senate, and more than seven "Years of the Woman" to reach equality in the House of Representatives. Moreover, the "year" of the woman ignores the two decades of steady progress and efforts by women who sought election to the state legislatures or to Congress, and of women who sought to elect them. The year of "the" woman suggests that the story is about successful women candidates, ignoring the role of women voters in primary and general elections, of women contributors who gave unprecedented amounts to help fund women's campaigns, of women activists who volunteered their time and skills, and of women's organizations which mobilized support for women candidates.

Commentators also noted that 1992 was not the "year of *all* women candidates." Some women incumbents were defeated by male challengers. Mary Rose Oakar of Ohio lost, at least in part because of the House bank scandal, and Elizabeth Patterson of South Carolina lost to a Republican backed by the Christian Coalition.[4] Nearly all women who challenged House or Senate incumbents lost, often by large margins.

The 1992 election was not the "year of *all* woman candidates" in another sense. Almost all of the women who won new seats in the House, and all new women in the Senate, were Democrats. Most Republican women who sought to win an open seat or to unseat an incumbent in the House or Senate were defeated. Some Republicans argued that a better phrase would be the "year of the liberal, Democratic woman." The successes of Democratic women were particularly galling to those Republicans who had worked hard to nominate women in their party, especially in light of the lack of success of several highly qualified Republican Senate challengers in 1990.[5]

Despite these important caveats, the term "Year of the Woman" does point to one important fact: women's gains in Congress were unprecedented. Figure 1.1 shows the percentage of women who served in the Senate and in the House in each term from 1977 through 1993, and the percentage of state legislative seats held by women in each year. The 1992 election brought a sharp increase in the numbers

FIGURE 1.1 Percent of Women in American Legislatures, 1977-1993

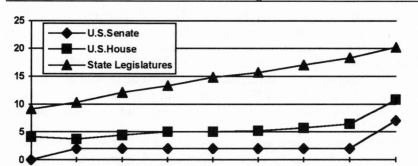

of women in both the Senate and the House. The increase of women in the U.S. Congress from 1991 to 1993 was the largest gain during this period. The gains in state legislatures, however, were part of a steady, incremental pattern of increasing numbers.

Explaining Women's Gains in 1992

Why did 1992 produce the large gains in women's representation that had been expected in so many previous elections? A number of factors combined to elect more women at the national level. These factors can be divided into three types: those that relate to the behavior of candidates, those that relate to the responses of political elites, and those that relate to the behavior of voters. Record numbers of women ran for the House and Senate in 1992, in part because of the opportunities presented by an unusually large number of open seats in the House, and in part because of special circumstances that motivated women to seek election to the Senate. Political elites responded to these candidates. PACs and party committees funneled large sums of cash to women candidates, allowing them to run competitive campaigns. Finally, the 1992 election hinged on issues such as education, health care, and unemployment—issues on which women have generally been perceived as more competent than men. The issues of the campaign, combined with an electorate interested in political change, resulted in increased votes for women candidates.

Women Candidates in 1992

Research suggests that women who seek election to the U.S. Congress do not face discrimination in the funding of their campaigns, nor do they face discrimination from voters. In an analysis of women candidates for open-seat primaries in the U.S. House, Barbara Burrell reported that women candidates in these races do as well as men. She concluded that "The fact that women hold few seats in the House is primarily due to the scarcity of their numbers in these races" (Burrell 1992: p. 507).

Part of the explanation for the record number of women elected to Congress in 1992 is that record numbers of women chose to run. Burrell (1993) reported that 218 women ran in their party's primary, a substantial increase from the previous record of 134 in 1986. Fully 108 women won their party's nomination for House elections, and eleven won nomination for a Senate candidacy. Why did so many more women seek election to the U.S. House and Senate in 1992? The explanations appear to differ for the House and Senate.

Throughout the 1980s, women continued to increase their numbers in state legislatures, city councils, and county commissions. Many of these women were anxious to run for national office whenever conditions were ripe. Dolan and Ford (1993) report that women elected to state legislatures in the 1980s were more ambitious than those women elected in previous years (but see also Freeman and Lyons 1992). Women and men with this kind of electoral experience are the most likely to win a seat in Congress: throughout the 1980s, most newly elected members of the House (both men and women) have previously held elected office.[6] By 1992, there existed a ready pool of ambitious, skilled women with solid political bases who were ready to seek election to Congress.

Jacobson and Kernell (1983) have argued that skilled politicians wait for the best year to mount a candidacy for the House of Representatives. A state legislator or county commissioner faces long odds in winning a House seat against an incumbent, and by mounting a challenge she frequently gives up her current office. She has a far better chance to win the seat if the incumbent has retired. If it seems likely that the incumbent will soon retire or seek higher office, many skilled politicians wait to run for the open seat. If it seems likely that the incumbent will continue to run for the House in the future, skilled politicians generally wait to run in a year in which political conditions favor their party, or until a scandal weakens the incumbent's political base.

The 1992 election provided an excellent opportunity for women (and men) in state legislatures and other state and local offices to seek election to the U.S. House. Redistricting forced many incumbents to campaign in areas they had never represented, and occasionally changed the partisan balance of the district to allow a more competitive election. Many incumbents were vulnerable because of their involvement in scandals, because they had voted for an increase in their own salaries, or because of a general electoral mood that favored change. Finally, a general anti-incumbency mood was evident in the early months of 1992, suggesting that even popular incumbents might be more vulnerable than in previous elections. Thus, strategic politicians who planned to run against an incumbent found 1992 a good year to mount their challenge. However, in 1992, most women who chose to challenge incumbents lost.

More importantly, redistricting created a number of new, open districts, and a record number of retirements brought on by redistricting, scandal, and campaign finance laws (Groseclose and Krehbiel 1993) created even more open seats. Fully fifty-two House incumbents retired in 1992, thirteen sought higher office, and two died prior to the election. Combined with newly drawn districts and incumbents who lost in party primaries, there were ninety-one open seats in the House in 1992, a far larger number than in most recent elections. For experienced women politicians who lived in these open districts, 1992 was likely to be their best shot for many years at a House seat. This was especially true for Democrats, for President Bush's popularity continued to drop during 1992, and the recession lingered. These conditions would normally lead experienced Democratic candidates to seek election to Congress, and 1992 was no exception. Redistricting allowed ambitious Democratic women and men to read these signals and declare relatively late candidacies.[7]

Thus, the candidacies of many of the women who sought election to the House were part of a normal pattern in politics, in which experienced politicians seek higher office in years in which national and/or local conditions maximize their chances for success. The 1992 elections provided a better opportunity than had most previous elections, and a record number of women responded to these conditions. Women's gains in the House in 1992 were due to the existence of opportunities, and of a large pool of skilled women politicians ready to exploit those opportunities.

Yet the record number of female House candidacies were also due in part to circumstances unique to the 1992 elections. As Robert Biersack and Paul Herrnson report in Chapter 9, the political parties made aggressive efforts to recruit women candidates in 1992, in part because polling data convinced party elites that these candidates would be especially attractive to voters. In addition, Roberts (1993) has reported that women's PACs made special recruitment efforts in 1992.

Because there are only thirty-three or thirty-four Senate elections in most election cycles, efforts to explain candidacy decisions frequently involve more idiosyncratic elements. Opportunities to seek election do not occur in every election in every state, and frequently prospective candidates must wait a number of years for the best opportunity to run. Most successful candidates for the U.S. Senate are those who have held important state office (e.g., governor), who have served in the U.S. House, or who have held executive office in the largest cities of the state. Like state legislators, these former state officeholders or incumbent House members generally bide their time, waiting for the best chance to challenge an incumbent or to run for an open seat.

Some of the Senate candidacies by women in 1992 fit this pattern. Dianne Feinstein had been a powerful and popular mayor in San Francisco, and she had lost a very close election for governor two years earlier. She had name recognition throughout the state, a ready list of volunteers to help her campaign, and recent experience in raising money for an expensive election. Barbara Boxer had served in the House for many years. Both women fit the normal profile of U.S. Senate candidates, and both women found 1992 a promising year to run for the Senate because of unique opportunities in their state. Feinstein took on an appointed incumbent who did not have the enthusiastic support of the conservative wing of his party, and Boxer sought election to an open seat created by the retirement of an incumbent. The 1992 election therefore posed the best opportunity to seek a Senate seat in California in several years. Had these opportunities occurred in an election a few years earlier or later, it seems likely that both women would have run.

Similarly, Geraldine Ferraro and Elizabeth Holtzman would have been strong candidates for the Senate in any year. As Craig Rimmerman notes in Chapter 6, Holtzman had narrowly lost a previous Senate bid primarily because a third candidate siphoned off some of her support, and Ferraro had been the Democratic vice-presidential nominee in 1984. Because New York has one incumbent Democratic senator, the chance to challenge the Republican incumbent Alfonse D'Amato only occurs every six years, and 1992 appeared to be a particularly good year because D'Amato had been politically damaged by scandal.

Thus, the New York and California candidacies fit a pattern of "normal politics," by which I mean that the women who sought to win Senate seats in 1992 did not appear to have been motivated by any special circumstances, but rather seized opportunities that happened to occur in 1992. As Sue Tolleson Rinehart notes in Chapter 2, however, once these women became active candidates their election campaigns were anything but "normal politics," because the media, the voters, and even the candidates interpreted their candidacies through the prism of gender. Similarly, the primary election battle between Ferraro and Holtzman was perceived differently by most observers because the two candidates were women.

Yet other women candidates for the Senate in 1992 had not served in Congress or as mayors of large cities. These women might not have been expected to run for the Senate, at least until later in their political careers. They claimed to be motivated by factors unique to the 1992 election—specifically by the Hill-Thomas hearings. The October 1991 confirmation hearings of Supreme Court nominee Clarence Thomas involved a televised session in which an all-white, all-male panel grilled Professor Anita Hill about her charges of sexual harassment. Several Republicans on the committee, including Arlen Specter of Pennsylvania, aggressively challenged Hill's testimony.

Although public opinion polls at the time suggested that both men and women were more likely to believe Thomas than Hill, the data also showed that professional women were more likely to believe Hill. Women who had struggled to advance in professional settings believed Hill's explanation of her contacts with Thomas after the alleged incidents of harassment. It made sense to them that Hill would remain in contact with someone who was an important professional connection, even if she had been offended by his conduct. Many of these professional women were deeply angered by the hearings, and encouraged other women to seek election to the Senate, promising financial and other support.

The candidacies of Lynn Yeakel in Pennsylvania (who challenged Specter), of Carol Moseley-Braun in Illinois, and of Patty Murray in Washington were each motivated in part by the powerful image of the all-male panel skeptically questioning a woman who had raised the charge of sexual harassment.[8] In each case, however, there were special opportunities in 1992. Jean Schroedel and Bruce Snyder note in Chapter 3 that in Washington, the candidacy of Murray was also motivated by the highly-publicized news stories that incumbent Brock Adams had sexually molested and harassed women, making Adams potentially vulnerable in his party's primary. Ted Jelen reports in Chapter 4 that the candidacy of Carol Moseley-Braun may have been motivated in part by the primary-election candidacy of millionaire Al Hofeld, which threatened to siphon off enough support from incumbent Dixon to make him vulnerable. Susan Hansen notes in Chapter 5 that in Pennsylvania, Specter faced a Republican primary challenger who would attack the incumbent from the right during the primary campaign and perhaps weaken his support in the party for the general election.

Yeakel, Moseley-Braun, and Murray (along with Geri Rothman-Serot, who narrowly lost to incumbent Senator Christopher Bond in Missouri) were making a relatively long leap to a Senate candidacy. Moseley-Braun, Murray, and Rothman-Serot had served in state legislatures (Murray for only one term), and Yeakel had no previous elected experience.[9]   The Yeakel, Moseley-Braun, and Murray campaigns made costly mistakes that may have been partly due to their lack of experience in high visibility national elections. Such a large political leap is not unheard of—indeed Russ Feingold of Wisconsin won a Senate seat in 1992 after having served in the state legislature, and Specter won his Senate seat in 1980 after having served as a prosecutor, a post to which he was defeated in a bid for reelection.[10]   Yet while Feinstein and Boxer followed a relatively common path to a Senate candidacy, Yeakel, Moseley-Braun, and Murray did not.

It is worth noting that of the eleven women who sought election to the Senate, none defeated an elected incumbent in a general election.[11] Feinstein beat an appointed incumbent whose party was divided, and Moseley-Braun defeated the incumbent Alan Dixon in a three-way primary election in which Dixon and challenger Al Hofeld traded a barrage of negative advertisements.[12] The power of incumbency was most evident in the contrast between the fortunes of the campaigns of Yeakel of Pennsylvania and Murray in Washington. As Susan Hansen argues in Chapter 5, Arlen Specter effectively used his advantages as a senator to defeat Yeakel. Yeakel arguably ran as effective a campaign as did Murray, but Murray ran for an open seat.

Moreover, Carole Chaney and Barbara Sinclair note in Chapter 7 that nearly all of the newly elected women in the House won open seats. Few incumbents were defeated in 1992 by male or female challengers. Fully 80 percent of newly elected men to the House ran for open seats, as did 92 percent of newly elected women. When women candidates opposed male candidates for House open seats, they won nearly two-thirds of the time. When they faced male incumbents, they almost always lost.

Thus, the large number of open seats in the House and Senate was crucial to the success of women candidates in 1992. Incumbency remains a powerful barrier to increasing the number of women in Congress. The 1992 gains by women were made possible by the existence of a pool of experienced women politicians who had been building their political bases for years, and the opportunities provided by the creation of new districts and the retirement of House and Senate incumbents.[13]

Although Sue Thomas reports in Chapter 8 that a record number of women also sought election to state legislatures in 1992, the increase was far smaller than for the House or Senate. Since large numbers of state legislative seats are open in any election cycle, potential candidates need not wait as long for a chance to run for an open seat. This means that 1992 did not offer as many special opportunities for state legislative candidates as for women who sought election to the House or Senate. It may be that some women missed an important opportunity, however, for there is evidence that women candidates in general may have enjoyed an advantage with voters in 1992, and this advantage probably extended to state legislative elections.

Although women now occupy 20 percent of state legislative seats, that average masks a wide diversity in statehouse representation by women. The 1992 elections raised the percentage of women in the Washington state legislature to 40 percent, but only 4 percent of the seats in the Kentucky state legislature are held by women. In general, Western states have the most women in state legislatures, Southern states have the least, and Midwestern states are closer to the national average. As Susan Hansen notes in Chapter 5, Pennsylvania more closely resembles a southern state in its low percentage of women in the state legislature than it does the surrounding states. If state legislators are the recruitment pool from which future members of congress are selected, then some states have a far larger pool than others.

Elite Response: Mobilizing Resources for Women Candidates

Although part of the explanation for the Year of the Woman lies in the decisions by women to seek office, these women benefited enormously by the activity of political elites. Party organizations encouraged women to run, provided them with valuable services, and helped introduce them to interest groups and contributors who would support their campaigns. Representative Jerry Lewis of California introduced Republican women House candidates to sympathetic PACs, and the Democratic Senatorial Campaign Committee established a Women's Council that raised substantial sums for women candidates.[14] Party committees provided both hard and soft money to help fund the campaigns. Such party resources have always been available to women who appeared to have a real chance of winning, but in 1992, party officials believed that women were more likely to win than in previous elections. Robert Biersack and Paul Herrnson report in Chapter 9 that the party committees did not contribute more or less money to women candidates than to men with similar levels of political experience who ran in similar types of districts or states. Thus, party support of women candidates did not represent a concerted effort to increase the number of women in Congress, but rather a normal effort to help candidates in close elections.

Perhaps more importantly, women elites provided crucial financial support to women candidates. Although women candidates, in the aggregate, have generally received less money than male candidates, research has shown that this past disadvantage was entirely due to differences in levels of political experience. Political money tends to flow to likely winners, and because a higher proportion of women candidates have historically lacked political experience and incumbency status, they have attracted less money. Once candidate experience and incumbency is controlled, women raise as much money as men (Burrell 1985; Uhlaner and Schlozman 1986). In 1992, however, women raised slightly more money than men with similar backgrounds. This increase in funding for women candidates was due to the mobilization of elite women into campaign finance activity.

Although historically women have been less likely than men to make sizable donations to political candidates (Powell with Brown and Hedges 1980; Wilcox, Brown, and Powell 1993), they have long constituted an important part of the direct-mail base of small gifts for progressive and Democratic groups. Democratic direct-mail expert Roger Craver estimated that in the 1980s, women provided 60 percent of the small donations to these groups. The *Webster* decision and the Anita Hill hearings led to a sharp increase in this direct-mail giving by women. Craver estimated that his clients added more than 2.5 million donors to their house lists, most of them women.[15]

Several of the women Senate candidates raised substantial funds from direct-mail solicitations to women donors. These women contributors were especially crucial in the early days of women's campaigns. According to one account, Lynn Yeakel received more than two-thirds of her money through June 1992 from women contributors, while Specter got more than three-quarters of his early cash from men.[16] The ratios were even higher for contributions from outside Pennsylvania. The *Washington Post* reported that approximately two-thirds of Boxer's contributors in the primary election were women.[17] After women won their party's primary, they were able to attract more money from male donors.

Women therefore provided vital funds by contributing to the direct-mail appeals of women candidates. Candice Nelson reports in Chapter 10 that Women's PACs also raised and distributed campaign monies. The receipts of EMILY's List, a PAC that contributes to pro-choice Democratic women candidates, increased four-fold in 1992. Yet the direct contributions of this PAC were only a fraction of the money it raised on behalf of these candidates. EMILY's List held fundraisers to benefit candidates, and asked its members to contribute directly to women seeking election to Congress. The PAC claims to have channeled more than $6 million to women candidates in 1992, much of it early in the campaign.[18]

Other established PACs and interest groups raised money for women candidates. The National Organization for Women, the Women's Campaign Fund, and other groups raised substantially more money than in previous elections, and gave it to a number of women candidates. A number of PACs formed in 1992 to help support women candidates, including the WISH List, a pro-choice Republican PAC that claimed to have contributed more than $450,000 dollars to women candidates either directly or through bundling (Rimmerman 1994).

These PACs also helped the female Senate candidates develop their direct-mail bases. Direct-mail campaigns raise a substantial portion of their funds from the "house list," a list of regular donors. Some of these women candidates built their house lists from members of women's PACs. The *Washington Post* reported that EMILY's List members contributed more than $300,000 to the campaign of Barbara Boxer, and these donors helped form the core of the early house list, which later expanded to more than 70,000 names.[19]

Women contributors, and women's PACs, provided crucial "seed money" that enabled women candidates to hire consultants, to take early polls, to develop a "PAC kit," and to the raise later funds from men and from other political groups. The value of such early money cannot be overestimated. George Gould of the Letter-Carriers' PAC indicated that Democratic women candidates in 1992 were far better prepared to solicit money from his PAC than in previous years, and that they were better able to address the issues of concern to labor. He attributed this preparation in part to the effective use of the seed money provided by women's PACs.[20] These direct contributions by women and women's PACs helped candidates later raise money from labor unions, environmental groups, and other sources. It is important to note that labor also provided substantial amounts of seed money to Democratic women candidates, however. Some labor PACs are members of EMILY's List, and their support was clearly important in helping many Democratic women candidates start their campaigns.

This financial activity by political elites helped women candidates get their message to the voters. Women candidates were well funded in 1992, especially in the general election. Barbara Boxer raised more money than any other candidates in 1992, including all Senate incumbents running. Dianne Feinstein had a $1 million fundraising edge over appointed incumbent John Seymour, and Carol Moseley-Braun raised more than three times the total of her Republican opponent in the general election, although her primary election campaign was poorly funded. Lynn Yeakel also raised substantial sums, and although Specter received more money overall, Yeakel outspent Specter in the final months of the campaign.

The promise of these funds helped persuade some women to run in 1992. Roberts (1993) reports that women's PACs and other feminist organizations actively recruited women candidates. These groups held workshops and training sessions for women candidates, and have worked within progressive networks to identify possible women candidates. Thus, elite support by women contributors, PACs, and party officials was an important part of the success in recruiting and ultimately electing women in 1992.

Voter Response

The record numbers of women elected in 1992 is partly a function of their decisions to run, and of elite support, especially in the form of financial aid. But ultimately women won elections because they received more votes than their opponents. In 1992, a combination of factors produced an electorate that was more eager to support women candidates than in previous elections.

Previous research has suggested that voters employ gender stereotypes in evaluating candidates. Women candidates are generally perceived as more competent to deal with "compassion" issues such as poverty, education, unemployment, and health care, while men candidates are perceived as better able to handle "force" issues such as crime and foreign policy (Sapiro 1981-1982; Mueller 1986; Alexander and Andersen forthcoming). Women are assumed to have greater sensitivity and warmth, and this translates into a perception that they will be better able to deal with the domestic issues that are especially salient during economic downturns, while perceptions of male aggressiveness and assertiveness leads voters to think of them as better able to resist foreign aggression and violent crime (Huddy and Terkildsen 1993).

In past elections, women have sought to portray themselves as having "masculine" traits. Feinstein's support for the death penalty is a case in point: political analysts argued that it enabled her to appeal to conservative men in the 1990 California gubernatorial election, and to appear "tough" enough to govern. Yet the 1992 election centered around exactly those issues on which women are perceived to be more able, while the defense issue that previously benefited male candidates was far less salient.

The lingering recession, the persistent media attention to gaps in health care for the uninsured, and nagging worries about the quality of America's schools were most salient to voters in 1992. The end of the Cold War and the collapse of the Soviet Union eliminated one of male candidates' persistent advantages during the 1980s—their perceived willingness to arm and defend the country against foreign threats. In 1992, gender role stereotypes played to the advantage of women candidates. Leonard Williams in Chapter 11 reports the result of his content analysis of television advertisements for men's and women's Senate campaigns. He noted that none of the ads explicitly focused on the need for military spending, and that both women and men sought to portray themselves as compassionate and caring.

Moreover, the electorate in 1992 was frequently characterized as seeking some sort of political change. Although few incumbents ultimately lost in congressional elections, more incumbents lost or won narrowly than in any election in the past decade. Prospective voters told pollsters and focus-group moderators that they wanted new faces in leadership, and a new approach to politics. With a Congress long dominated by men, electing women clearly represented change. A variety of polls showed that although most voters professed an indifference to candidate gender, more women and men voters preferred a generic woman candidate to a generic male candidate.[21] In California, a Field Poll showed that Democratic voters before the June primary favored a generic female candidate over a male candidate by five to one, and that Democratic women voters preferred a woman candidate by seven to one. Women form a substantial 56 percent majority of California Democratic voters, and their larger numbers and stronger preference created an advantage for women candidates in the primary (DiCamillo 1993).

Thus, the electorate in 1992 focused on issues on which women are perceived as especially strong, and didn't care much about the issue on which women have traditionally been disadvantaged. The contrast with the 1990 election is instructive. In November 1990, America prepared to go to war in the Persian Gulf against Saddam Hussein. In Colorado, Josie Heath's Senate campaign floundered at least in part because she had called for a 50 percent cut in the defense budget while Hank Brown had a record of support for the volunteer military. In a time when America was building towards its first major land war in nearly two decades, candidates who projected strength on foreign and defense matters were advantaged (Barone and Ujifusa 1991). But in 1992, the Persian Gulf War was a distant memory for most voters, and the domestic economy, health care, and education were far more salient.

Yet despite the numerous polls that showed that voters preferred hypothetical female candidates to hypothetical men, in the general election, women House candidates do not appear to have received an electoral advantage because of their gender. Rather, Democratic primary voters seemed to prefer women, allowing them to win their party's nomination to relatively safe open seats. In the general election, partisanship and ideology are more important than the gender of the candidate.

Elizabeth Adell Cook reports in Chapter 12 that during the primary elections, many Democratic women Senate candidates benefited from a gender gap in vote choice. When party (and to a lesser extent ideology) were constants, women voters preferred to support women candidates. During the general election there was a gender gap in these Senate elections as well in most states where women sought Senate election. Barbara Boxer won her Senate seat by carrying the woman's vote, and Lynn Yeakel carried a majority of women's votes in the Pennsylvania Senate election. This gender gap was partly due to partisanship, for women were more likely than men to vote for Democratic candidates in most Senate elections, regardless of the gender of the candidates. A variety of studies have shown a growing gender gap in partisanship and presidential vote choice over the past decade, and this gender gap has been evident in many Senate elections as well. Indeed, in past elections women provided the margin of victory for some male Democrats who defeated female Republican candidates, including Herbert Kohl of Wisconsin in 1988 and Bill Bradley of New Jersey in 1990, and few Republican women candidates have received more votes from women than from men. Voters (both male and female) generally vote for candidates who share their partisanship and who best represent their views on issues, regardless of gender.

Yet in 1992, women voters appear to have decided that gender is a relevant factor in vote choice. A series of news stories ranging from the Hill-Thomas hearings to the Tailhook scandal raised concerns among many women that male politicians did not understand their needs. A *Newsweek* poll taken immediately after the election showed that more than two-thirds of women believe that most men do not understand the issues that concern women most.[22] The same survey showed that 51 percent of women believed that Anita Hill been harassed by Justice Thomas, a sharp increase from the 27 percent who believed Hill in October 1991.

Does Electing Women Matter?

Soon after the 1992 election, a Republican woman seized the opportunity created by the appointment of Lloyd Bensten as secretary of the treasury to run for an open Senate seat in Texas. In June 1993, Kay Bailey Hutchison handily defeated Democrat Bob Krueger, who had been appointed to fill the Senate seat until a special election could be held. Her election increased the number of women in the Senate to seven. Hutchison was the sitting state treasurer, and her candidacy fit the pattern of "normal politics" described above: she seized the opportunity of an open seat to seek election to higher office. Her victory brought the second Republican woman to the Senate.

Hutchison's election raises important questions about the importance and meaning of electing women to the House and Senate, for many women who worked hard to elect Democratic women to the Senate in 1992 did not support her candidacy. Gloria Steinem called Hutchison a "female impersonator," and Krueger received money from the Hollywood Women's Caucus and NARAL PAC.[23] Hutchison will likely take positions in the U.S. Senate that differ widely from those of Boxer, Feinstein, Murray, Moseley-Braun, and Mikulski, and are similar to those of Nancy Kassebaum. She was endorsed by the Christian Coalition, despite her moderate stance on abortion.[24] Polls suggested that women voters were less supportive of Hutchison than were men.

If Hutchison's vote will frequently cancel that of a Democratic woman, is her election a victory for women? More generally, why is electing more women important? The scholars who have contributed to this volume offer different answers to this question.

First, there may be some value in having a Senate that "looks like America." Sue Thomas in Chapter 8 and Susan Gluck Mezey in the conclusion both suggest that there is value in having more women in office because they bring a certain diversity of opinion and experience into the policy process. Thomas also suggests a symbolic value of having women in public office. These arguments refer to what Sue Tolleson Rinehart calls virtual representation and what Susan Mezey calls descriptive representation. To the extent that diversity and symbolism are important, then more women in political office is a good regardless of their policy positions.

Yet Tolleson Rinehart suggests that virtual representation is important in part because of the assumption that it is linked somehow to substantive representation—what Mezey calls "acting for" women. Both Thomas and Mezey report the results of studies that suggest that in the aggregate, women in public office have different policy priorities than men. Thomas quotes one state legislator who credits the number of women in her state House and Senate with helping pass comparable worth, abortion rights, and ERA legislation. In August 1993, the five Democratic women senators used their knowledge of Senate rules to kill a rider that would have barred coverage of most abortions in the health care plans offered to federal workers.

Yet Mezey notes that women do not always "act for" women, citing a vote by Nancy Kassebaum against the Family and Medical Leave Act. Many men voted for the bill, presumably acting for women. If a vote for family leave is a vote "for women," then many men voted for women, and one woman senator voted against their interests. Kay Bailey Hutchison would presumably have voted with Kassebaum. Had there been more Republican women in the Senate instead of Democratic men in 1993, the bill might not have passed. Similarly, eleven (mostly Republican) women voted in the House in July 1993 to retain the ban on federal funding of abortions for poor women. Although, in general, elected women may be more supportive than men of policies of special interest to women, partisanship is a better predictor of legislative voting than gender.

Moreover, male legislators can be strong supporters of the feminist agenda. Sue Tolleson Rinehart notes that the men who ran against Feinstein and Boxer in the California primary had strong feminist credentials, and Hansen reports that Arlen Specter had a strong record of support for abortion rights and other women's issues. Tolleson Rinehart quotes with some skepticism Jane Hasler Henick, vice president of the National Woman's Political Caucus, who argued that "A man cannot speak for a woman in Congress."

Of course, "acting for" or "speaking for" women is a somewhat ambiguous concept. Susan Mezey suggests that acting for women involves support for feminist positions on a variety of issues. But some non-feminist and even anti-feminist women (and men) in state legislatures and in Congress doubtlessly believe that they are acting in the best interests of women. The thousands of women who contributed to the presidential campaign of Pat Robertson would argue that feminist senators act *against* their interests.

If acting for women means promoting policies such as abortion rights, family leave, and comparable worth, then the election of Bill Clinton in the 1992 presidential election is an important part of the year of the woman. Within a few weeks, Clinton accomplished what additional Democratic women in the Senate could not have done had Bush won reelection. Clinton signed the Family and Medical Leave Act that Bush had vetoed, and signed executive orders reversing twelve years of pro-life policies by the Reagan and Bush administrations. He appointed women to prominent positions in his cabinet, to the U.S. Supreme Court, and in other advisory positions such as the Council of Economic Advisers.

In Chapter 13, Mary Bendyna and Celinda Lake argue that the election of Clinton was an important victory for women. They show that college-educated, employed women were an important anchor for Clinton's electoral coalition, supporting him throughout the campaign. Women were more likely than men to vote for Clinton, and although Clinton won a plurality of men's votes as well, he owes much of the magnitude of his victory to women voters. Women were especially attracted to Clinton's policies designed to address the "social deficit" on health care and education.

Conclusion

The 1992 election represented an important change from the pattern of incremental gains by women candidates throughout the 1980s. Yet women in the national legislature in the U.S. continue to represent only a small proportion of all members. After tripling their numbers in the Senate in 1992 and electing an additional woman in 1993, women occupy only 7 percent of the seats. After dramatically increasing their numbers in the House, women occupy fewer than 11 percent of the seats. After a decade of steady progress in state legislatures, women occupy only 20 percent of the seats. Even after an election proclaimed as the "Year of the Woman," American legislatures are overwhelmingly dominated by men.

Figure 1.2 puts these numbers in a comparative context. After an election in which women greatly increased their numbers in the House, the U.S. still lags behind many of the Protestant nations of Northern Europe, and behind Catholic Italy and Spain in the percentage of women in the lower legislative chamber. Although it is not shown in Figure 1.2, many developing nations also have a greater

FIGURE 1.2 Percentages of Women in Legislatures in Western Democracies

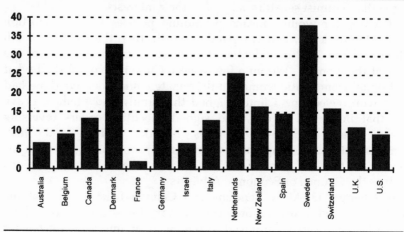

Source: APSA Legislative Studies Section Newsletter, 16: 1.

representation of women in their legislatures than the U.S. Had we constructed this figure in 1990, the U.S. would have ranked nearer the bottom of this list, so the newly elected women in 1992 and 1993 did improve America's ranking. But despite recent gains, the U.S. still trails many nations in electing women to its legislature.

A comparative perspective allows us to focus on why America lags behind many other nations in increasing the numbers of women in Congress. The U.S. has a relatively large and well-organized feminist movement, and there is widespread agreement on the norm of political equality for women. Most Americans claim to be willing to vote for a woman candidate for president, and presumably would do so for lower offices (Welch and Sigelman 1982). This suggests that the explanation may not lie in the voters, but perhaps in political institutions.

Scholars have pointed to the importance of national differences in electoral systems in explaining variations in the proportion of women in national parliaments (Norris 1985; Lovenduski 1986; Randall 1987). Countries with proportional representation frequently have more women in their legislatures, because party officials can assure the election of women by placing them higher on party lists. Randall notes that in most countries, national party leaders are more predisposed to back women candidates than are local party elites, and that any elections in which national party leaders play a large role are therefore more likely to produce a woman candidate than those in which the local party officials are more important. It was the national party elites who placed women candidates high on the party lists in Scandinavian countries, and national elites who help elect more women in the by-elections in Britain.

In the U.S., most women must win two elections to become a member of Congress—a primary election within their party and a general election against an opponent of the other party. National party elites are almost always neutral in party primaries, so they do not give special assistance to women candidates seeking the nomination, although they may encourage them to run. In the U.S., then, neither national nor local party officials promote the nomination of women, although they do sometimes encourage women to run. Instead, women must win their nomination and their ultimate victory in a system that is clearly skewed toward reelecting incumbents, who are usually male.[25]

If the U.S. electoral system makes progress toward gender equality in political representation slow, how likely is it that gains of the magnitude of those of 1992 will occur again soon? Of the various factors that led to the "Year of the Woman," some are special and may not recur. The Anita Hill hearings provided an unprecedented stimulus to women candidates and contributors, for the image of an all-male panel refusing to believe a woman who claimed to have been sexually harassed carried a powerful emotional charge. Of course, there will continue to be scandals relating to sexual harassment. Soon after the 1992 elections, the *Washington Post* published a series of stories that charged that Senator Robert Packwood of Oregon had harassed women who worked for or lobbied him.

The *Post* later revealed that one out of nine women who serve on congressional staffs have been harassed by a member of Congress, and one in three reported harassment by co-workers, supervisors, lobbyists, or members.[26] Nearly two out of three women complained of unequal pay, and more than half believed that they faced a "glass ceiling" that limited their advancement. These sorts of stories will continue to galvanize the attentive public, but to date none have had the emotional impact of the Anita Hill hearings, nor are they likely to match that earlier event in their power to motivate candidacies and contributions.

Some of the factors that help explain women's success in 1992 are intermittent events that occur occasionally, but not frequently. The very large number of open seats in 1992 will not be matched in any election soon, and the next redistricting is a decade away. Incumbents do retire or seek higher office, and over the course of a decade a substantial number of House seats come open. Yet the opportunities of the 1992 election are unlikely to be repeated in the near future.

Finally, some parts of the explanation for women's successes are likely to endure, at least in the near future. The voters' interest in domestic issues will probably survive for a few years, and I hope the lack of a foreign policy threat will continue as well. This suggests that women candidates may continue to face an electorate that is especially appreciative of what it perceives to be their unique abilities and interests.

Many of the women who are now on the mailing lists of various direct-mail vendors will continue to contribute money to women candidates, although the record amounts contributed in 1992 are unlikely to be repeated. Women's PACs will continue to solicit money, and continue to find ways to encourage and support women candidates. Perhaps most importantly, as women continue to make gains in state legislatures, the pool of skilled women with political bases will continue to expand, and these women will be ready and willing to seek higher office when the opportunity appears, and to use the resources provided by these women's PACs and women contributors to mount competitive campaigns.

All of this suggests that women will make incremental gains in Congress over the next several election cycles, gradually increasing their numbers. It also suggests that women are poised to take advantage of opportunities whenever they arise.

Notes

1. The 1990 election did result in the election of women as governors, including a Democratic woman governor of Texas. In Chapter 2, Sue Tolleson Rinehart argues that Ann Richards's victory in that election helped make women credible candidates in rough-and-tumble contests in 1992.

2. See, for example, Susan Faludi's essay in *Newsweek*, December 28, 1992, p. 31.

3. Her response was "Try again."

4. See the analysis by Megan Rosenfeld in the *Washington Post*, November 12, 1992, p. D1.

5. Lynn Martin and Claudine Schneider gave up House seats to challenger incumbent Democratic men, and both lost badly. Patricia Saiki gave up a House seat to run for an open Senate seat in Democratic Hawaii, and lost a somewhat closer race. None of these women candidates benefited from a gender gap.

6. Those who have not held elected office frequently have held appointed office, been party officials, or had some celebrity status that gave them name recognition in the district.

7. Although in most election cycles, the best non-incumbent candidates declare their candidacy very early (Wilcox 1987; Wilcox and Biersack 1990), in years when House districts are redrawn quality candidates can declare later in the cycle and still have a reasonable chance of success. In 1992, the uncertainties of redistricting allowed many winning candidates to declare later in the election cycle. More than half of the House non-incumbents who raised at least $400,000 in 1992 declared their candidacy after March 1, a figure greater than in any election in the 1980s.

8. At least a few House candidates were also partly motivated by the Hill-Thomas hearings. See *Washington Post*, October 28, 1992, p. D1.

9. Jelen notes that the office Moseley-Braun held at the time of her election — recorder of deeds for Cook County, was far more important than its name implies, since it involved a number of patronage jobs that could help a candidate mobilize Chicago voters.

10. Other incumbent senators have made fairly large political leaps. Carl Levin of Michigan won a Senate seat from the Detroit city council, and Herbert Kohl of Wisconsin had held no elected office before his Senate victory. Yet such cases are the exception, not the rule.

11. This point was noted by Jeffrey L. Katz and Ceci Connolly in *Congressional Quarterly Weekly Report*, November 7, 1992, 3557-3562.

12. It is worth noting that although Moseley Braun won the primary because Dixon and Hofeld traded negative ads, Feingold in Wisconsin won his primary for the same reason.

13. The year 1992 could also be called the "Year of the Outsider." The record number of open seats allowed not only women, but also minorities to greatly increase their representation. Record numbers of African-Americans and Hispanics were elected, and the U.S. Senate elected its first Native American. The Year of the Woman is therefore part of a larger phenomenon, in which the opportunities of the 1992 election allowed new groups to win access to power.

14. See story by Charles Babcock in the *Washington Post*, October 22, 1992, p. A1.

15. Ibid.

16. See story by Beth Donovan in *Congressional Quarterly Weekly Report*, October 17, 1992, 3269-3723.

17. *Washington Post*, October 22, 1992, p. A1.

18. Federal Election Commission figures do not support the EMILY's List claim, although the FEC does not record bundled contributions of less than $200. When the likely magnitude of these gifts is considered, the claims by EMILY's List seem reasonable.

19. *Washington Post,* October 22, 1992, p. A1.
20. Personal interview with the author.
21. See article by George Will in *Washington Post,* September 20, 1992, p. C7.
22. *Newsweek,* December 28, 1992.
23. Women's groups did not universally back Krueger, however, for Hutchison received money from the Republican PAC WISH List.
24. Hutchison supported choice through viability (the first twenty-four weeks), but also supported state legislation to limit access to abortion, such as parental notification and consent, and mandatory waiting periods.
25. Burrell (1992) notes that primary elections for open seats in the U.S. House are critical to electing more women to Congress. In 1992, more women won those elections.
26. See story by Richard Morin in the *Washington Post,* February 21, 1993, p. A1.

References

Alexander, Deborah, and Kristi Andersen. Forthcoming. "Gender Role Beliefs as Frameworks for Candidate Evaluation." *Political Research Quarterly.*
Barone, Michael, and Grant Ujifusa. 1992. *The Almanac of American Politics 1992.* Washington D.C.: National Journal.
Biersack, Robert, Paul S. Herrnson, and Clyde Wilcox. 1993. "Seeds for Success: Early Money in House Elections." Forthcoming, *Legislative Studies Quarterly.*
Boles, Janet. 1993. "The Year of the Woman—Continued (Or, the Return of the Puritan Ethic?)" Presented at the annual meeting of the Midwest Political Science Association, Chicago.
Burrell, Barbara. 1985. "Women's and Men's Campaigns for the U.S. House of Representatives, 1972-1982: A Finance Gap?" *American Politics Quarterly* 13: 251-272.
— — —. 1992. "Women Candidates in Open-Seat Primaries for the U.S. House: 1968-1990." *Legislative Studies Quarterly* 17: 493-508.
— — —. 1993. "'Just a Mom in Tennis Shoes': Exploring the Distinctiveness of Women's Campaigns for National Office in 1992." Presented at the annual meeting of the Midwest Political Science Association, Chicago.
Congressional Quarterly Weekly Report. October 17, 1992. 3269-3273.
— — —. November 7, 1992. 3557-3562.
DiCamillo, Mark. 1993. "How 1992 Truly Became 'The Year of the Woman' in California Politics." Presented at the annual meeting of the American Association for Public Opinion Research, St. Charles, IL.

Dolan, Kathleen, and Lynne E. Ford. 1993. "Changing Times, Changing Styles: The Professionalization of Women Legislators." Presented at the annual meeting of the Midwest Political Science Association, Chicago.

Duerst-Lahti, Georgia. 1993. "Year of the Woman, Decade of Women: Wisconsin Legislative Elections." Presented at the annual meeting of the Midwest Political Science Association, Chicago.

Freeman, Patricia, and William Lyons. 1992. "Female Legislators: Is There a New Type of Woman in Office?" In Gary F. Moncrief and Joel A. Thompson, eds. *Changing Patterns in State Legislative Careers.* Ann Arbor: University of Michigan Press.

Groseclose, Timothy, and Keith Krehbiel. 1993. "Golden Parachutes, Rubber Checks, and Strategic Retirements from the 102nd House." Presented at the annual meeting of the Midwest Political Science Association, Chicago.

Huddy, Leonie, and Nayda Terkildsen. 1993. "Gender Stereotypes and the Perception of Male and Female Candidates." *American Journal of Political Science* 37:119-147.

Jacobson, Gary, and Samuel Kernell. 1983. *Strategy and Choice in Congressional Elections.* New Haven: Yale University Press.

Krebs, Timothy, and Michael Walsh. 1993. "The Success of Nonincumbent Female Candidates in U.S. House Elections 1972-1992: A Test of the 'Year of the Woman' Thesis." Presented at the annual meeting of the Midwest Political Science Association, Chicago.

Lovenduski, Joni. 1986. *Women and European Politics.* Amherst: University of Massachusetts Press.

Mattlin, Jay. 1993. "The Gender Gap Revisited: Do Voters Apply the Same Standards to Male and Female Candidates?" Presented at the annual meeting of the American Association for Public Opinion Research, St. Charles, IL.

Mueller, Carol. "Nurturance and Mastery: Competing Qualifications for Women's Access to High Public Office?" In G. Moore and G.Spitze, eds. *Women and Politics: Action, Attitudes, and Office-Holding.* Greenwich, CT: JAI Press.

Newsweek, December 28, 1992.

Norris, Pippa. 1985. "Women's Legislative Participation in Western Europe." *West European Politics* 8: 21-45.

Powell, Lynda with Clifford Brown, Jr. and Roman Hedges. 1980. "Male and Female Differences in Elite Political Participation: An Examination of the Effects of Socioeconomic and Familial Variables." *Western Political Quarterly.* 18: 333-358.

Randall, Vicky. 1987. *Women and Politics: An International Perspective* (2nd Edition). Chicago: University of Chicago Press.

Rimmerman, Craig. 1994. "New Kids on the Block: National Gay and Lesbian Victory Fund and WISH List in 1992." In Robert Biersack, Paul S.

Herrnson, and Clyde Wilcox, eds. *Risky Business: PAC Decisionmaking in the 1992 Elections.* New York: M.E. Sharpe.

Roberts, Susan. 1993. "Further Feminism and Female Representation? The Role of Women's PACs in Recruitment." Presented at the annual meeting of the Midwest Political Science Association.

Sapiro, Virginia. 1981-1982. "If U.S. Senator Baker Were a Woman: An Experimental Study of Candidate Images." *Political Psychology* 2: 61-83.

Uhlaner, Carole Jean, and Kay Lehman Schlozman. 1986. "Candidate Gender and Congressional Campaign Receipts." *Journal of Politics* 48: 30-50.

Washington Post. Articles as noted in text. 1992-1993.

Welch, Susan, and Lee Sigelman. 1982. "Changes in Public Attitudes toward Women in Politics." *Social Science Quarterly* 63: 312 -322.

Wilcox, Clyde. 1987. "The Timing of Strategic Decisions: Candidacy Decisions in the U.S. House in 1982 and 1984." *Legislative Studies Quarterly* 12: 565-572.

Wilcox, Clyde, and Robert Biersack. 1990. "Research Update: The Timing of Candidacy Decisions in the House, 1982-1988." *Legislative Studies Quarterly* 15: 115-126.

Wilcox, Clyde, Clifford Brown, Jr., and Lynda Powell. 1993. "Sex and the Political Contributor: The Gender Gap among Presidential Contributors in 1988." *Political Research Quarterly.* 46: 355-376.

2

The California Senate Races:
A Case Study in the
Gendered Paradoxes
of Politics

Sue Tolleson Rinehart

"If we can build bombers, we can build buses. If we can build submarines, we can build subways."

— Barbara Boxer

"Two percent may be good for milk, but it's not good for the U.S. Senate."

— Dianne Feinstein

The California Senate elections of 1992 would have been unusual in any case. Very, very rarely are a state's two seats contested in the same election; the most frequent occurrences of such races have been those in which a new state, upon entering the United States, chooses its first two senators -- something that has not happened in some time. But Alan Cranston's retirement created an open seat, and Senator Pete Wilson's victory over Dianne Feinstein in the 1990 gubernatorial race created another opening. In 1991, now-Governor Wilson appointed Republican John Seymour to hold the seat until 1992, when Seymour would campaign with the advantages of an incumbent in a special election which would determine who would hold the seat for the final two years of the term.

That was the expectation, at any rate. But Dianne Feinstein, the former mayor of San Francisco, upset well-laid Republican plans. She moved quickly, after the narrowest of defeats in the 1990 gubernatorial election, to declare herself a candidate for the "short term" seat. Barbara Boxer, a five-term member of Congress from Marin County, also declared herself to be a Senate candidate: in 1991, she said she would compete for the Senate seat long held by Alan Cranston. For the first time in forty-two years (when Helen Gahagan Douglas lost a monumental struggle for the Senate against Richard Nixon in 1950 -- see Scobie 1992), it appeared that a woman would be a credible party standard bearer in a California Senate contest, raising once again all the confounding problems of gender and gender roles in the campaign. When it began to seem more and more certain that not one but *two* women would carry the Democratic flag into battle, the state and the nation were enthralled.

Political scientists and observers should remain enthralled, for the two California Senate races raise extraordinary challenges to our understanding of voting behavior, political ambition, and gender politics. The conventional wisdom about these races proved to be folly in a number of ways. But this was much more than a surprising pair of outcomes. It illustrates many of the symbolic, affective, cognitive, and policy paradoxes surrounding political women and those who judge them. The epigraphs with which this essay begins illustrate two of the paradoxes: the general problem of what Virginia Sapiro (1993) calls the "political uses of symbolic women" -- how are women perceived through the prisms of gender? What kinds of leaders will women be? -- and the more specific questions of whether women in office differ in their policy orientations from their male counterparts, and whether women are thus agents of "change."

An Analytical Adventure

As we consider the California Senate races, we need to think not only about how these two women succeeded, but about how their success challenges us to consider the prisms of gender and their effects on virtually all of our assumptions about voting behavior and candidate recruitment.

Here it might be useful to remind ourselves of the differences between *sex* and *gender*, and their expression in democratic theory as *virtual* and *substantive* representation. People are either biologically female or male. When we talk about differences in the share of elective offices that women and men hold, we are making this simple biological distinction; we are talking about the *sex* of officeholders, even though it is fashionable today to replace all uses of "sex" with "gender." When we ask "How many women...?" in the U.S. Senate, or in state legislatures, or in any institution, we are asking questions about sex, not gender. We are asking the question out of interest in the *virtual* representation, or the actual presence in a political assembly of members of different groups. But we are usually at least implicitly asking these questions because we expect that men's and women's differences will be reflected in genuinely different leadership behavior, or in the advocacy of different policies. This expectation relates to *gender* and *substantive* representation. Biological sex is the starting point for the social construction of "appropriate" male and female gender roles in all the world's cultures, and most of those cultures expect that, having learned their gender roles, women and men will act on them, and will act differently from one another. If they do behave differently, then in terms of democratic theory, we will expect differences in *substantive* representation, or the representation in a political assembly of different issues or different points of view. So we are interested in the *virtual* representation of women -- how many are there? -- not only out of simple justice, but usually because we expect them to be different, to add new forms of *substantive* representation. The rush to replace all uses of "sex" with "gender" has obscured the fine shades of difference in these questions.

Had Boxer and Feinstein been men, we might simply have argued that they pursued the normal paths to higher office, and then correctly bided their time, waiting for the right opportunity to run (e.g., Jacobson and Kernell 1983; Fowler and McClure 1989). Had they been men, we might have used any combination of voting behavior theories to explain Californians' reactions to them. We might argue that they matched most voters' desire for change in a specific direction, even if the policy positions of each were not necessarily spatially closest to those of individual voters and, especially, even if the candidates themselves were not spatially proximate (e.g., Rabinowitz and MacDonald 1989). We might conclude that they successfully engaged voters' image-driven "running tallies" of candidate evaluation (e.g., Lodge, McGraw, and Stroh 1989), or that both Boxer and Feinstein were correctly positioned to trigger either "pocketbook" or "sociotropic" voting on economic issues (Lewis-Beck 1988). We might contend that short-term forces and weak partisanship left voters anchorless, ready to be mobilized by unusual (and unusually appealing) candidates, despite voters' weak propensities to turn out to vote at all (e.g., Miller 1992; and for a superb general review of the vote determinant literature that nonetheless fails to consider gender, see Niemi and Weissberg 1993).

But each of these broad groups of theoretical perspectives on what makes someone run for office, and what makes people vote for that person, must be stretched if we are to ask what makes a *woman* run, and what makes voters choose (or reject) that woman. The literature on candidate recruitment, candidate pools, and political ambition generally features a near total absence of attention to gender. An exception is the work done by Fowler and McClure (1989). They there make the very good point that, even when a woman correctly positions herself to run for higher office, it is quite likely that, should she win, there will be few women available at levels below hers to move up and contend for the office she has left for a higher one. That wrinkle in the problem of candidate pools, and of the timing of candidacies, shows why sex and gender should not be overlooked in "general" studies. In 1990, for example, three successful Republican congresswomen, Lynn Martin, Claudine Schneider, and Patricia Sakai, risked -- and lost -- their House seats through unsuccessful challenges to incumbent Democratic senators. One might see this as a problem of partisan balance in the House, but we should also view it as a problem for the Republicans in another way. Their share of *women* House members was significantly reduced, and this has important consequences for the Republicans' competitiveness, given the increasing "feminization" of the Democratic party (see Chapter 7, on gender and partisanship in the 1992 House elections).

Similarly, the "image-driven" model of candidate evaluation makes a good deal of theoretical and intuitive sense (Lodge, McGraw, and Stroh 1989), but it too begs for more use of what we have learned about sex and gender. We know that voters have distinct reactions to and expectations about women candidates (see, for example, Sapiro 1982; Pierce 1989; Huddy and Terkildsen 1993; Huddy and Terkildsen forthcoming). Voters make particular, gendered assumptions about women's issue competence, decision-making strengths, toughness, and their presumed leadership style. As more and more women run for office at all levels, scholars cannot afford to neglect these phenomena in their models of candidate affect and evaluation.

In the area of voting behavior, we have entered our second decade of "gender gaps." If women are now turning out in absolute numbers at rates higher than those of men (Kenski 1988), and have voiced fairly consistent modal policy preferences that differ from the modal preferences of men, then gender gaps matter. But they also matter because they challenge orthodox thinking: it begs the question simply to argue that women are more "liberal," but the question of whether women's and men's gender role socialization may stimulate differing policy orientations (sometimes liberal, sometimes conservative: the point here is to ask toward what position the *roles* themselves would direct a man or woman, and not to try to force the roles into the old unidimensional ideological scale; see Conover 1988) begs for more serious attention. Exactly the same question can be posed to scholars of partisanship. We need not ask *whether* more women have become more Democratic as much as we need to ask *why*, and to ask what *effect* this will have on party competition. Certainly, all of these considerations should be borne in mind as we look at the elections of Dianne Feinstein and Barbara Boxer.

A Brief Story of the Campaign

The Primary

Dianne Feinstein emerged from a terribly close 1990 gubernatorial race (where it is estimated that she lost by less than three votes per precinct outside of her disastrous showing in Orange County), went through a remarkably quick period of mourning for her defeat, and declared her Senate candidacy in 1991. "I think in the governor's race my being a woman was a disadvantage, not an advantage," she said in an interview. She continued:

> *In the Senate race, I believe it is an advantage. I think people have doubts, still, about women in high executive offices, whether they can be the kind of managers that a man can be.... They don't doubt women in terms of their ability to advocate program change or public policy, which is, after all, the role of a legislator.*[1]

Research suggests that Feinstein was right (see, for example, Huddy and Terkildsen forthcoming): while voters are obviously and steadily warming to women candidates, there is still a lingering preference for women in stewardship or representative roles rather than in executive mansions. Ann Richards's almost astonishing Texas gubernatorial victory in 1990, at the same time that Feinstein went down to defeat in California, changed many things -- her success may have helped make 1992 the "Year of the Woman" by making women candidates in even the toughest political crucibles seem credible -- but the Richards-Williams race was at the same time more brutal and more idiosyncratic than the race between Feinstein and Wilson. Richards won in part because the words and actions of her opponent, Clayton Williams, increasingly made him seem ill-equipped to hold an executive position himself, while Richards's almost ruthless competence had become the stuff of legend (Tolleson Rinehart and Stanley 1994). In contrast, Pete Wilson, Feinstein's opponent in 1990, was eminently competent if not charismatic, and the two shadows of the Persian Gulf War and California's catastrophic budget woes dimmed any hope of electing a *woman* governor. These unserendipitous events struck a campaign organization that had not learned the lessons of face-to-face mobilizing of Californian voters in any case (Morris 1992) -- although it is to the 1992 Feinstein campaign's credit that it became an astute pupil of the lessons of the 1990 defeat. In 1992, however, with foreign affairs obscured in the long shadows of economic and domestic concerns, both Feinstein and Boxer were eminently suited to appeal to voters' desire for change (see Chapter 9 on the "efficiency" of the cues that women candidates' sex represented for voters).

Feinstein positioned herself from the beginning of the 1992 campaign *as a woman*, and even as a feminist, to a much greater extent than she had done in 1990 (see Morris 1992). One of the most striking features of 1992, in fact, is the notable number of women candidates at all levels who ran *as* women, and as pro-feminist. This is in the starkest contrast to the way women candidates had felt (apparently correctly) that they must de-emphasize their sex and, especially, any feminist orientations they might hold, in the 1970s (Carroll 1984; 1985). But Feinstein could not have been presented as having ever been in the feminist vanguard, if she also could never have been tarred with the brush of antifeminism. She had never been active in feminist organizations, or an advocate of "women's issues," but neither had she ever obviously opposed either women or "women's issues." If this were to be the Year of the Woman, how could Feinstein's feminism, mild as it might previously have been, be brought out in higher relief? Barbara Boxer had, if anything, the opposite problem: in her House career, she had so aggressively taken feminist positions that she entered the campaign with a feminist identification so strong that the conventional wisdom (supported by earlier findings that a feminist woman would be perceived as making much too narrow a representative appeal) suggested that she would have difficulty winning. Boxer would be herself, of course. And so, presumably, would Feinstein. But how would those selves be presented?

Feinstein began by quickly taking strong feminist positions on women's issues, appealing directly to feminist sentiments, and also appealing to "sisterhood." Audiences responded warmly to Feinstein's celebratory approach: one Orange County Republican woman who had voted for Ronald Reagan and George Bush said "Even though it sounds like a very unintelligent thing to say, and it's not a general rule with me, I will probably vote for Dianne because she's a woman. I think women have been scrutinized so much that they have to be better than men to get where she is."[2] Feinstein herself sounded the tocsin in May: "Can we, if we stand together, be true sisters in the fight for equality and can we begin to make some changes?" When asked if this amounted to an endorsement of Barbara Boxer she quickly said "No, no," but, after a wry smile, added "It came pretty close, didn't it?"[3]

A formidable implicit challenge was offered to Boxer's and Feinstein's male Democratic primary opponents: run against a woman who runs *as* a woman if you dare. The men did not dare; instead they began a contest to see who, man or woman, was the "best feminist." In truth, all the Democratic candidates had strong records on "women's issues," and even John Seymour, the incumbent Republican senator currently holding the short term seat, was pro-choice on abortion -- although only 20 percent of the voters knew that he took this position.[4] But voters do not conduct cool intellectual inventories of candidate issue positions vis-a-vis their own. Instead, voters call up a "summary tally" composed of images, affect, ideology, partisanship, and imperfect knowledge of candidates' stands on issues (Lodge, McGraw, and Stroh 1989). In this campaign, and especially on the question of who would best represent women on substantive questions such as abortion, and who would be the best agents of "change," Boxer and Feinstein were able to present the most pleasing totality of characteristics to inquisitive voters. And surely, on the question of the virtual representation of women, in a year when that appeared to be more desirable than it had been in the past, the male candidates were at a distinct disadvantage.

John Seymour later, and no doubt unintentionally, introduced questions of the virtual representation of various groups (and sizism?) as problems for *men* when he wistfully compared his 5'6" to the height of Senator Bill Bradley of New Jersey in the course of using a basketball analogy to describe his Senate activities to a group of women supporters. Scholars and journalists have not yet paid enough attention to appearance and carriage and their influence on voters' candidate evaluation; usually we have assumed that women are disadvantaged in this contest, since even in terms of the "best" physical stereotypes of masculinity and femininity, handsome men are thought to be smart and capable candidates, while attractive women are not expected to be competent (Bowman 1984). The journalist Molly Ivins points out that Ann Richards's sharp humor and attractiveness, even sexiness, was a challenge to many Texans in the 1990 gubernatorial campaign (Tolleson Rinehart and Stanley 1994), but consider also the kind of problem that Michael Dukakis faced in 1988, campaigning against the much taller, more athletic-looking George Bush. In the California general election it was Dianne Feinstein who was the taller candidate, and much was made of her "commanding but not threatening presence;" note the careful joining of "masculine" and "feminine" traits, and note too that here our gendered expectations about the physical appearance of leadership were stood on their heads.

Barbara Boxer lacks Feinstein's particular kind of physical presence, but has manufactured a considerable presence built of dynamism and a warm and engaged personality. Boxer was consciously, if implicitly, acknowledging the complications inherent in the question of virtual representation by sex when she said "The U.S. Senate needs a dose of reality, and that dose comes in this package." The dose comes in a physically female package, different from almost all the packages we have seen in the past, and presumably in a different package of political orientations and styles as well. Jane Hasler Henick, vice president of the National Woman's Political Caucus, dismissed the charge that primary candidate Gray Davis was a better feminist than Dianne Feinstein with the assertion that "A man cannot speak for a woman in Congress,"[5] thereby uniting virtual and substantive representation in a single sweeping statement.

This unusual simultaneous campaign for two Senate seats, then, began raising every question about gender roles, gender stereotypes, and women's paths to elective office that scholars have thought to ask, and it began raising those questions at a very early stage. Both the frontrunning candidates were women, but what does that mean? Do we really wish to agree with Hasler Henick that a man *cannot*, or at least cannot always, speak for women? If we do, then given women's level of virtual representation in Congress, the representation of women's *interests* will remain endangered. But there is yet another consideration, even in the realm of virtual representation. Are these two women, as virtual representatives, each supposed to be everywoman? If not, how different can they be from one another and still run *as* women? Consider this encapsulation of the two women:

> *Indeed, the styles of Feinstein and Boxer are studies in contrast. The better known Feinstein, 58, is a tall, cool-tempered, reassuring figure who many consider commanding but not threatening. Boxer, 51, is a small woman who*

is usually seen as a pugnacious, energetic politician who elicits strong emotions from her audiences. Feinstein cut her political teeth in the executive branch of government... Boxer is serving in the legislative arena.... [6]

Two men thus described would not have been expected to run as a pair, and there is no question that each would not have been expected to be "everyman." The women were expected to do so, by the media, by their joint supporters, and most importantly, by themselves.

Boxer and Feinstein do share some characteristics: they are of the same generation, they are both Jewish, and both are from northern California. They both have long experience in politics, including the experience of political success in years that most emphatically were *not* "years of the woman." They are both, broadly speaking, progressive Democrats, although Boxer is certainly much more liberal and idealistic, while Feinstein is more pragmatic and less ideological (she had sometimes angered various constituencies when, as mayor of San Francisco, she had chosen the prudent rather than the visionary alternative: see Morris 1992). Both must be called feminists, even if Boxer is more emphatically so, and even if the question of Feinstein's feminism engaged considerable debate before it was settled in favor of declaring that she is. Both are the skilled campaigners (Feinstein's ability to learn from her 1990 gubernatorial campaign cannot be overestimated) and proven fundraisers who are most likely to be able to take advantage of opportunities when they arise (in these ways, at least, their candidacies were "normal politics").

But there the similarities end: their ideological and policy orientations, their whole approaches to politics, have differed markedly. Nor had the two women been close allies in the past. In prior elections, each had endorsed the other's opponents,[7] and neither ever actually endorsed the other during the primary campaign, although as Feinstein herself wryly noted, they came close. Both, however, were intelligent and observant enough, and no doubt genuinely sincere enough, to see the remarkable challenge with which they were jointly faced. And the exhilaration as the primary campaign unfolded was unquestionable: Californians, and indeed, people (especially women) all over the country, seemed struck by this race to a degree that few other primary contests could ever achieve. The novelty of two experienced women competing for two Senate nominations at the same time, and what can only be called the thrill that many women felt as they contemplated the success of *both* Boxer and Feinstein, made what would have been an unusual campaign in any circumstances positively a delight. Politics was interesting again, no matter who one was going to vote for.

Feinstein and Boxer received the lionesses' share of money and media attention during the primary campaigns: the novelty of the races meant that the media and, apparently, the public, conceived of the campaigns as "Feinstein/Boxer and their opponents." And in contrast to the hands-on, forthcoming, positive campaign style that each adopted, Mel Levine and Gray Davis, the principal male opponents of Boxer and Feinstein, respectively, appeared remote, and even lazy (both appealed to large donors and did less pressing of the flesh) and negative (both were perceived to have gone on the offensive against their female opponents). Any male candidates would have had a hard time in this milieu, no matter how carefully they orchestrated their campaigns, but Levine and Davis would appear not to have made the best of a difficult situation. Thus Dianne Feinstein and Barbara Boxer won their primary contests handily. Exit polls suggested that voters saw both women as harbingers of change -- despite their differences, and differences among voters, each was deemed the appropriate choice both in terms of issue direction and representation (see again Rabinowitz and MacDonald 1989, for explanations of how directional rather than spatial models of voting behavior are better suited to explain unusual cases like the present one). The Republican primary victors, John Seymour in the short term seat, and Bruce Herschensohn for the full term seat, might have felt that they were about to inherit the problems of Levine and Davis. They would have been right. The big banner headline in the *Los Angeles Times* the day after the primary was "Feinstein, Boxer Win Easily."[8] Coverage of the California Senate primary in the *New York Times* ran to a full page, including a news analysis piece and two long profiles of Boxer and Feinstein, but with less than two complete paragraphs for discussion of Seymour and Herschensohn.[9] An op/ed piece by Bill Bress in the *Los Angeles Times* two weeks after the primary lauded both Feinstein and Boxer for clean and "honest" campaigns: "The twin victories... also represent a rejection of the aloof, money-driven bad mouth political campaigns waged by their principal Democratic opponents.... Barbara Boxer and Dianne Feinstein weren't the only ones who won on Tuesday. We all did."[10] Given such a public mood, John Seymour and Bruce Herschensohn began, incredibly enough, as underdogs, even though both were the candidates of the majority party, in terms of California's recent national voting behavior, even though one was the incumbent, with close ties to a sitting governor and President Bush, and the other was, like the women, initially seen as a candidate of "integrity" and "change." Underdogs they would remain.

The General Election Campaign

Through the summer and into the fall, both Feinstein and Boxer retained commanding leads, and their respective opponents, Seymour and Herschensohn, made little progress in impressing themselves on voters' minds. The conventional wisdom had earlier maintained that voters would not award *both* Senate seats to women (this assumption is indirectly supported by research on women's routes to elective office, where it is repeatedly found that multi-member or party list election systems benefit women, presumably precisely because one can vote for a given *woman* without "giving away" all the legislative power to *women* (see, for example, Welch and Studlar 1990). Further, there was the fact that Boxer had a much more liberal record than Feinstein: would voters choose both a moderate and someone on the left? The difficulty for voters, if there was one, would be either confounded or ameliorated by the presence of a similar (but isotopic) ideological disparity on the Republican side, with Herschensohn, vehemently anti-abortion and pro-defense spending, considerably to the right of the much more moderate Seymour. But polling results throughout the summer continued to suggest that voters wanted "change," and saw both Boxer and Feinstein as being best able to bring that about.

Boxer and Feinstein carefully protected their frontrunner positions into the fall. Boxer said in October, "I have to act as if I was twenty points behind.... Politics is tough. It can change."[11] She would prove to be more prophetic than, perhaps, she had bargained for. Seymour and Herschensohn began the autumn still dismally trailing, each prepared to launch attacks in October -- perhaps too late, since most experts were by then concluding that voter opinion was crystallizing in the women's favor.

Nonetheless, attack the men did, and with some early effect. On October 8, the *Los Angeles Times* chided Boxer (rather mildly) for avoiding a debate with Herschensohn that could have blanketed the state on television (the first debate between the two had been seen only by watchers of C-SPAN).[12] Herschensohn had attempted without success during the first debate, in September, to portray Boxer as soft and even incompetent on national security. This, though, gave Boxer an opportunity to display her experience in other than "women's" or feminist issues:

At one point, the two disputed each other's facts while debating the development of the Patriot missile. Boxer said the Patriot was never part of the Strategic Defense Initiative, or "Star Wars" program. Herschensohn said

it was and told Boxer "Every step of the way, you fought SDI." Boxer retorted
in a chill, firm tone: "I am on the Armed Services Committee. I will show
you."[13]

Herschensohn, exasperated, later explained his readiness to go on the
offensive by saying "You've got to win.... There's only x-many weeks
(sic) before the election, five and a half or something like that."[14]
Things got much nastier from there.   Herschensohn's vigorously
negative television ads, following thickly upon one another,
apparently served to close the gap between him and Boxer to ten
points in October, from fourteen points a month before. He became
increasingly personally critical of her, especially for her bad checks in
the House bank imbroglio.   He may, however, have damaged his
strategy by carrying it too far.   In a fundraising letter that received
considerable press coverage, Herschensohn called Boxer a "'radical
left-wing' congresswoman with 'little use for religious values or even
traditional family values'" -- a charge he would have difficulty
substantiating.[15]   He would continue to hammer away at Boxer's
("radical") liberalism, her bounced checks, and her congressional
perks throughout October, working especially hard at depicting her as
a high-living, perk-abusing congressional celebrity.[16] He seemed to
achieve a considerable amount -- his ads may well have stimulated the
already angry mood of anti-incumbency -- judging from the narrowing
of the gap between the two and Boxer's own nervous lowering of
expectations about her race.[17] But two things converged to brake his
momentum, and not a moment too soon from Boxer's perspective.

First, Boxer was cleared by the Justice Department of any
wrongdoing in the House bank scandal,[18] and Herschensohn's
continued attacks on her had the effect of increasing the fervency of
her supporters.[19]   Boxer was criticized at the time for not having
responded to Herschensohn's attacks earlier, and for having allowed
herself to be outspent by Herschensohn from July 1 to mid-October.[20]
The Boxer campaign staunchly maintained that this had been an early
strategic decision, and one they were determined to stick to, risky as it
might seem to let attacks go unanswered while resources are
husbanded for the last stage.   And Boxer *is* shrewd, skilled, and
unafraid of risk.[21] There is, furthermore, a striking precedent among
recent women's candidacies, and that is once again the 1990 Texas
gubernatorial campaign of Ann Richards. In the autumn of 1990,
Richards, in a far more urgent situation as the underdog in the race,
was also being roundly criticized for allowing the summer to pass
without advertising on television, or responding to her opponent
Clayton Williams's attacks. But the Richards campaign insisted that,

from the beginning, their strategy had been to shepherd their resources for the last leg, no matter what transpired in the summer. Hard as it was for them to do so in the face of relentless criticism, they stuck to their risky strategy (Tolleson Rinehart and Stanley 1994). Like Boxer's campaign, Richards's campaign also had to endure charges that it was neither well-managed nor effective.[22]   But in any event, both the Richards and Boxer risks seemed worth it. Richards surged from ten points down in October to victory in 1990, and Boxer stabilized her slide, barely holding her lead in 1992.

Neither woman could have seen her gamble pay off, however, without help from her opponent.   For Ann Richards, it was the October revelation that the billionaire Clayton Williams had paid no income taxes in 1986, during a Texas recession when very much poorer people, strapped by taxes, still paid them.   For Boxer, a revelation about Herschensohn's behavior threw the second, and probably critical, obstacle in the path of his momentum. On October 30, the news broke that Herschensohn had patronized a Hollywood nude dance club and an adult newsstand -- quite startling activities on the part of a man who had so insistently campaigned on "religious" and "traditional family" values. The story received national coverage. Herschensohn's immediate reaction was an angry denial; his second reaction helped him less. He admitted the acts and promptly accused Boxer herself of having orchestrated a smear campaign:

> *"It is trash, it's slime, it's sleaze, it is smearing and it is selective spying,"*
> *Herschensohn said at a hastily called news conference in San Diego during*
> *which he acknowledged visiting the two establishments. "Barbara Boxer to me*
> *represents the worst of political life."*[23]

Herschensohn offered no evidence to support his allegation, and indeed, none ever appeared linking Boxer or her campaign to the release of the story, although a statewide Democratic party official was held responsible.

So, while voters are increasingly embracing women candidates, they are by no means doing this in an ungendered way. Traditional gender role stereotypes abound in voters' and pundits' (and candidates') assumptions that women in office will be more compassionate, accountable, cooperative, responsive, and the like, even while we also expect women to be strong and tough -- to demonstrate the characteristics of leadership.   But so, too, it is traditional gender role socialization that causes us to recoil when a male candidate is verbally savage to or insulting about his female opponent. For many men, it must seem close to hitting a woman. As terrible as violence against women is in this country, it is committed by a minority of men, and it is regarded, officially at least, as beyond the pale. Men who are not abusers rightly regard violence against women (when they can be made to see it) as abhorrent, whether they are at all sympathetic to feminism or not. A male candidate insulting a female candidate is a far cry from violence against women, but it nonetheless triggers a number of the same gendered orientations, especially those concerned with the rules a gentleman must obey in his conduct toward a lady. And yet politics is a scrappy, often highly uncivil business. If women want to play, should they not also be able to "take it"? The most successful women candidates are those who present clear images of their strength; in the Richards and Boxer cases, I would argue that, having proved their toughness, they then also could be the beneficiaries of some measure of chivalry. The lesson is stark but paradoxical. In the terrible heat of political crucibles like Texas or California, women candidates must be tough. And men must be careful.[24]

For Dianne Feinstein, the crucible does not seem to have become even uncomfortably warm. With extremely high statewide recognition, money, and a large pre-existing base of support as the benisons of her wrenchingly close defeat in 1990, her campaign in 1992 looked more and more like what journalist Lou Cannon called an impending coronation. The two Feinstein-Seymour debates revealed much more ideological distance between the candidates than their moderate images and the conventional wisdom had suggested. Feinstein presented herself as unmistakably interventionist in her beliefs about government, and Seymour looked more like a Reaganite "less government" Republican than some had previously thought him. The debates also revealed that Seymour's attack strategy would be one of casting doubt on Feinstein's sincerity and commitment -- in short, on her character.[25] This strategy seems, in retrospect, to have been a mistake, even given that Seymour, the colorless underdog, would have had few options other than to attack. Though much milder than the attacks of Bruce Herschensohn, Seymour's charges were not penetrating enough to mobilize new Seymour supporters, but probably were negative enough to stimulate greater intensity (men's atavistic chivalry, women's sisterhood) on the part of Feinstein's supporters. Her own counterattacks do not seem to have alienated many voters. In exit poll data, more people thought that Seymour had aired the most unfair ads than thought this of Feinstein.

Seymour claimed on October 23 that his own polls showed him having closed the gap to 5 percent: "I don't believe those polls... but I sure do trust the direction and momentum."[26] Seymour, in the honorable tradition of underdogs everywhere, made a brave showing. But the reality was that virtually nothing could stop Feinstein now.

And her insuperable lead plus, perhaps, the completion of a change of heart begun in 1990, gave Dianne Feinstein the chance to do what she had not done in the primary. She endorsed Barbara Boxer:

> With Boxer's once commanding lead eroding nearly to nothing in several polls, Feinstein and Democratic party officials were eager to extend some coattails to the Marin County congresswoman. Team was the catchword of [election eve, at the final campaign rallies], and Feinstein referred to herself and Boxer as the "new Cagney and Lacey."[27]

"Cagney and Lacey" did it. "Lacey" swept to an easy victory, and "Cagney," buoyed by a very high turnout, also but more narrowly succeeded.[28] Their wins, joined to Bill Clinton's seizure of California's fifty-four electoral votes, gave the Democrats their biggest electoral sweep of the state since 1958.[29] Seymour was gracious in defeat. Herschensohn was not, taking his loss very bitterly.[30]

Exit poll data showed -- astonishingly, given that both women won -- that voters choosing the Democratic pair ranked abortion rights, the scarcity of women in the U.S. Senate, the need for "change" (that so useful euphemism), and the environment as the four most important issues influencing their decisions.[31] It is not surprising that some, perhaps many, voters would voice such concerns. It is very surprising indeed that a *majority coalition* of such issue orientations would form, and that it would be so freely (even comfortably?) linked with sex (via the virtual representation of women) and gender (via the "women's issues" and issues women are thought to be "best" at handling). In California, at least, the days of women candidates who must be "closet feminists" in order not to alienate voters (Carroll 1984) appear to be over. Table 2.1 also suggests that, while Feinstein exceeded her share of the 1990 vote in 1992, Boxer managed to hold onto Feinstein's 1990 coalition, and did better among the well-educated and affluent than Feinstein did in 1990, as, indeed, Feinstein herself did in the second go-round. Significant gender gaps, especially among white Californians, are of course also very markedly in evidence.

The success of the two women among groups of voters who have the means to donate money to candidates -- whether they do so or not -- implicitly directs us to another domain in which women candidates' fortunes appear to have been transformed. That domain is the getting of money. Boxer and Feinstein ranked first and fourth, respectively, among *all* 1992 Senate candidates in the success of their fundraising,[32] not least because large numbers of women are now putting their

TABLE 2.1 Comparisons of Vote Share, 1990 and 1992[a]

| | 1990 share in percent: | | 1992 share in percent: | | | | |
	Feinstein	Wilson	Feinstein	Seymour	Boxer	Herschensohn	Clinton
All voters	**50 (49.7)**	**50 (50.3)**	**57**	**39**	**50**	**44**	**47**
Sex of voter:							
Male	43		50		43		43
Female	57		64		57		51
Whites only:							
Male	38		45		38		39
Female	53		60		54		46
Race:							
White	46		52		46		42
Black	84		88		84		83
Hispanic	67		66		61		65
Asian	43		61		52		39
Age:							
18-29	49		53		48		50
30-44	53		58		53		46
45-59	49		57		52		46
60 plus	46		58		43		47
Education:							
hs grad	52		55		43		45
some coll	49		54		51		44
coll grad	46		58		51		43
postgrad	55		68		62		55
Family Income:							
<$15,000	63		65		59		63
15-29999	54		61		53		50
30-49999	52		53		47		41
50-99/75	47		54		45		45
>100/75	38		54		52		41

Voted Bush 88	22	34	26	20
Family finances:				
Better	43	49	36	33
Same	58	51	43	41
Worse	51	68	64	58
National economy:				
Excellent	50	0	0	0
Good	32	19	14	5
Not so good	52	57	48	45
Poor	65	72	66	61
Importance of woman gov/sen:				
Most/very	49	79	75	72
Imp/somewhat	67	52	43	38
Not/not very	46	28	20	20
Abortion:				
legal all	64	73	66	62
legal some	40	54	49	42
not legal	37	34	24	26

Source: Voter Research and Surveys General Election Exit Polls, California Files, 1990, 1992.

[a]Note that a slash indicates differences between 1990 and 1992 question wording or categories: 50-99/75, for example, means the category ran from $50,000 to $99,999 in 1990, but from $50,000 to $75,000 in 1992, and >100/75 means that the top category in 1990 was over $100,000 and $75,000 in 1992. On attitudes toward women candidates: in 1990, responses were "single most important factor in decision," "one of several important factors;" In 1992, choices were "very important" or "somewhat important;" remaining responses of "not important" in 1990; "not very important" in 1992.

money where their votes (and hearts) are (see Chapter 9 on party support of women candidates, and Chapter 10 on women's PACs such as EMILY's List). As we have entered the decade of the 1990s, gender gaps have become significant not only because women have thoroughly mobilized themselves as voters but, now that more women have the income to do it, as donors as well. Boxer raised approximately $10 million, and Feinstein raised about $8 million (they did not surpass the all-time record set by Jesse Helms in 1984, who raised $16.5 million for his reelection bid).[33] Both Boxer and Feinstein outraised and outspent their general election opponents, while both had efficiently won their primaries spending *less* per primary vote than did their principal opponents.[34]

Ann Richards, who had shown in 1990 that a woman can win in the most difficult of circumstances (and who believes that her candidacy was immeasurably benefited by the early money she received from EMILY's List) came to California in October 1992, to help raise money for Feinstein and Boxer. Feisty, funny Governor Richards made an unashamed appeal to old gender role stereotypes in the cause of promoting women in office, who could then challenge many aspects of those old stereotypes:

> *With this kind of crisp breeze in the air, I thought, hmm, hmm, it is going to be nice to start wearing some wool suits, and I need to get myself a new pair of shoes.... This fall, what I want you to do, is write Barbara Boxer and Dianne Feinstein a check for just one good pair of Ferragamo shoes. You might even stretch it out to an Ellen Tracy jacket and an Anne Klein pair of slacks. Feel good about yourself!*[35]

Women by the thousands had written Ann Richards a check for one pair of shoes, Ferragamo or otherwise, in 1990 (Tolleson Rinehart and Stanley 1994). Now she came to California to beseech women to do the same for the Senate candidates.[36]

Women candidates could not hope to succeed by relying *only* on women donors, of course. But women candidates, like men who run, face the chicken-and-egg problem of needing to look credible in order to raise money, and needing to raise money in order to look credible. "Credible" women candidates, particularly incumbents, have been more successful as fundraisers than is usually acknowledged (Carroll 1985). The change we may be witnessing now, though, is that more women candidates look credible, or at least trigger optimism, at earlier points in their candidacies, to women *voters*, who then send a check to the candidate, or to bundling groups like the Democratic EMILY's List, or the new Republican WISH List. Women's early support of one another may, for the moment, be resolving the chicken-and-egg dilemma that money has always caused in American politics. This is yet another facet of the prisms of gender.

Conclusion

Just a week after the 1992 general election, ultraconservative (and vehemently anti-feminist) Orange County Republicans William Dannemeyer and Robert K. Dornan indicated that they would be challenging Dianne Feinstein for her Senate seat in 1994.[37] Should either of these two men win the Republican primary, we will have yet another opportunity to watch sex and gender insinuate themselves into the competition over choosing leaders. But Feinstein won her election with enough of a margin to give her a safe seat, and her appointments to the Senate Appropriations and Judiciary Committees will surely benefit the new senior senator from California. Her sex is more likely to disadvantage a Dannemeyer or a Dornan than to disadvantage her. Boxer, with a very much more marginal victory, has six years in which to establish her incumbency, and she too won a very important committee appointment, to Banking, Housing, and Urban Affairs.[38] What will the two women do with their new positions? What kinds of leaders will they be? How will they differ from men? They join four other women in the U.S. Senate, and six women, even if they were all alike, and all utterly committed to the same agenda, could still not transform the institution. They will be *expected* to be different from men, though. They also seem to expect it from themselves.

Feinstein and Boxer campaigned, at the end, as the "team for change." They will not ignore the realities of the institution they have entered, and must thus work for "change" within its formidable constraints. And while they are both women, they are not "woman." They differ significantly from one another in their styles, in their ideological intensity, in a number of their policy preferences. They have, in the past, been rivals, even opponents of one another. But the past breach between them seems genuinely to have been healed; Boxer seems sincerely convinced now that Feinstein is a feminist (or enough of one), and pragmatic Feinstein no longer seems to see Boxer as too ideological to be effective. The healing of the breach began in the 1990 general election campaign for governor, when Boxer took to the hustings for Feinstein. In the 1992 campaign, Feinstein came to Boxer's aid at a critical point. Observers say that "Cagney and Lacey" have not merely struck a bargain to work together, but have "bonded in a remarkable way."[39]

And although six women could not revolutionize the Senate, the two women from California can change some of the ways things are done. Feinstein is, technically, the senior senator from California, and would, according to Senate norms, traditionally have the power to recommend to the president all judicial nominees to the federal bench in California. She has chosen instead to share that power with Boxer: they will take turns making recommendations.[40] This is a modest piece of evidence on which to erect an edifice of women's differences in leadership style from that of men: a similarly situated man might well feel that his seniority was too slight to permit him any heavy-handedness in such a case. What is notable, though, is that Feinstein's decision was rapid, pragmatic, sensible, and cooperative, and did not seem to require a struggle to relinquish ego or self-aggrandizement. Boxer returned the favor, allowing Feinstein to take credit for introducing the California Desert Protection Act, even though Boxer has built much of her reputation on her environmentalism.

"Cagney and Lacey" are certainly *beginning* their tenures as a team. They are too smart and too experienced not to know that, in many ways, they are going to have to play by the usual rules. Those rules emanate from a gendered institution; they are, if you will, "men's rules," and both Feinstein and Boxer will be judged by how well they learn and use them. But they also are committed to representation of women and of gender differences. They are highly conscious (as are we all) of their status as virtual representatives of women. They assume as well that policy orientations are gendered, and expect to bring that substantive representation to bear in their legislative agendas. Finally, they know that, in the eyes of many, these two forms of representation converged in one image, in the physically female "package" that Boxer had alluded to, to make Feinstein and Boxer appear to be agents of change. Their victories were exuberantly greeted, and they have begun well. Their continued success will help stretch "years of women" far beyond 1992.

Notes

1. *Los Angeles Times*, April 28, 1992, p. A1.
2. *Los Angeles Times*, May 17, 1992, p. A3.
3. *Los Angeles Times*, May 31, 1992, p. A3.
4. *Washington Post*, October 19, 1992, p. A1.
5. *Los Angeles Times*, April 22, 1992, p. A1.

6. *Los Angeles Times*, May 27, 1992, p. A1.

7. *Washington Post*, October 19, 1992, p. A1.

8. *Los Angeles Times*, June 3, 1992, p. A1.

9. *New York Times*, June 4, 1992, p. A12.

10. *Los Angeles Times*, June 16, 1992.

11. *Los Angeles Times*, October 5, 1992, p. A3.

12. *Los Angeles Times*, October 8, 1992, p. B6.

13. *Los Angeles Times*, September 13, 1992, p. A3.

14. *Los Angeles Times*, September 23, 1992, p. A3.

15. *Los Angeles Times*, October 8, 1992, p. A3.

16. *Los Angeles Times*, October 29, 1992, p. A3.

17. *Los Angeles Times*, October 23, 1992, p. A1.

18. *Los Angeles Times*, October 10, 1992.

19. *Los Angeles Times*, October 8, 1992, p. A3.

20. *Los Angeles Times*, October 23, 1992, p. A1.

21. *Los Angeles Times*, October 6, 1992, p. A1.

22. Research shows that, ceteris paribus, women's campaigns are no worse (nor, perhaps, better) managed than those of men; see Carroll 1985, for evidence of this even in the 1970s, and Darcy, Welch, and Clark 1987, for more recent evidence. Nonetheless, it is striking how often women's campaigns are accused of being *badly* run when, in fact, they may only be *differently* run than what the "experts" and the campaign orthodoxy would demand.

23. *Los Angeles Times*, November 1, 1992, p. A1.

24. Political analyst Sherry Bebitch Jeffe, far more knowledgeable about California politics than am I, warns me not to make too much of any chivalrous response to Herschensohn's attacks.   But this remains a researchable question: the exit poll data do show that while 38 percent of all voters (regardless of for whom they voted) felt that both Boxer and Herschensohn had aired unfair ads, a significant 4 percent more felt Herschensohn alone had been unfair (19 percent) than felt this about Boxer (15 percent). The difference is not overwhelming, and California is not Texas, but in a close race, the difference could be very important indeed.

25. *Los Angeles Times*, October 11, 1992, p. A3; October 12, 1992, p. A33.

26. *Los Angeles Times*, October 24, 1992, p. A24.

27. *Los Angeles Times*, November 3, 1992, p. A1.

28. Those with fond memories of the "Cagney and Lacey" television series will immediately know who I have identified as whom. Those who do not know the program may now have a reason to catch a rerun: which California senator is which New York cop?

29. *Los Angeles Times*, November 4, 1992, p. A1.

30. *Los Angeles Times*, November 5, 1992, p. A3.

31. *Los Angeles Times*, November 4, 1992, p. A3.

32. Republican incumbents Arlen Specter of Pennsylvania and Alfonse D'Amato of New York ranked second and third, respectively.

33. *Los Angeles Times,* December 21, 1992, p. A3.

34. *Los Angeles Times,* October 6, 1992, p. A3; December 21, 1992, p. A3.

35. *Los Angeles Times,* October 21, 1992.

36. This author vividly remembers hearing then-State Treasurer Ann Richards, in the spring of 1990, asking a small gathering of (mostly) women in Lubbock, Texas, for their support. She said that she had gotten a note, and a check, from an old friend, who said that after looking at what she spent on clothes, she was ashamed not to send a similar amount to Richards. I believe this event may be the origin of the kind of appeal Governor Richards has since made on behalf of other women candidates as she did for Boxer and Feinstein.

37. *Los Angeles Times,* November 11, 1992.

38. *Los Angeles Times,* January 10, 1993, p. M4; January 27, 1993, p. A1.

39. *Los Angeles Times,* November 8, 1992, p. A1.

40. *Los Angeles Times,* January 27, 1993, p. A1.

References

Bowman, Ann. 1984. "Physical Attractiveness and Electability: Looks and Votes." *Women & Politics* 4: 55-65.

Carroll, Susan J. 1984. "Women Candidates and Support for Feminist Concerns: The Closet Feminist Syndrome." *Western Political Quarterly* 37: 307-323.

------. 1985. *Women as Candidates in American Politics.* Bloomington, IN: Indiana University Press.

Conover, Pamela Johnston. 1988. "The Role of Social Groups in Political Thinking." *British Journal of Political Science* 18: 51-76.

Darcy, Robert, Susan Welch, and Janet Clark. 1987. *Women, Elections, and Representation.* White Plains, NY: Longman, Inc.

Fowler, Linda L. and Robert D. McClure. 1989. *Political Ambition: Who Decides to Run for Congress.* New Haven: Yale University Press.

Huddy, Leonie and Nayda Terkildsen. 1993. "Gender Stereotypes and the Perception of Male and Female Candidates." *American Journal of Political Science* 37: 119-147.

------. Forthcoming. "Contrasting Stereotypes of Women and the 'Ideal' Politician at Different Types and Levels of Office." *Political Research Quarterly.*

Jacobson, Gary and Samuel Kernell. 1983. *Strategy and Choice in Congressional Elections.* New Haven: Yale University Press.

Kenski, Henry C. 1988. "The Gender Factor in a Changing Electorate." In Carol M. Mueller, ed. *The Politics of the Gender Gap.* Beverly Hills: Sage.

Lewis-Beck, Michael S. 1988. *Economics and Elections: The Major Western Democracies.* Ann Arbor: University of Michigan Press.

Lodge, Milton, Kathleen M. McGraw, and Patrick Stroh. 1989. "An Impression-Driven Model of Candidate Evaluation." *American Political Science Review* 83: 399-419.

Los Angeles Times. 1992-93. Articles as noted in text.

Miller, Warren E. 1992. "The Puzzle Transformed: Explaining Declining Turnout." *Political Behavior* 14: 1-44.

Morris, Celia. 1992. *Storming the Statehouse: Running for Governor With Ann Richards and Dianne Feinstein.* New York: Charles Scribner's Sons.

New York Times. June 4, 1992, p. A12.

Niemi, Richard and Herbert Weissberg. 1993. "What Determines the Vote?" In Niemi and Weissberg, eds. *Controversies in Voting Behavior,* 3rd ed. Washington, DC: CQ Press.

Pierce, Patrick A. 1989. "Gender Role and Political Culture: The Electoral Connection." *Women & Politics* 9: 21-46.

Rabinowitz, George and Stuart Elaine MacDonald. 1989. "A Directional Theory of Issue Voting." *American Political Science Review* 83: 93-121.

Sapiro, Virginia. 1982. "If U.S. Senator Baker Were A Woman: An Experimental Study of Candidate Images." *Political Psychology* 3: 61-83.

------. Forthcoming. "The Political Uses of Symbolic Women: An Essay in Honor of Murray Edelman." *Political Communication.*

Scobie, Ingrid Winther. 1992. *Center Stage: Helen Gahagan Douglas, A Life.* New York: Oxford University Press.

Shapiro, Robert Y. and Harpreet Majahan. 1986. "Gender Differences in Policy Preferences: A Summary of Trends from the 1960s to the 1980s." *Public Opinion Quarterly* 50: 42-61.

Tolleson Rinehart, Sue and Jeanie R. Stanley. Forthcoming, 1994. *Claytie and the Lady: Ann Richards, Gender, and Politics in Texas.* Austin: University of Texas Press.

Washington Post. October 19, 1992, p. A1.

Welch, Susan and Donley Studlar. 1990. "Multi-Member Districts and the Representation of Women: Evidence from Britain and the United States." *Journal of Politics* 52: 391-412.

3

Patty Murray:
The Mom in Tennis Shoes
Goes to the Senate

Jean R. Schroedel
and Bruce Snyder

Luck is the residue of design.
— Branch Rickey, President and General Manager of the
Brooklyn Dodgers

Luck is what happens when preparation meets opportunity.
— Darrell Royal, Head Football Coach at the University of Texas

While sports aphorisms are often trite and overused, they can sometimes be applied with accuracy beyond the playing field. Certainly, athletic contests and political campaigns are thematically, and metaphorically, related. Most importantly, both are constrained by time, and winning and losing are quantitatively determined (almost always immediately at the conclusion of the competition).

It is especially ironic that witticisms from the sex-segregated pastimes of baseball and football apply so nicely to the circumstances surrounding the election of Patty Murray as Washington State's first female United States senator in November 1992. Undoubtedly, there were elements of luck—in the sense of "being in the right place at the right time"—in her victory. Murray was part of a significant national and even more noteworthy statewide trend in favor of women in the

1992 elections, and she also benefited from the electorate's perception of her as an "outsider" in a year when such an image was a political asset. Yet, at the same time, her success was the product of design and preparation as well. In order to win, Murray had to put herself in a winning position, and it was "political ambition" that led her there. We will examine the factors that contributed to Murray's victory, with special emphasis on the concept of political ambition that has been used to explain why so few women have attained elected office.

Basic Facts About the Campaign

By 1992, one-term incumbent Senator Brock Adams, a liberal Democrat, had been rendered somewhat electorally vulnerable by a 1988 allegation of sexual molestation, for which charges were never filed.[1] Adams' weakness attracted a large and highly qualified field of early Republican challengers, led by five-term U.S. Representative Rod Chandler of Bellevue, King County (Seattle) Executive Tim Hill, and State Senator Leo Thorsness of Renton. Among Democrats, however, only Murray, a one-term state senator from the Seattle suburb of Shoreline, challenged the incumbent of her own party, formally announcing in early December. Only after Adams withdrew from the race in March, following new allegations of sexual harassment, did prominent and experienced Democratic potential candidates emerge.[2] Following a period of intense speculation, both retiring Governor Booth Gardner and former Congressman Mike Lowry decided not to run in what suddenly became an open seat race. Former Congressman Don Bonker, who served in the House of Representatives from 1975 to 1989, had initially declared his candidacy for state lands commissioner but entered the Senate race in early May.

Washington's primary election was held on September 15, much later than most states'. Its open primary format, known colloquially as a "jungle primary," is also unusual, because it puts all candidates, regardless of party, on the same ballot. The state has no party registration, and voters are free to vote for any candidate. The top vote-getters of each qualified party then face off in the November general election. In the crowded field of five major and six minor candidates, Murray was the clear overall winner, with nearly 29 percent of the vote, outdistancing Bonker by more than 10 percent. The Republican victor, Chandler, garnered slightly less than 20 percent, about 3 percent more than his closest GOP rival.

Murray thus began the relatively short general election campaign with a significant edge in popular support over Chandler. On

November 3, she maintained that edge, beating Chandler 55 percent to 45 percent to become the first woman to represent Washington in the United States Senate. At forty-two years of age, she is the third youngest member of the Senate and the youngest of its six women.

The How and Why: A Tale of Political Ambition, Opportunity, and Preparation

Patty Murray's political roots can be traced to her early activities in the Shoreline area, a largely suburban, white, middle-class region characterized by political pros as "swing to Democratic" that comprised most of the State Senate's First District. Her family's own health and welfare was probably the single most important factor in her political development. In the early 1980s, she began a grassroots lobbying campaign to urge the state legislature to do something about pesticides that blew into her yard as her young son played. She became involved in local education issues as well. Shortly thereafter, she served as a member and eventual president of the Shoreline School Board.

In 1988, the First District's incumbent state senator was Republican Bill Kiskaddon, who, according to several state political figures, was a competent political moderate with a record blemished primarily by his relatively frequent absences and missed roll-call votes.[3] It was generally assumed that a prominent Seattle-area trial lawyer would be Kiskaddon's Democratic challenger, but Murray got the jump on him with a relentless door- to-door campaign in December and January. Murray's early campaigning effectively "scared off" the erstwhile frontrunner and all other Democratic challengers, and she developed a reputation for tenacity and hard work. Because Murray was only outpolled by Kiskaddon 53 percent to 47 percent in the primary,[4] the "smart money" poured into her general election campaign, and it turned into one of the most expensive state legislative races that year. The issues in the general election—education, the environment, and her opponent's spotty attendance—were ones that Murray was well-positioned to use to her advantage. By virtue of hard campaigning, she reversed the primary results and defeated the incumbent.

Murray's most memorable experience in the State Senate, which some believe apocryphal but which for her was politically apocalyptic, occurred upon her arrival, when an unnamed legislator dismissed her as "just a mom in tennis shoes." Once there, however, Murray apparently made an impact. The forty-nine member State Senate was, according to insiders, a rather stifling place for Democrats in 1988 — a place where Republicans maintained a numerically slim but politically solid majority. Many senators had been around for a long time, and, because two State House of Representatives districts were "nested" into each State Senate district, the typical road to the Senate was through the House. As a young and female first-termer with only local school board experience, Murray was unusual. One Senate staffer recalled that some of her woman colleagues, as well as some (male) legislative leaders, resented her occasional unwillingness to abide by norms of hierarchy and deference. Her style was informal and hands-on, facilitating a collegial atmosphere with staff and often reminding others that her name was "Patty" and not "Senator." "She didn't act like a freshman," said the staffer.

Her four-year record in Olympia comported with her campaign positions. Above all, Murray was a very hard worker who rarely missed a vote, despite a daily commute of close to 130 miles from her Shoreline home to the state capital. Examination of her voting record reveals that Murray missed eight (six excused absences) out of 888 floor votes on bills in her first year and nine (all excused) out of 511 in her last year (when she was running for the U.S. Senate). Murray concentrated legislatively on the same issues that formed the core of her campaign: education, the environment, housing, and labor. Most of the bills she introduced dealt with these core issues, and her committee assignments exhibited a similar focus: Economic Development and Labor, Education, and Transportation in 1989-1990, and Commerce and Labor, Education, and Ways and Means in 1991-1992.[5]

Notwithstanding the resentment felt toward her by some colleagues, Murray was a star on the rise. Halfway into her term, she was named minority whip, the fourth-ranking position in the Democratic leadership, at least partly because, as one staffer noted, "She was here all the time." Perhaps more noteworthy, however, was Murray's standing in an informal "poll" of thirty-two political insiders — lobbyists, legislators, legislative staff, local officials, and the like — conducted by the *Seattle Times* after the 1989 session. In ratings of the fifty-three State Senate and House members from the Seattle area, Murray ranked fifth overall after only one year in office. Again, her personal style, hard work, and integrity were cited as particular strengths.[6]

Why would a person held in such high regard, new on the job, and clearly eager and diligent, voluntarily depart after only one term? In the broadest sense, there are two plausible explanations, both of which probably contributed to Murray's decision.

First, the Democrats' long-standing status as a minority party in the State Senate was a continuing source of frustration to her. With a Democratic governor and a sizable numerical advantage in the State House of Representatives, the solidarity of the slim Republican majority created, at least in the minds of many Democrats, a disheartening gridlock that stymied most policy initiatives. Much of Murray's own legislative agenda, such as minimum wage reform, assistance for public school teachers, and environmental protection, never even got to the Senate floor. As one who was elected as a grassroots activist and reformer in 1988, Murray felt stymied by the GOP's grip on the institution and its legislative program.

Her tenacity—some would say stubbornness—affected her behavior in the State Senate and contributed to her sense of disappointment. In separate interviews, four people who work in or with the State Senate described Murray as a "pit bull", someone who would seize an issue and not let go. An example frequently mentioned was her open—and ultimately successful—defiance of her party's leadership by continuing to push on the floor for stronger provisions in a family leave bill. However, some of her colleagues opined that, in some of her actions, perseverance became self-righteousness which, especially in her first two years, made her seem "uppity." Some state Democrats also felt her decision to vacate her State Senate seat, thereby hurting the party's ability to achieve majority status, showed her disregard for the "team." Murray said, "I felt I could leave because people like me were beginning to get into the State Senate, but I didn't see anyone like me in the [United States] Senate."[7] Regardless, she was not reluctant to challenge the institution or its leaders.[8]

A second and more personal reason for Murray's decision was her apparently strong political ambition. The concept of political ambition has been discussed by a number of scholars who have tried to explain the seeming incongruity between, on the one hand, the rise of feminism and the electoral "gender gap," and on the other, the continued paucity of women in Congress (Bernstein 1986; Bledsoe and Herring 1990; Burrell 1988; Costantini 1990; Fowler and McClure 1989). Whether defined as a drive for personal advancement (Bernstein 1986, 157) or as "the desire for political power, prestige and profit" (Costantini 1990, 746), political ambition is generally considered a key characteristic of successful politicians, especially among higher elective officeholders. It is the "fire in the belly" that often separates winners from losers.

Because studies have shown no voter bias against women congressional candidates (Darcy and Schramm 1977; Zipp and Plutzer

SCCCC - LIBRARY
4601 Mid Rivers Mall Drive
St. Peters, MO 63376

1985), minimal, if any, sex-based differences in political fundraising (Burrell 1985), and little evidence that parties treat women candidates as sacrificial tokens relegated to hopeless races (Gertzog and Simard 1981), scholars have recently focused on the "political opportunity structure" through which incumbents win elections and men tend to be the incumbents (Burrell 1988; Carroll 1985a).[9] If challenging incumbents is always difficult and usually quixotic, the politically ambitious candidate would generally prefer to run in an open seat race.[10] Such races provide the best opportunity for personal political advancement (i.e., victory).

Bernstein (1986) demonstrates that women candidates for the House have enjoyed increasing success in winning challenger nominations (against incumbents) and decreasing success in gaining open seat nominations, a trend that results in too many hollow victories and too few bona fide ones. Burrell (1988) duplicates those results in her study of the 1984 House elections. This phenomenon may be attributable to the greater ambition of male candidates in open seat races; the less ambitious candidates — disproportionately female — are left to fight it out for spots against sitting incumbents.

The root cause of women's lower political ambition has not been well explored or documented. In fact, some research suggests that women officeholders (as opposed to non-elected elites) are no less ambitious than their male counterparts (Carroll 1985b). Nonetheless, it is clearly a fundamental issue, and several reasons have been offered, including biology (Rossi 1983), gender role socialization (Ruble 1983; Sapiro 1983) and socioeconomic situation (Welch 1978). A panel study of the pursuit of higher office among city council members found that self-described ambitious women are less likely to seek higher office than those without ambition, although such a finding may have been attributable to "sex-based differences in response tendencies" (Bledsoe and Herring 1990, 217-218). In any event, an exposition of the fundamental causes of sex-based differences in ambition, political or otherwise, is beyond our purview. Rather, our task is to place the experience of Patty Murray into the context of political ambition.

Notwithstanding the uncertainty over causality, various indicators have been used to assess the political ambition of particular political actors. Age is among the key indicators. Age has been used as an "indirect measure" of the political ambition of U.S. House members and candidates (Bernstein 1986). Older candidates are less likely to "express ambitions to advance, to seek advancement, or to advance" (Hain 1974, 269).[11] A rational choice model of the ambition of sitting U.S. senators, operationally defined as deciding to run for president, looked at relative costs, liabilities, and propensity to take risks as categories of predictors. Costs were classified as high if a senator was up for reelection; liabilities included being a first-term senator, being too young or too old, being minority or female, and, more subjectively, having suffered a prior political failure; and risk-taking propensities were accorded those who either challenged an incumbent or ran in a state deemed safe for the opposition party the first time they ran for the Senate (Abramson, Aldrich, and Rohde 1987).

Obviously, these factors are not ideal indicators of ambition in seeking a U.S. Senate seat; different institutional, structural and procedural considerations would apply. However, the use of these measures of House and Senate ambition as somewhat crude analogues for the ambition of a particular state senator—Patty Murray—could not have predicted her election to or candidacy for the U.S. Senate. From her perspective in late 1991, her risk was high, because she was up for reelection and sacrificed her State Senate seat. Her liabilities were many, including her status as a first-term state senator, as a woman, and, arguably, as too young. However, she was a risk-taker, having challenged a two-term Republican incumbent in her 1988 State Senate victory. Prospectively, her decision in 1991 to run for the U.S. Senate was not rational, or perhaps it was irrationally ambitious.

The conventional wisdom holds that the impetus for the "Year of the Woman" was the Senate Judiciary Committee's hearings, in October 1991, concerning Anita Hill's allegations against Supreme Court nominee Clarence Thomas. However, in Murray's case, the initial catalyst was her own desire for upward political mobility. Interviews with some of her confidantes indicated that she began thinking about a 1992 run for governor or senator as early as the summer of 1991. In the early fall, around the time of the Thomas hearings, she had meetings and telephone conversations with political allies, seeking advice about which office to seek. Her initial preference, based on interviews, was the governor's seat. When popular two-term Democratic incumbent Booth Gardner, in a decision rumored for months, announced on October 22 that he would not run again, Murray said she was "'at the cliff,' considering a leap into the [governor's] race."[12] Whatever moral outrage Murray initially felt about the treatment of Hill by the Judiciary Committee and the 2 percent female representation in the Senate was either generalized to the entire political system or secondary to her personal political ambition to attain higher office.

Within six weeks of Gardner's announcement, however, Murray formally declared her candidacy for the U.S. Senate, thereby targeting a sitting incumbent of her own party rather than an open seat for an office in which she had expressed strong public and private interest. The decision illustrated Murray's political acumen. Some of her close allies suggested that she was more activist than manager, and that she was better suited for a legislative than executive position. Moreover, private early polls apparently showed that Senator Adams was vulnerable, and preliminary public polls found his support to be no higher than 25 percent.[13] However, the source of Adams' weakness was as important to Murray as its very existence, and it made him a particularly inviting target to a woman on the rise. Public allegations of sexual harassment against Adams dating back to 1988 continued to dog him, personalizing and reinforcing among Washington voters the issue that had received such widespread national attention in the Thomas hearings. Murray, in an interview four months after the election, said the Thomas hearings were critical to her decision to run, and she downplayed the effect of Adams' problems. Nonetheless, even before the March 1 *Seattle Times* exposé that forced Adams to withdraw, his image—right or wrong—as a U.S. Senator who sexually harassed women was tailor-made for a "mom in tennis shoes."

Murray's announcement in early December 1991, of her candidacy for the Senate received little media attention. In fact, her declaration was overshadowed by speculation that more "prominent" Democrats, such as former U.S. Representative Mike Lowry, were considering entering the race.[14] The only extended print attention accorded Murray in the very early days of the campaign was itself a mixed blessing. A December 29 story on Murray, buried on page A14 of the *Seattle Times*, was headlined "A Very Long Shot in a `Woman's Year'" and began: "Common sense and political wisdom say Patty Murray is the longest of long shots in next year's race to unseat U.S. Senator Brock Adams."[15] In this and other early reports, Murray was generally portrayed as a feisty but overmatched candidate who was simply not ready for a Senate race or seat.[16]

Murray was at least partially responsible for the perpetuation of that image. Her early campaign was notable mainly for its self-proclaimed "mom in tennis shoes" theme, an intentional effort to cast herself as the underdog. That the slogan also evoked images of family, the middle class, and womanhood was more than a tangential benefit. Interviews with Murray's staff and with other observers of Washington state politics reveal that the frequency with which she used the slogan declined as the campaign progressed, an observation supported by a review of newspaper articles on the race. However, she continued to stress, albeit more obliquely, the same traits of motherhood, middle class, and political outsider.

Another aspect of the early campaign also benefited Murray. The "will he or won't he?" game of political musical chairs, played primarily by Gardner and Lowry, the state's leading male Democrats, set Murray further apart from the pack. Their ambivalence, played out in public for months, suggested a lack of political ambition (or, at least, courage) and a feeling that political offices are interchangeable. Murray, whose own ambivalence was brief, relatively private and essentially unreported, was comparatively clear and resolute in her political aspirations. She announced and never looked back.

On the other hand, although there is no direct evidence that the ultimate decisions of Lowry and Gardner not to run for the Senate helped Murray, it is difficult to believe otherwise. After two months of active campaigning, Murray stood at 3 percent in a statewide poll on the Senate race. Taken from February 14 to February 16, the Elway Poll showed that Adams led with 25 percent, followed by Lowry with 14 percent, Chandler with 11 percent, and four minor Republicans with less than 4 percent. While such early polls are usually little more than exercises in name identification, the results demonstrated several things. First, as an incumbent with only 25 percent, Adams was in serious trouble. Second, two months of preliminary campaigning had not generated much enthusiasm or support for Murray, who could not break out of the pack of also-rans. Finally, with 37 percent undecided and the traditional volatility of early poll data, all the candidates had ample time and opportunity to build viable support.[17]

Over the next few months, almost every new development in the campaign worked to Murray's advantage. Adams dropped out on March 1, the day the *Seattle Times* published a story in which eight women accused him of sexual misconduct. If one candidate stood to profit from such a gender-based issue, it was Murray. After repeated claims he would enter the race in March, Mike Lowry did announce his candidacy on March 23 — for governor. On April 28, EMILY's List, the national fundraising organization that assists only selected pro-choice, Democratic candidates, announced its endorsement of Murray. It had refused to consider Murray while Adams, an incumbent whose votes and policy positions were, ironically, consistently pro-woman, was still a candidate. Two days later, Gardner announced he was not a candidate for the Senate. Less than an hour after that, Don Bonker, who had previously indicated he was running for state lands commissioner, announced he was running for the Senate seat. As Murray said on May 1, "Certainly the cards have fallen in place."[18]

When the smoke finally cleared in early May, Murray and Bonker were the only two serious Democrats in the race. Bonker's relatively late entry and the prolonged jockeying among the other erstwhile putative candidates manifested the pervasive skepticism with which political insiders viewed Murray. They were not especially reluctant to express their doubts, either. Republican Rod Chandler, reacting to Adams' withdrawal, overlooked Murray when he said his chances were much better against "Lowry or a late entry" than they were against Adams.[19] Adams himself implicitly discounted Murray when he voiced his opinion that Gardner would be a better Senate candidate than Lowry.[20] In words and deeds, both Lowry and Gardner signified their disregard for Murray.[21] Finally, in officially kicking off his campaign on May 6, Bonker said, "I can't stand idly by and watch this seat go to a Republican," not so subtly insinuating that Murray was a loser.[22] Even the press sometimes viewed her as "battling the impression she's the, um, less filling Senate candidate."[23] All the while, Murray was plugging away in a campaign that, for her, began in early December.

While both the primary and general election campaigns generated some discussion over ideology and policy, the candidates devoted much of their energies to the development of personal and symbolic images of themselves and their opponents.[24] Bonker tried to identify with Paul Tsongas, who endorsed his candidacy. In the general election campaign, Chandler tried to paint Murray as a left-liberal. Both portrayed Murray as inexperienced and naive, labels that Murray seemed to embrace.[25] She hammered away at both opponents as typical "blue suits" responsible for the country's problems, reinforcing the themes of gender and change that set her apart. Bonker's acknowledged expertise on trade issues and Chandler's position on the House Ways and Means Committee, normally political assets, seemed to matter little. Chandler, also a former television news anchor, was by most accounts the "winner" in his four debates with Murray. However, the debates were not held in prime time and received limited television coverage. In fact, the most memorable moment was an exchange of non-sequiturs in the first debate, when Chandler inexplicably closed by singing the last two lines from the old Roger Miller song "Dang Me."[26] In response, Murray said simply, "Rod, that's just the kind of attitude that got me into this race." Neither Chandler nor Bonker were able to find an effective way to campaign against Murray. Their frustration was captured in Bonker's comment to a reporter: "I feel like I'm running against a movement, not a person. If it was Pat Murray, it wouldn't be a contest . . . ."[27]

Without doubt, women were largely responsible for Murray's victory. First, and most fundamentally, they apparently voted for her in large numbers. Polls conducted the day before the primary and general elections indicated she had a two to one edge among women over her closest rival in the primary, and women favored her by 48 to 35 percent over Chandler in the pre-general election poll.[28] A general election exit poll showed that women voted for Murray by a 58 to 42 percent margin, while only 51 percent of men voted for her.[29] A "gender gap" of such magnitude is approximately the same as that which has been discovered in recent presidential elections and in the other major 1992 statewide elections in Washington.[30]

Women literally put their money where their votes were, contributing to Murray's campaign in disproportionately high numbers and amounts. Analysis of contributions to Murray, Bonker, and Chandler reveals several important fundraising differences. Official reports filed with the Washington Public Disclosure Commission for calendar year 1992 show that individual contributions accounted for 43 percent of Chandler's receipts, 67 percent of Murray's and 84 percent of Bonker's. Most (61 percent) of Murray's individual contributions came from people who gave less than $200, compared to 34 percent of Bonker's and only 30 percent of Chandler's individual contributions.[31] By law, contributors of $200 or more ("large contributions") must be itemized, and we identified, where possible, the sex of each such contributor.[32] As evaluated by amount and by contribution, differences among the campaigns were striking. In amount, women gave $205,650 (54.2 percent) in large contributions to Murray, while men gave $173,900 (45.8 percent). Comparable totals were: for Chandler, $128,540 (17.9 percent) from women and $585,795 (82.1 percent) from men; and for Bonker, $41,480 (22.4 percent) from women and $143,655 (77.6 percent) from men. The sex breakdown of the number of large contributions yields even more dramatic differences. Of contributions of at least $200 to Murray's campaign, 620 (61.6 percent) came from women and only 387 (38.4 percent) came from men. Chandler got 1,427 (85.5 percent) and Bonker 253 (78.3 percent) of their large contributions from men, and only 242 (14.5 percent) and seventy (21.7 percent), respectively, from women.[33] See Figure 3.1 for a breakdown of large contributions by sex.

Bonker's protestations about a "movement" were not merely sour grapes complaints of a soon-to-be-defeated candidate. Not only were women generally much more willing to open their checkbooks for Murray than for Bonker or Chandler, but much of that money came

FIGURE 3.1   Number of Large Individual Contributions by Sex

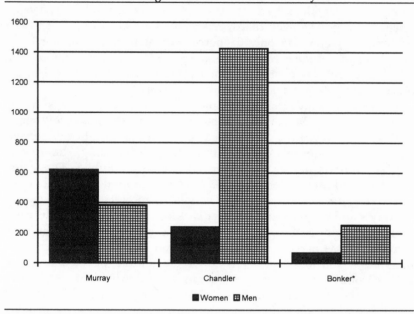

*Contributions lower, in part, because campaign ended with September 15 loss in primary.

from women outside the state. Fully 30 percent of Murray's large contributions (and 28.6 percent of the total amount of such contributions) came from out-of-state women. Only 2.3 percent of Chandler's and 7.7 percent of Bonker's large contributions emanated from the same source. Bonker relied heavily on out-of-state men, who accounted for almost 29 percent of his large contributions. Males from Washington accounted for nearly half of his large contributions and 72 percent of Chandler's, whose out-of-state money came largely in the form of PAC, rather than individual, contributions.[34]   See Figure 3.2 for a depiction of in-state and out-of-state contributions by sex.

It has been calculated that members of EMILY's List accounted for about $230,000, or 23 percent, of total individual contributions to the Murray campaign.[35]   The publicity and notoriety that attended the group's April 28 endorsement, coupled with the support of NOW, the National Women's Political Caucus, and other women's groups, helped make Murray a national candidate. Two months before the hotly contested September primary, Murray received an unusual amount of attention at the Democratic National Convention.[36]   Ellen Malcolm, the president of EMILY's List, reported that the group's

FIGURE 3.2   Percent of Large Individual Contributions by Sex and Origin

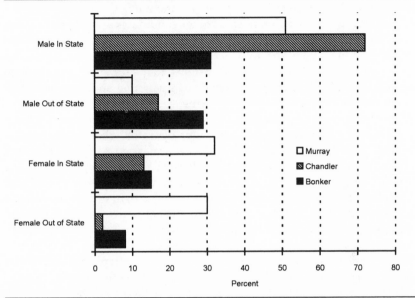

nationwide membership grew from 3,000 before the Thomas-Hill hearings to 24,000 in November 1992, and that those members contributed over $6.1 million to House and Senate candidates across the country.[37] Although Murray received a relatively small portion of that money, EMILY's List and other groups helped mobilize women in support of her and other women candidates.

Ultimately, what seemed to matter was that Washington voters seemed to want change and that they also seemed to view women (and Democrats) as the agents for change. Murray was swept into office on a tidal wave of electoral victories by women and Democrats in the state. Democratic women won races for insurance commissioner, attorney general, and lands commissioner; a woman won the non-partisan race for superintendent of public instruction; Democrats, including two women, won eight of the nine congressional races, and a Republican woman won the other; Lowry won the governor's race; Democratic majorities were restored to both houses of the state legislature; and the percentage of women elected to the state legislature was the largest in the country. Another example of Washington voters' desire for change was H. Ross Perot's 24 percent showing—ninth highest in the country.[38] Exit polls show that most (54 percent) of the Perot vote went to Murray, indicating that "change," however amorphous and ephemeral, was a part of her message that resonated. Murray was certainly not an anomaly.

Yet, Murray was different from other candidates—her opponents as well as her new women colleagues in the Senate, a point she less than artfully made when she told a reporter during the campaign, "I'm different from the Ferraros and Feinsteins, that's for sure. I came from the real world. Barbara Boxer's been campaigning so long, I'm afraid she won't be able to talk when she wins. . . . Those are women whose main function in life is raising money."[39] Murray, her two teenaged children and her husband, a computer operator who worked at the port of Seattle and to whom she has been married for almost twenty years, are a decidedly middle-class family. At the beginning of the 103rd Congress, Murray, at 42, was three years younger than Carol Moseley-Braun and at least ten years younger than any other woman senator. She was also the only woman senator whose children were still living at home.[40] Four months after the election, Murray obliquely acknowledged her political distinctiveness when she stated, "Government ought to be people like me."[41] Perhaps more than any other Senate candidate, Murray symbolized the admixture of change and middle-class themes that captured the mood of the country in 1992.

Conclusion

Patty Murray is an unusual politician. Throughout the eleven months of her Senate campaign, she somehow retained her image as a down-to-earth mother of two who struggled to balance the family checkbook and serve her community. Many people, including seasoned political observers, thought she was too naive, too unsophisticated, or too "slow" to become a U.S. Senator. Even after she raised almost $1.5 million, after she challenged a sitting incumbent of her own party, and after she won two statewide elections against seasoned opponents, a State Senate staffer remarked:

> She never struck me as the type of politician you see down here all the time . . . with burning ambition necessarily — on the surface . . . although it must have been there. That's not your impression when you first meet her. She's very down-to-earth, very hard-working, very dedicated, but I never thought . . . .You see a lot of people down here drooling at the mouth about U.S. Senate seats for years [who] don't quite have the guts to get into a primary. She's kind of rare . . . . Most politicians are thinking about their careers — about the next step.

The paradox is that Murray can act in ways that manifest very strong ambition without seeming ambitious. Seemingly non-political, she succeeded in a highly political environment. Perhaps because gender roles condition society to view women as nurturing care-givers, the image of an ambitious—as opposed to "feisty"—mom in tennis shoes is difficult to assimilate. Murray, and many other female candidates in Washington State and around the country, seemed to benefit from being women without facing the obstacles women normally confront. Was her election an aberration or the beginning of a new era of young, ambitious women politicians?

Notes

Data on campaign contributions for the 1992 Washington Senate race were obtained from the Washington Public Disclosure Commission. All analyses, computations and interpretations of such data are the responsibility of the authors.

Face-to-face interviews were conducted with twelve people in Seattle and Olympia from January 4 through January 8, 1993. They included lobbyists, Republican and Democratic campaign workers, a state legislator, State Senate staff, and Senator Murray's Washington staff. Several additional telephone interviews were conducted in January and February 1993. Senator Murray was interviewed by phone on March 11, 1993.

1. Adams had served in the House from 1965 to 1977, and from 1977 to 1979 as Transportation Secretary in the Carter Administration. His steadfast liberalism was evidenced by his ADA ratings, consistently in the ninetieth percentile; his pro-labor record was illustrated by AFL-CIO and COPE ratings between 77 and 100. Brief biographical sketches can be found in Barone and Ujifusa (1991) and Duncan (1989).

2. The new allegations involved a series of incidents over twenty years, involving eight different women. The *Seattle Times* (March 1) broke the story. A good perspective on both the 1988 allegation and the new accusations can be found in the *Washington Post*, March 22, 1992, p. F1.

3. Information on the 1988 State Senate race, as well as on many aspects of the 1992 U.S. Senate campaign, was obtained from a series of interviews conducted in Washington State with people in government and politics, including legislators and legislative staff, lobbyists, campaign workers and consultants, and officials in both political parties. Except as noted otherwise, the interviewees wish to remain anonymous. Of course, regardless of attribution, interviews will be noted as sources of information wherever applicable.

4. Because Kiskaddon was the only Republican and Murray the only Democrat in the jungle primary, their combined vote was 100 percent of the total vote cast, and they were automatically pitted against each other in the November general election.

5. Information on Murray's State Senate voting, bill sponsorship, and committee membership was obtained from the State Senate in Olympia.

6. The results were published in the *Seattle Times* on January 7, 1990, page A1. Seventeen out of the fifty-three legislators in the study were women, and five were ranked in the top ten overall. Murray was the only state senator, however.

7. Telephone interview with Senator Murray, March 11, 1993.

8. In their use of the term "uppity," Murray's colleagues did not mean elitist. Even supporters acknowledged that she sometimes "bent the framework" through populist appeals that emphasized her youth, her sex, and her non-traditional style.

9. Although the preponderance of this literature has centered on the House of Representatives, both the empirical data and the underlying rationales seem to apply to the Senate as well.

10. Jacobson (1987, 28-29) documents reelection rates for House and Senate incumbents from 1946-1984. While incumbent senators were more vulnerable than their House counterparts, they still enjoyed an advantage, and it reached 90 percent in the 1980s.

11. Regardless of individual attitudinal responses to surveys of political ambition, women generally seem to have behaved less ambitiously than men. Traditional career patterns, family roles and gender socialization have apparently caused women to delay their candidacies "until such an age that their ambition is more constrained than is that of the [younger] men with whom they are competing" (Bernstein 1986, 158).

12. *Seattle Times*, October 23, 1991, p. A1.

13. *Seattle Times*, December 6, 1991, p. D1; February 13, 1992, p. A1.

14. One of the clearest examples of Murray's status as the "unknown candidate" was a December 6, 1991 *Seattle Times* article that speculated about Lowry's possible candidacy. The headline read "Lowry's Looking Like a Candidate—It's All But Declared; He'll Challenge Fellow Democrat for Senate." The text of the article left no doubt that the singular "Democrat" was Adams, who had not yet announced his intention to seek reelection; Murray, less than one week after her formal announcement, was not even mentioned until the third from the last sentence. See *Seattle Times*, December 6, 1991, p. D1.

15. According to several of our sources, the article was written by a reporter whom they described as an early and ardent Murray supporter among the media. Her pro-Murray orientation apparently caused some problems at the *Times*. Interviews indicate that she tried to orchestrate an

editorial board endorsement of Murray in the general election without having the candidate interviewed by the board. Murray's Republican opponent had already met with the board, and when the publisher heard of the phantom endorsement, he demanded that Murray appear as well. Ironically, following that meeting, the relatively liberal *Times* endorsed Chandler.

16. While the media treatment of Murray changed somewhat as the campaign continued (and as she became more successful), it was in many ways consistent with the findings of a recent study. Kahn (1992) conducted an experiment that tested for the effects of media coverage and candidates' gender in hypothetical U.S. Senate races. She found that media coverage of males portrays them as more viable candidates, while females are viewed by readers — regardless of portrayal — as more honest and better able to deal with women's issues.

17. Results of the poll were published in the *Seattle Times*, February 29, 1992, p. A8.

18. Although not directly related to the Washington Senate race, Lynn Yeakel's upset of Lieutenant Governor Mark Singel in Pennsylvania's April 28 Democratic Senate primary, coupled with Carol Moseley-Braun's earlier win over Illinois incumbent Senator Alan Dixon, also had to give hope to Murray.

19. *Seattle Times*, March 2, 1992, p. A1.

20. *Seattle Times*, March 4, 1992, p. D1.

21. The ballyhooed March 23 Lowry-Gardner meeting, following which Lowry reversed field and announced his gubernatorial candidacy, leaving Gardner as the undeclared senatorial frontrunner, is a good example.

22. *Seattle Times*, May 7, 1992, p. E2.

23. *Seattle Times*, August 10, 1992, p. B2.

24. Interest group ratings demonstrate the ideological differences among the three. During the 1980s, Bonker's CCUS (Chamber of Commerce of the United States) ratings varied from 17 to 40, while Chandler's ranged from 71 to 95 (Duncan 1989). The roughly equivalent score for Murray in the State Senate, from the Association of Washington Business, was as low as 0 (*Seattle Times*, October 30, 1992, p. A1).

25. For example, a late campaign commercial for Chandler told voters, "She's just not ready," implying that being a "mom in tennis shoes" is not sufficient experience for the United States Senate.

26. For those who don't remember, the song ends: "Dang me, dang me, they oughta take a rope 'n hang me — hang me from the highest tree. Woman, would ya weep for me?" Although he apologized at the next debate for the "lame attempt at humor," Chandler's gaffe gave Murray confidence, and she improved in the subsequent debates. See the *Seattle Times*, October 15, 1992, p. B1; October 20, 1992, p. C1; October 22, 1992, p. A3.

27. *Seattle Times*, September 3, 1992, p. A1.

28. *Seattle Times*, September 16, 1992, p. A1; November 4, 1992, p. A1.

29. Exit poll data were provided by Voter Research, Inc.

30. See, for example, discussions in Carroll (1987), Miller (1987), and Mueller (1991). Voter Research, Inc. reported the gap was 6 percent for Bill Clinton and 7 percent for Mike Lowry in the 1992 Washington elections, indicating that women voters seemed to favor both male and female Democratic candidates. Men split 50 percent-50 percent in the gubernatorial race, while women favored Lowry 57 percent to 43 percent. In the presidential election, 42 percent of Washington men voted for Clinton, 31 percent for Bush, and 27 percent for Perot; the breakdown for women was 48 percent-31 percent-21 percent.

31. Another indicator of Murray's grass roots support is that only 30 percent of her cash came from political action committees (PACs), compared to slightly over half of Chandler's cash contributions. PAC money tends to be "smart money," with the lion's share usually directed to probable winners — usually incumbents (Magleby and Nelson 1990, 48-51). Approximately 25 percent of the average Senate winner's total contributions came from PACs in 1988; in the previous two Washington Senate races, victors Slade Gorton (1988) and Brock Adams (1986) each received a little more than a third of their money from PACs (Makinson 1990, 15; 176-177; 252-253).

32. Some contributors were identified only by initials, while others had names that were not sex specific. They were excluded from this analysis.

33. It should be noted that these figures represent contributions, not contributors. In other words, we counted each contribution of $200 or more as a separate contribution, whether or not it came from a person who had already given. For example, if Mary Smith gave $250 on July 20 and $250 more on October 20, it equals two female contributions. A curious, but tangential, finding is apparent from these data. For Murray, the average female contribution was $332, while the average male contribution was $449. For the two male candidates, however, the average female contribution was larger than the male contribution (Chandler: $531 female, $411 male; Bonker: $593 female, $568 male). Given national sex-based differences in wealth and income, and women's apparent enthusiasm for Murray, these figures for Chandler and Bonker are somewhat paradoxical.

34. An early analysis of Lynn Yeakel's campaign revealed that "fully 71 percent of her out of state money and nearly two-thirds of her Pennsylvania money [as of July 15] came from women—a figure that may be unprecedented" (Donovan 1992, 3270). Slightly more than 71 percent of Murray's out of state money, but only 42.7 percent of her Washington money, came from women.

35. Because most of EMILY's List donors contributed less than $200, and thus were not "large contributions" that had to be publicly reported, this

information was obtained in a telephone interview with Eugenia Higgins, Murray's campaign treasurer, on April 7, 1993.

36. At a July 13 reception held by the Women's Council of the Democratic Senatorial Campaign Committee and attended by all twelve prospective Democratic women Senate candidates, Senator Howard Metzenbaum proclaimed 1992 the "Year of the Woman." The implicit support of the national party and the national spotlight of the convention gave Murray the kind of credibility that most candidates in her position would not have received. See the *Seattle Times*, July 14, 1992, p. A5.

37. Transcript of November 5, 1992 news conference at the National Press Club, Washington, DC, from NEXIS and the Federal News Service.

38. *Seattle Times*, November 4, 1992, pp. A1, C6, C9; *Congressional Quarterly Weekly Report*, November 7, 1992, 3552.

39. *Seattle Post-Intelligencer*, July 15, 1992, p. 5. According to interviews, these comments elicited an admonishment from Ellen Malcolm and a promise not to repeat them from Murray.

40. When the 103rd Congress was sworn in, Barbara Boxer was 52, Barbara Mikulski was 56, Dianne Feinstein was 59 and Nancy Kassebaum was 60. See *Congressional Quarterly Weekly Report*, January 16, 1993, Supplement to No. 3, 160-168.

41. Murray interview.

References

Abramson, Paul R., John H. Aldrich, and David W. Rohde. 1987. "Progressive Ambition among United States Senators: 1972-1988." *Journal of Politics* 49: 3-35.

Barone, Michael and Grant Ujifusa. 1991. *Almanac of American Politics 1992.* Washington, DC: National Journal.

Bernstein, Robert A. 1986. "Why Are There So Few Women in the House?" *Western Political Quarterly* 39: 155-164.

Bledsoe, Timothy and Mary Herring. 1990. "Victims of Circumstances: Women in Pursuit of Political Office." *American Political Science Review* 84: 213-223.

Burrell, Barbara C. 1985. "Women's and Men's Campaigns for the U.S. House of Representatives, 1972-1982: A Finance Gender   Gap?" *American Politics Quarterly* 13: 251-272.

— — —. 1988. "The Political Opportunity of Women Candidates for the House of Representatives in 1984." *Women & Politics* 8: 51-68.

Carroll, Susan J. 1985a. *Women as Candidates in American Politics.* Bloomington, IN: Indiana University Press.

— — —. 1985b. "Political Elites and Sex Differences in Political Ambition: A Reconsideration." *Journal of Politics* 47: 1231-1243.

— — —. 1987. "Women's Autonomy and the Gender Gap: 1980 and 1982," in Carol Mueller (ed.), *The Politics of the Gender Gap.* Newbury Park, CA: Sage.

Congressional Quarterly Weekly Report. November 7, 1992. 3552.

— — —. January 16, 1993. Supplement to No. 3. 160-168.

Costantini, Edmond. 1990. "Political Women and Political Ambition: Closing the Gender Gap." *American Journal of Political Science* 34: 741-770.

Darcy, R. and Sarah Schramm. 1977. "When Women Run Against Men." *Public Opinion Quarterly* 41: 1-12.

Donovan, Beth. 1992. "Women's Campaigns Fueled Mostly by Women's Checks." *Congressional Quarterly Weekly Report,* October 17: 3269-3273.

Duncan, Phil. 1989. *Politics in America 1990.* Washington, DC: Congressional Quarterly.

Fowler, Linda L. and Robert D. McClure. 1989. *Political Ambition: Who Decides to Run for Congress.* New Haven: Yale University Press.

Gertzog, Irwin and Michele Simard. 1981. "Women and `Hopeless' Congressional Candidacies: Nomination Frequency, 1916-1978." *American Politics Quarterly* 9: 449-466.

Hain, Paul. 1974. "Age, Ambitions and Political Careers: The Middle-Age Crisis." *Western Political Quarterly* 27: 265-274.

Jacobson, Gary. 1987. *The Politics of Congressional Elections.* Boston: Little, Brown.

Kahn, Kim Fridkin. 1992. "Does Being Male Help? An Investigation of the Effects of Candidate Gender and Campaign Coverage on Evaluations of U.S. Senate Candidates." *Journal of Politics* 54: 497-517.

Magleby, David B. and Candice J. n. 1990. *The Money Chase: Congressional Campaign Finance Reform.* Washington, DC: Brookings Institution.

Makinson, Larry. 1990. *Open Secrets: The Encyclopedia of Congressional Money and Politics.* Washington, DC: Congressional Quarterly.

Miller, Arthur. 1987. "Gender and the Vote: 1984," in Carol Mueller (ed.), *The Politics of the Gender Gap.* Newbury Park, CA: Sage.

Mueller, Carol. 1991. "The Gender Gap and Women's Political Influence," in Janet K. Boles (sp. ed.), *American Feminism: New Issues for a Mature Movement,* May 1991, Annals of the American Academy of Political and Social Science. Beverly Hills: Sage.

Rossi, Alice. 1983. "Beyond the Gender Gap: Women's Bid for Political Power." *Social Science Quarterly* 64: 718-734.

Ruble, Thomas L. 1983. "Sex Stereotypes: Issues of Change in the 1970s." *Sex Roles* 9: 397-402.

Sapiro, Virginia. 1983. *The Political Integration of Women* Urbana, IL: University of Illinois Press.

Seattle Post-Intelligencer. July 15, 1992, p. 5.

Seattle Times. 1990-92. Articles as noted in text.

Washington Post. March 22, 1992, p. F1.

Welch, Susan. 1978. "Recruitment of Women to Political Office: A Discriminant Analysis." *Western Political Quarterly* 38: 464-475.

Zipp, John F. and Eric Plutzer. 1985. "Gender Differences in Voting for Female Candidates: Evidence from the 1982 Election." *Public Opinion Quarterly* 49: 179-197.

4

Carol Moseley-Braun:
The Insider as Insurgent

Ted G. Jelen

On October 15, 1991, the United States Senate voted by a fifty-two to forty-eight margin to confirm Clarence Thomas for the United States Supreme Court. Senator Alan Dixon (D-Illinois) announced his intention to vote in favor of Thomas, despite the fact that Thomas's nomination had been tarnished by allegations of sexual harassment by University of Oklahoma Law Professor Anita Hill.[1] In defending his vote, Dixon argued that the American system is based on the presumption of innocence, and that Thomas was therefore entitled to the "benefit of the doubt." [2]

Just over five months later, Senator Dixon's political career came to an abrupt end when he lost a primary election for the Senate nomination to a previously little-known African-American woman. Carol Moseley-Braun, the new Democratic nominee for Illinois's Senate seat, had given up the obscure, but politically consequential post of Cook County recorder of deeds to take on what was regarded as a hopeless challenge to Alan Dixon. In the November election, Moseley-Braun easily defeated Republican Richard Williamson to become the first black woman elected to the United States Senate.

Dixon's carefully calculated, but politically disastrous vote on the Thomas nomination was a proximate cause of Moseley-Braun's spectacular upset election. Without this public, self-inflicted wound, it is entirely likely that Dixon would have been reelected to the Senate rather easily. Dixon's vote was apparently the main consideration in Moseley-Braun's decision to run for the Senate, and without her candidacy, Dixon would likely have defeated the somewhat quixotic primary challenge of Al Hofeld without much difficulty.

Nevertheless, Dixon's political vulnerability, and Moseley-Braun's surprising electoral strength, resulted from a variety of circumstances, strategic calculations, and blunders on the part of a number of people. Even in retrospect, there was nothing inevitable about any aspect of Carol Moseley-Braun's victory.

The Emergence of a Challenger

In order to understand how Carol Moseley-Braun was positioned to take advantage of the somewhat unusual circumstances surrounding her election, it is necessary to analyze the unique configuration of Democratic and racial politics in the city of Chicago. Moseley-Braun's quick emergence as a credible challenger to Alan Dixon can be attributed, in part, to the fact that she held an important position in Chicago politics, and was regarded by insiders as a candidate with enormous potential.

In the beginning, there was the machine: the fabled Democratic organization of Cook County. This once legendary institution was capable of making and unmaking mayors, governors, and U.S. senators, and was frequently regarded as a force in national politics. The structure of the organization was quite simple. Candidates were "slated" or selected for election by the Cook County Democratic Central Committee. Once slated, candidates could count upon a veritable army of precinct and ward committee members working on their behalf. The incentive that these party workers had for their campaign activities was patronage: employment at municipal jobs which were relatively well-paying and often undemanding. Patronage was dispensed by the Office of the Mayor (see Royko 1971; O'Connor 1975; Rakove 1975).

The machine (to use the less euphemistic term) was a formidable force in Illinois politics as long as the Cook County Democrats and the mayor's office were working together. When conflict arose between the two pillars of the machine, organization candidates were typically most vulnerable. The organization reached a high point during the administration of Richard J. Daley (1955-1976), who, throughout his terms as mayor, was simultaneously chairman of the Democratic Central Committee. While this concentration of authority was regarded by many as "dictatorial," it did have the effect of enhancing the electoral power of the machine.

The influence of the machine began to wane after Mayor Daley's death in 1976. Unwilling to submit to the same sort of party discipline in the post-Daley era, Chicago Democrats reached an important power sharing agreement between Aldermen Michael Bilandic and Edward "Fast Eddie" Vrdolyak. The two aldermen had some difficulty working together, and the personal animosity between them resulted in Bilandic's defeat in the 1979 mayoral primary by Jane Byrne. In its first mayoral election since Daley's death, the fabled Chicago Democratic machine failed to deliver.

For the first time since the mayoral election of 1955, the party's slating apparatus was formally severed from the mayor's patronage powers during the Byrne administration. Moreover, a federal court ruling forbade firing municipal employees for purely political reasons. Given the inhospitable climate of city politics during the early 1980s, party chairman Vrdolyak attempted to increase his influence by engineering an upset in the 1982 gubernatorial election in Illinois. Republican Governor James Thompson held a wide lead over former U.S. Senator Adlai Stevenson III. Vrdolyak's means of narrowing Thompson's lead was to organize a massive voter registration drive in the black wards of Chicago. Vrdolyak's attempted coup was nearly successful, as the expected Thompson landslide turned into a very narrow Thompson victory.

The results of Vrdolyak's black voter registration drive were quite ironic. While Vrdolyak failed to unseat Governor Thompson, he managed to set in motion events which led to the defeat of Mayor Byrne in 1983. Byrne ran for reelection in the 1983 mayoral primary against two opponents, Richard M. Daley, the son of the late mayor, and Harold Washington, a respected African-American member of the U.S. Congress, who represented the city's far South Side. In a very divisive race, in which Byrne and Daley ran primarily against each other, Washington won the primary with less than 40 percent of the vote. Washington was assisted by a very high black turnout, made possible by Vrdolyak's successful registration drive of the previous year. After defeating Republican Bernard Epton in the general election, Washington became Chicago's first black mayor.

Harold Washington quickly realized that he was unlikely to replicate the unusual circumstances of his 1983 victory. Taking thought for the morrow, Washington set about forming his own political organization with whatever meager post-machine resources he could muster. In so doing, Washington began recruiting African-

American candidates to run for those municipal offices which retained substantial powers of appointment.

After Washington's reelection in 1987 (in which he easily defeated Vrdolyak), veteran State Representative Carol Moseley-Braun was recruited to run for Cook County recorder of deeds as part of Washington's "Dream Ticket" for the municipal elections of 1988. The post of recorder of deeds, while not normally an office of high visibility, does retain extensive patronage powers. Moseley-Braun, a graduate of the University of Illinois at Chicago and the University of Chicago Law School, had represented the Hyde Park section of Chicago (which contains the University of Chicago) for over a decade.[3]

Moseley-Braun was elected recorder rather easily, but, by the time the 1988 elections occurred, the political situation in Chicago had changed drastically. Mayor Washington had died of a sudden heart attack in late November 1987, and was replaced by Eugene Sawyer. This African-American alderman had been selected interim mayor by the City Council, with a special election to fill Washington's unexpired term scheduled for 1989. In 1989, Richard M. Daley defeated Sawyer in the Democratic primary, and then defeated Alderman Timothy Evans (an Independent African-American) and Edward Vrdolyak, who had by this time turned Republican. In a bid for his own full term in 1991, Daley defeated Evans and Danny K. Davis, a black alderman, in the Democratic primary. He then defeated African-American candidate R. Eugene Pincham of the newly created Harold Washington party (Barone and Ujifusa 1991).

The ascendancy of the younger Daley to the mayor's chair created a genuine tactical difference among African-American candidates in Chicago. While some counseled accommodation within the regular Democratic party, others operated within the Harold Washington party. Flexibility between these two alternatives was difficult because of a peculiarity of Illinois election law. Under Illinois's "sore loser" law, a candidate may not lose a party primary, and then proceed to run as an independent or as the candidate of another party in the general election. Thus, a decision to run in a Democratic primary, or as the candidate of the Washington party had to be made well in advance of a given electoral season.

Carol Moseley-Braun's strategy during this period was to operate within the Democratic party while seeking to maximize black influence within the party. Thus, in the 1991 Democratic mayoral primary, Moseley-Braun endorsed Timothy Evans, but endorsed Daley over Pincham in the general election.[4] During the 1990 general election, Moseley-Braun maintained her regular Democratic credentials by campaigning actively for U.S. Senate candidate Paul

Simon.[5] Moseley-Braun's loyalty to the Democratic party has occasionally generated severe criticism from other black leaders.[6]

Moseley-Braun's stature as a potential African-American candidate grew as the result of Daley's two mayoral victories. In winning the special election of 1989 and a full term in 1991, Daley had defeated virtually every prominent African-American candidate in the city of Chicago. In the wreckage following Daley's defeats of Sawyer, Evans (twice), Davis, and Pincham, only two black politicians in Chicago were mentioned as having the stature to mount a credible campaign for mayor: Water Reclamation District Commissioner Joseph Gardiner and Cook County Recorder of Deeds Carol Moseley-Braun. By virtue of her election to the patronage-rich position of recorder, and because of the two mayoral elections held due to Washington's death, Moseley-Braun had risen to the front rank of black politics in Chicago. Moseley-Braun was widely regarded as a plausible candidate for either mayor of Chicago or for the U.S. House of Representatives.[7] Her surprising decision to run for the U.S. Senate resulted from a unique opportunity created by Senator Alan Dixon.

The Primary Election

Belleville attorney Alan J. Dixon had been among the most successful elective politicians in the history of Illinois. His election to the United States Senate in 1980 — running counter to a Republican landslide at the presidential level — was the fulfillment of a career as a successful candidate which had begun with his election as police magistrate of Belleville in 1949. His decisive reelection in 1986 seemed to confirm Dixon's status as a nearly unbeatable incumbent (Barone and Ujifusa 1991).

Throughout his political career, Alan Dixon had been generally regarded as a conservative Democrat. Indeed, one *Chicago Tribune* poll, conducted in late 1991, showed that Dixon's approval rating was significantly higher among self-identified Republicans than among Democrats.[8] Dixon had generally been a pro-labor, pro-civil rights senator who supported high levels of defense spending. He had taken generally conservative positions on divisive social issues, and, as Illinois's senior senator, was regarded as having been quite effective in bringing federal money home to Illinois (Barone and Ujifusa 1991). Thus, Dixon had carefully cultivated the image of a "sensible" conservative Democrat, with few ties to the party's left wing. However, Dixon had been quite careful to maintain ties to key Democratic constituencies, such as organized labor and African-

Americans. Indeed, some analysts have suggested that Dixon's vote on the Thomas confirmation was calculated to appeal to blacks, who seemed to Dixon to be a more formidable electoral force than feminist women (Overby et al. 1992).[9]

Thus, as the 1992 election season began, Dixon's renomination and reelection seemed quite secure. It was no surprise, then, that the first declared opposition to Dixon's renomination came from a political novice, who was perhaps too inexperienced to "know" that Dixon could not be defeated. Al Hofeld, a multimillionaire personal-injury attorney, entered the Democratic primary against Dixon as the result of the general "anti-incumbency" mood which characterized late 1991 and early 1992. Prior to the 1992 Senate campaign, Hofeld's sole political experience had been to chair the Chicago Board of Ethics, a position to which he had been appointed by Mayor Richard M. Daley.[10] While some analysts regarded Hofeld as running to the political left of Senator Dixon, Hofeld's campaign (financed mostly with several million dollars of his own money) emphasized Dixon's "insider" status, and pointed to a general need for change in Washington.[11] Hofeld did not provide particular examples of malfeasance by Dixon, but made the general charge that Dixon's twelve years in Washington had put him "out of touch" with the voters of Illinois.[12]

Hofeld's declaration took place on November 17, 1991, just over a month after the Senate vote on the Thomas nomination. Hofeld did not mention Dixon's vote, and spokespersons from Hofeld's campaign suggest that Dixon's Thomas vote was not a consideration in Hofeld's decision to enter the primary. On the same day that Hofeld declared, Carol Moseley-Braun announced her intention to formally declare her candidacy for the Senate.[13] Unlike Hofeld, Moseley-Braun explicitly raised the Thomas hearings as a rationale for her candidacy.

The possibility of a female challenger to Dixon had been discussed in the Chicago press since Dixon's vote on the Thomas nomination. Three names had been mentioned most frequently: Cook County Recorder of Deeds Carol Moseley-Braun, former federal judge Susan Getzendamer, and Democratic National Committee member Marjorie Benton.[14] Among this trio of prominent Democratic women, Moseley-Braun had several assets which made her seem most attractive as a candidate. First, she was African-American; a characteristic which could be expected to offset the pro-Thomas support Dixon expected to receive among Illinois blacks. Second, Moseley-Braun was the only prominent Democratic woman in Illinois with recent experience in running for elective office. Third, her office at the recorder of deeds provided the nucleus of a political organization, which the other contenders would have had to construct from scratch. Fourth, her candidacy may have had the tacit approval of Mayor Richard M. Daley, who appeared to regard her challenge to Dixon as hopeless. A loss in the Senate primary would force Moseley-Braun to give up her position as recorder, and would tarnish her as a mayoral candidate in 1995.

The most important consideration, however, was Moseley-Braun's relatively quick decision to join the race after Hofeld had entered. Hofeld's well-financed candidacy may have suggested to Moseley-Braun that the Senate race was perhaps winnable and no less improbable than a mayoral bid in 1995. With the office of mayor in the hands of a potential adversary, Moseley-Braun appears to have regarded herself as somewhat underemployed as recorder of deeds.[15]

The primary campaign itself was quite unmemorable. Hofeld continued his anti-Washington, anti-incumbent message, while Dixon emphasized his long "experience," his "years of public service," and the tangible benefits he had brought to Illinois. Throughout the primary, Moseley-Braun's campaign was all but invisible. With a war chest of just over $200,000 (as opposed to $5 million for Hofeld and a comparable amount for Dixon), Moseley-Braun confined her campaign to Chicago and its suburbs, aside from a few brief trips downstate. Unlike Dixon and Hofeld, who spent lavishly on television advertising, Moseley-Braun was confined to local radio outlets and whatever "free media" her campaign events could generate.[16] It was therefore something of a surprise when polls taken close to the election showed that Moseley-Braun had pulled even with her better-known, better-financed opponents. The surprise was even greater when, on primary election day, Moseley-Braun had polled 38 percent of the Democratic primary vote, compared to 35 percent for Senator Dixon and 27 percent for Hofeld.[17] In a relatively even three-candidate race, a candidate needs just over one-third of the vote to gain a plurality. By barely exceeding that threshold, Carol Moseley-Braun had unseated the previously invincible "Al the Pal" Dixon.

Analysis of the final primary returns suggests that the two most important aspects of Moseley-Braun's primary victory were the mobilization of women who had previously been electorally inactive, and the effects of Hofeld's attacks on Dixon. Predictably, Moseley-Braun received the bulk of her primary vote in the city of Chicago, and received most of her Chicago total from the black areas on the city's South and West Sides. However, she ran surprisingly well in the suburban "collar" counties—Lake, McHenry, DuPage, Kane, and Will—as well. Moreover, turnout in the Democratic primary was quite high in these traditionally Republican areas. While some analysts attributed this showing to a crossover vote among Republican women, analysis of the vote totals demonstrates that the votes cast in the Republican primary did not show a noticeable decline from 1988. Exit poll data suggests that many suburban women who voted for Moseley-Braun had not voted in previous primary elections.

None of this would have mattered had Dixon been able to deliver his traditional base of downstate support. It was in the portions of Illinois outside the Chicago area that the effects of the Hofeld campaign were most strongly felt. While Moseley-Braun ran quite poorly downstate, Hofeld made a sufficiently strong showing to deny Dixon victory. Indeed, for the first time in Dixon's career as a statewide candidate, he failed to receive a majority in the ninety-six-county downstate area.[18]

While the outcome of the Democratic senatorial primary was affected by the unusually large number of candidates, the Republican primary was characterized by a dearth of plausible candidates. Because the incumbent's reelection was regarded as a foregone conclusion by most Republicans, few Republicans wished to challenge Dixon. Republican Governor James Edgar showed no interest in running, and, after a period of public hesitation, Labor Secretary Lynn Martin declined to enter. Having lost a one-sided race for the U.S. Senate to Paul Simon in 1990, Martin had no inclination to risk repeating electoral defeat at the hands of Dixon, who was perceived as an even stronger candidate than Simon.

Faced with a lack of experienced, well-known candidates to run for the Senate, Illinois Republicans formed a search committee to recruit a Senate candidate. The committee approached several potential candidates (including one Democrat) without success.[19] Finally, mere days before the deadline for filing for the Illinois primary, Chicago lawyer Richard Williamson agreed to declare his candidacy.[20]

Richard Williamson had some experience in national politics prior to his 1992 Senate bid. He had served as a White House aide under President Reagan, and had served the Bush administration as the American ambassador to United Nations organizations in Europe. Williamson's credentials in the White House and the State Department were offset by a complete lack of experience in electoral politics and a decided lack of photogenic or telegenic qualities.[21] Moreover, despite having held high appointive offices, Williamson was virtually unknown among Illinois voters. Williamson's apparent deficiencies as a candidate did not seem particularly important, as his candidacy was widely regarded as a sacrificial victim to the inevitable Dixon landslide. With these modest expectations, Richard Williamson won the Republican primary, running unopposed.

The General Election

An important factor in Carol Moseley-Braun's victory in the general election was the failure of prominent Republicans, such as Governor Edgar or Secretary Martin, to enter the senatorial primary. (For a general account of the strategic motives of congressional candidates and contributors, see Jacobson and Kernell 1981). Moseley-Braun's campaign was characterized by many analysts as disorganized, and as unable to settle on a coherent set of themes or issues. Moreover, the beginning of October saw the revelation of a potential financial scandal which dominated coverage of the Senate election for the final month of the campaign.[22] Nevertheless, Richard Williamson was unable to capitalize on these opportunities, and Moseley-Braun won a decisive victory in the general election. For the most part, the contest between Moseley-Braun and Williamson consisted of a series of non-events, or, alternatively, a number of unrealized possibilities.

Moseley-Braun entered the general election campaign with a sizable lead over her Republican challenger: most early polls put Moseley-Braun between thirty and thirty-five points ahead of Williamson. Unlike her primary campaign, Moseley-Braun's effort in the general election was well-financed: as a suddenly-likely winner, with the added novelty of being a black woman, Moseley-Braun was able to attract a large number of out-of-state campaign contributions from feminist and civil rights organizations and their members. Moseley-Braun received a great deal of money from women's political action committees, and also ran an effective direct mail campaign. By contrast, most Republican donors had committed their resources elsewhere, since they expected Dixon to win an easy reelection (see Jacobson and Kernell 1981). When Moseley-Braun emerged as the Democratic nominee, her huge early lead appears to have discouraged potential contributors to the Williamson campaign. With Bill Clinton running well ahead of President Bush in Illinois (which, as a Rust Belt state, had been hit hard by the 1991-1992 economic recession), the state seemed very forbidding territory for Republican candidates in 1992. Unknown and underfinanced, Williamson began a nearly hopeless campaign against Moseley-Braun.

Given his somewhat desperate circumstances, Williamson resorted to an unrelievedly negative campaign. Williamson charged Moseley-Braun with being "just another machine politician," with having made complimentary statements about the positive contributions of the notorious El Rukin street gang, and with having supported former Congressman Gus Savage (an ally of black separatist leader Louis Farrakhan and the object of frequent accusations of sexual and financial improprieties) some years earlier.[23] Aside from attempting to distance himself from President Bush, and arguing for a version of "supply-side" economics, Williamson had little to offer an electorate disillusioned with Republican economic policies.

It is not entirely clear why Williamson's attack strategy did not have a greater effect. Some analysts have argued that, as a woman, Moseley-Braun was less threatening than male black leaders such as Jesse Jackson or Harold Washington.[24] Another possibility is that Williamson's attacks were inconsistent: one can be a "machine politician" in Illinois (a state in which the Democratic organization has traditionally been dominated by whites), or one can be a radical African-American leader. However, many voters may have perceived the difficulty of both charges being simultaneously accurate. Moseley-Braun's careful balancing act between African-American forces and the remains of the Democratic organization made claims that Moseley-Braun supported either former Congressman Savage or street gangs seem quite implausible. Moreover, with President Bush being criticized nationally for his negative campaign against Bill Clinton, Williamson received pointed criticism for his tactics by the Chicago news media.[25] As a virtual unknown, Williamson simply did not appear to have the credibility required to carry a negative campaign against Carol Moseley-Braun.

All of this should not suggest that Moseley-Braun's campaign was in any way above criticism. She was regularly characterized by the news media as having a superficial grasp of important issues,[26] and of "sitting on her lead" by avoiding controversial statements. Moseley-Braun avoided issues such as sexual harassment and feminism, and concentrated her campaign on general economic themes of unemployment, investment, and worker retraining.[27]

On a tactical level, Moseley-Braun's campaign was often described as "disorganized" and "chaotic," with the candidate herself displaying a notorious lack of punctuality about her public appearances.[28] Her campaign manager and boyfriend, Kgosie Matthews, was reputed to have an authoritarian manner, which resulted in many resignations from the staff.[29] Matthews was also accused of sexually harassing several female volunteers during the course of the campaign.[30] Despite these problems, Moseley-Braun maintained a strong (twenty-five to thirty point lead) in most polls between March and September.

Near the beginning of October, the Moseley-Braun campaign was faced with its most serious crisis. Television station WMAQ (Chicago's NBC affiliate) broadcast a story alleging that Moseley-Braun's mother, who was living in a nursing home supported by Medicaid, had received an inheritance disbursement of just under

$30,000 the previous year, and had divided the money equally among her three children. Neither the original disbursement nor the gifts had been reported to either Medicaid authorities or the Internal Revenue Service.[31]

What stands out about the public aspects of this financial "scandal" was its duration. WMAQ first broadcast the story on October 1, but it was not until a few days before the election that Moseley-Braun reached a settlement with Medicaid authorities. For most of the month of October, Moseley-Braun's financial problems dominated news coverage of the Senate campaign. Moseley-Braun did not deal with this issue effectively, as most good candidates are successful in getting negative publicity off the front page as soon as possible.

While Moseley-Braun's Medicaid problem was a public issue, her lead in the polls shrank to roughly ten points, but Williamson was unable to draw any closer. Why was the allegation of financial impropriety not more damaging to Moseley-Braun's candidacy? Two considerations seem most important. First, the WMAQ story came too late in the campaign to do Williamson much good. While Williamson claimed that the allegations were having a salutary effect on his fundraising, most potential contributors had committed their resources elsewhere by October.[32] It seems entirely possible that, had the story emerged earlier in the campaign, the allegations might have affected the outcome. Second, by October, Williamson had established for himself a public image as a negative campaigner. Ironically, Williamson's earlier efforts to portray Moseley-Braun as a machine hack or a black radical seem to have backfired, as his attempts to capitalize on Moseley-Braun's Medicaid problem were seen as "just another attack" by a chronic negative campaigner. Thus, despite what would seem a golden opportunity, Williamson never succeeded in making the race competitive.

On election day, Carol Moseley-Braun received 53 percent of the popular vote, to 43 percent for Richard Williamson. (Most of the remaining 4 percent went to the Libertarian candidate.) Geographically, most of Moseley-Braun's margin came from the city of Chicago, although she also received a solid majority of the vote downstate. Even in the five suburban "collar" counties surrounding Chicago, she made an unusually strong showing for a Democrat, carrying over 40 percent of the vote. She also benefited from an unusually high turnout in Chicago. According to exit polls, Moseley-Braun ran best among her two main constituencies: she received 95 percent of the black vote, and 58 percent of the votes cast by women.[33]

She was able to deliver her geographical and demographic base handsomely, while making substantial inroads into constituencies which rarely support Democratic candidates in statewide races. While, as noted, Moseley-Braun ran impressively ahead of Williamson among women and blacks, she also received 48 percent of the white vote, and 49 percent of the votes cast by men. Moseley-Braun attracted the votes of 58 percent of self-identified Independents, and 18 percent of the votes of Republican identifiers (Williamson received 14 percent of the Democratic vote.)[34] Moseley-Braun ran particularly well among suburban women, and, quite surprisingly, carried the ninety-six-county downstate area. Downstate, Moseley-Braun ran best in university towns such as Champaign, Carbondale, and DeKalb, but also showed impressive strength in traditionally Republican areas. For example, in a six-county area in western Illinois normally carried by the Republicans, Williamson carried each county by an average of just under seventy-five votes.[35]

Thus, the Senate victory of Carol Moseley-Braun was won across geographical and demographic lines. She ran ahead of most Democratic candidates for statewide office among virtually every group of voters. What can account for so impressive a showing by a most improbable candidate? First, to the extent that there exists anything resembling a "coattail effect," Moseley-Braun clearly benefited from the strong race run by Bill Clinton in Illinois and the relative unpopularity of President Bush. The Bush campaign conceded Illinois to Clinton relatively early in the election season. Clinton won Illinois rather handily, and it seems likely that the high Democratic turnout was quite helpful to the Moseley-Braun candidacy. While political scientists continue to debate the effects of national political forces on congressional elections (see Gant and Luttbeg 1991), any effects of the presidential election would have assisted the Moseley-Braun candidacy.

Second, despite the problems which her candidacy later developed, Carol Moseley-Braun exhibited some personal characteristics which may have inoculated her against Williamson's attacks and the Medicaid story. Aside from her sex, Moseley-Braun's careful cultivation of both black and white forces within the Democratic party (while eschewing overt cooperation with the Harold Washington party) seems to have made the charge of radicalism difficult to sustain. Early in the campaign, Moseley-Braun appeared to have made a difficult, but strategically important decision to hold Jesse Jackson at arm's length, and to limit Jackson's overt role in her election effort. Moreover, Moseley-Braun's successful handling of the mundane, but important job of recorder of deeds may have enhanced her reputation for personal responsibility, and may have limited the damage of the Medicaid story. Moseley-Braun's decision to emphasize issues of economic investment, rather than those of race or gender discrimination, perhaps made her candidacy more acceptable to white voters than might have been the case otherwise. Certainly, Moseley-Braun could not have carried the downstate area had she been perceived as the "black candidate," rather than the Democratic candidate who happened to be black. Moreover, Moseley-Braun's personal appearance was pleasant and non-threatening. She dressed fashionably, but conservatively, and was quite careful to plan virtually all of her on-camera appearances. Moseley-Braun's "now-famous, face wide grin" made quite an appealing television image.[36]

Another consideration in explaining the Moseley-Braun victory appears to have been the Williamson candidacy itself. Republican leaders expected to face a strong Dixon bid for reelection, and so were unable to recruit a strong, visible, "high quality" candidate. Williamson was, in effect, asked to serve as token opposition to a certain Dixon victory. Lacking the characteristics of a strong contender for an unexpectedly open Senate seat, Williamson was unable to marshal the resources necessary to exploit the opportunities presented by Moseley-Braun's often amateurish campaign. Moseley-Braun's strong showing among women suggests that issues such as gender discrimination, abortion, and sexual harassment may have been quite salient to female voters in Illinois. Perhaps a pro-choice female Republican candidate, such as Lynn Martin or Loleta Didrickson, might have made a much stronger showing against Moseley-Braun. It seems quite likely that an experienced, visible Republican candidate might well have been able to take advantage of some of Moseley-Braun's electoral liabilities.

Conclusion

Carol Moseley-Braun's election was the result of the juxtaposition of a favorably situated candidate, albeit one with extensive electoral liabilities, meeting a number of extraordinarily favorable circumstances. Moseley-Braun's early calculation of maintaining ties with the Cook County Democratic party, while seeking to increase African-American influence within the party, was certainly a strategic decision of cardinal importance. Her credibility with both black and white factions of the Democratic party enhanced her reputation as a "serious" candidate, and may have served to inoculate her from charges of reverse racism, radicalism, and other divisive aspects of racial politics in Illinois.

Of equal importance is the somewhat inexplicable decision of Al Hofeld to contest Alan Dixon's renomination in the Democratic primary. Hofeld's well-financed attacks on Senator Dixon (which Moseley-Braun herself could never have afforded) served to weaken Dixon's image in precisely the area in which Dixon was strongest: the downstate region of Illinois, where voters are traditionally suspicious of Chicago politics, and of "professionalism" in politics generally. Hofeld's relatively strong candidacy made it possible for Moseley-Braun to be nominated with much less than a majority of the primary vote.

In part, Moseley-Braun owes her general election victory to the relatively low quality of the Williamson campaign. Richard Williamson began his campaign with few personal or financial resources, and was unable to engage in successful fundraising during his campaign. His early decision to run an "attack" campaign against Moseley-Braun had little effect in the early stages of the general election, and may have diminished his credibility when the Medicaid story presented him with a genuine opportunity.

What all this suggests, of course, is that Carol Moseley-Braun may have difficulty gaining reelection to the Senate in 1998. Given the role of circumstance in Moseley-Braun's 1992 election it may be that attractive candidates will seek the Republican senatorial nomination in 1998, and that potential Republican contributors could regard Moseley-Braun as vulnerable. It seems unlikely that Moseley-Braun will be able to replicate the fortuitous circumstances of the 1992 election.

Of course, Moseley-Braun's reelection chances in 1998 will depend crucially on her performance as junior senator from Illinois, and on the public perception of that performance. As this chapter was written, Carol Moseley-Braun had just assumed office, and it is much too early to attempt an assessment of her service. However, some of the post-election publicity that she has received has been quite negative. Dubbed by one reporter as "Our Lady of the Long Siestas,"[37] Moseley-Braun's work habits have come under criticism. Moseley-Braun has also been criticized for appointing ten new members to the staff of the recorder of deeds immediately prior to her resignation from that office.[38]

The importance of these allegations will only be established with the passage of time. Certainly, the Constitution provides incoming senators with a six-year respite from the day-to-day minutiae of campaigning. Nevertheless, the fact that these stories have been so widely circulated so soon after Moseley-Braun's election suggests that the 1998 senatorial campaign may have already begun.

Notes

1. *Chicago*, October 1992, pp. 64-69, 120-127.

2. *Chicago Tribune*, October 18, 1991, sec. 1, p. 1. Dixon was perhaps demonstrating confusion over the minor difference between a criminal trial and a confirmation hearing.

3. *Chicago Tribune*, November 4, 1992, sec. 1, p. 19.

4. *Chicago Tribune*, November 8, 1992, sec. 2, p. 1.

5. *Chicago Tribune*, January 30, 1992, sec. 1, p. 3.

6. *Chicago Tribune*, October 22, 1992, sec. 1, p. 1.

7. *Chicago Tribune*, April 7, 1991, sec. 1, p. 1; November 4, 1992, sec. 1, p. 19.

8. *Chicago Tribune*, November 24, 1991, sec. 1, p. 4.

9. See also *Chicago Tribune*, October 20, 1991, sec. 1, p. 3.

10. *Chicago Tribune*, November 18, 1991, sec. 1, p. 3.

11. *Chicago Tribune Magazine*, December 6, 1992, pp. 14-24.

12. *Chicago Tribune*, March 22, 1992, sec. 1, p. 1.

13. *Chicago Tribune*, November 18, 1991, sec. 1, p. 3.

14. *Chicago Tribune*, October 18, 1991, sec. 1, p. 1; October 20, 1991, sec. 1, p. 3.

15. *Chicago Tribune*, November 4, 1992, sec. 1, p. 19.

16. *Chicago*, October 1992, pp. 64-69, 120-127.

17. *Chicago Tribune Magazine*, December 6, 1992, pp. 14-24.

18. *Chicago Tribune*, March 22, 1992, sec. 1, p. 1; *Chicago*, October 1992, pp. 64-69, 120-127.

19. *Chicago Tribune*, December 4, 1991, sec. 1, p. 1.

20. *Chicago Tribune*, December 17, 1991, sec. 1, p. 5.

21. *Chicago Tribune*, October 22, 1992, sec. 1, p. 1.

22. *Chicago Tribune*, October 22, 1992, sec. 1, p. 1; *Chicago Tribune Magazine*, December 6, 1992, pp. 14-24.

23. Ibid.

24. *Chicago Tribune*, November 8, 1992, sec. 2, p. 1.

25. *Chicago Tribune Magazine*, December 6, 1992, pp. 14-24.

26. *Chicago*, October 1992, pp. 64-69, 120-127; *Chicago Tribune*, December 31, 1992, sec. 1, p. 10.

27. *Chicago*, October 1992, pp. 64-69, 120-127; *Chicago Tribune*, November 8, 1992, sec. 2, p. 1.

28. *Chicago Tribune Magazine*, December 6, 1992, pp. 14-24.

29. *Chicago Tribune*, March 22, 1992, sec. 1, p. 1; *Chicago*, October 1992, pp. 64-69, 120-127.

30. *Chicago Tribune*, December 31, 1992, sec. 1, p. 1.

31. *Chicago Tribune*, October 22, 1992, sec. 1, p. 1.

32.   Robert   Biersack,   Federal   Election   Commission,   personal
communication, 1993.
33. *Chicago Tribune*, November 5, 1992, sec. 1, p. 1; November 8, 1992,
sec. 2, p. 1.
34. *Chicago Tribune*, November 5, 1992, sec. 1, p. 1.
35. *Chicago Tribune*, November 8, 1992, sec. 2, p. 1.
36. *Chicago*, October 1992, pp. 64-69, 120-127.
37. *Chicago Tribune*, January 3, 1993, sec. 5, p. 2.
38. *Chicago Tribune*, December 31, 1992, sec. 1, p. 1; December 31, 1992,
sec. 1, p. 10.

References

Barone, Michael and Grant Ujifusa. 1991. *The Almanac of American Politics
    1992.* Washington, DC: National Journal.
Chicago. October 1992, pp. 64-69, 120-127.
Chicago Tribune. 1991-93. Articles as noted in text.
Chicago Tribune Magazine. December 6, 1992, pp. 14-24.
Gant, Michael M., and Norman R. Luttbeg. 1991. *American Electoral Behavior.*
    Itasca, IL: Peacock.
Jacobson, Gary, and Samuel Kernell. 1981. *Strategy and Choice in Congressional
    Elections.* New Haven: Yale University Press.
O'Connor, Len. 1975. *Clout: Richard J. Daley of Chicago.* Chicago: H. Regnery.
Overby, L. Martin, Beth M. Henschen, Julie Strauss, and Michael H. Walsh.
    1992. "Courting Constituents? An Analysis of the Senate Confirmation
    Vote on Justice Clarence Thomas," *American Political Science Review* 86:
    997-1003.
Rakove, Milton. 1975. *Don't Make No Waves, Don't Back No Losers.*
    Bloomington, IN: Indiana University Press.
Royko, Mike. 1971. *Boss: Richard J. Daley of Chicago.* New York: Dutton.

5

Lynn Yeakel Versus Arlen Specter in Pennsylvania: Why She Lost

Susan B. Hansen

1992 was widely touted in the media as the "Year of the Woman" in American politics. A record number of women (119) ran for Congress; forty-seven were elected to the House and six to the Senate (including the first black woman senator.) The proportion of women in state legislatures rose less dramatically, to over 20 percent. Yet in Pennsylvania, Lynn Yeakel failed to unseat Senator Arlen Specter, a two-term incumbent whose prosecutorial role in the Hill-Thomas hearings led to her candidacy. Why was Yeakel not successful? The answers to this question can tell us a great deal about the advantages of incumbency, Pennsylvania politics, the role of the media, and the reasons why women still have a long way to go to reach more equitable levels of representation in American state and federal legislatures.

Yeakel's loss was hardly unique; Year of the Woman rhetoric aside, most women running for state or national elective office in 1992 *lost*. Huckshorn and Spencer's (1971) study of congressional campaigns was entitled "The Politics of Defeat" because so many challengers lost, and their analysis is still valid for most women congressional candidates. Incumbents indeed have formidable advantages which help them defeat female and male challengers.

Yet Yeakel shares the blame for her defeat. The U.S. Senate seldom welcomes amateurs who have never before sought elective office, who make crucial errors in campaign strategy and tactics, and who fail to cultivate the grassroots.   As the Midwestern traveling salesman concluded in *The Music Man*, "You've got to know the territory." And Pennsylvania remains distinctly unfriendly territory for women.

Pennsylvania: A Tough State for Women

Pennsylvania has historically been inhospitable to female candidates for public office.   In 1992, the state elected its first woman to Congress since 1963 — and the only women elected before that date were widows of congressmen.   In 1992, Pennsylvania ranked forty-third out of fifty in the proportion of women state legislators, and last among non-Southern states.   Although the Commonwealth elected one more woman state legislator in 1992, it actually dropped in rank as other states increased their proportion of women legislators at faster rates (Center for the American Woman and Politics 1993).

Why has Pennsylvania elected so few women?   Previous research has suggested four main explanations.   First, the state's political culture is, in Elazar's conceptualization, "individualistic," stressing politics as a route to advantages for oneself and one's social group. Most officeholders have sought either full-time political careers or a boost to their careers as lawyers, teachers, or lobbyists.   "Moralistic" states, with more emphasis on public service and the public interest, have been more accepting of women's active involvement and of combining politics with other interests (Hill 1981).

Second, the state has long had a strong party system.   Until recently, the party endorsement was considered crucial to primary victories in Pennsylvania, a pattern which holds in few other states. And both the Republican and Democratic parties in the state have tended to use elective office as rewards for (male) party regulars:

> *The dominant political parties do not nominate women for political office if there is any chance of winning.   Political offices are the assets of the political machine.   In general, they are too valuable to be given to women.   They are used to pay political debts or to strengthen the party (Breckinridge 1933, cited in Darcy, Welch, and Clark 1987, 65).*

Newcomers have to buck not only incumbents but party designees if they attempt to run.   Several women recently elected to executive or judicial office (Mayor Sophie Masloff of Pittsburgh, State Treasurer Catherine Baker Knoll, Commonwealth Court Judge Doris Smith) had to run against the party's endorsed candidate in the primary, or (as with Auditor General Barbara Hafer's failed bid for governor in 1990) with little party support in the general election. While Knoll's, Smith's, and Masloff's victories demonstrate that the party's endorsement is worth far less than it used to be, lack of party backing does not help in recruiting or financing strong female candidates. Further, under Pennsylvania law, the losing candidates in a primary are not permitted to run as Independents for the same office, which further augments the importance of parties.

Third is the importance of incumbency. Incumbents can (and do) use the prerogatives of office (patronage, gerrymandering, constituency service, state appropriations) to maintain their seats. Jewell and Breaux (1988) reported that between 1968 and 1986, most (75 to 85 percent) of Pennsylvania's General Assembly incumbents sought reelection. Of those who did, 94 percent of State Senate and 97 percent of State House candidates were successful, by margins averaging 79 and 81 percent respectively. Such rates of incumbency success are among the highest of the fourteen states Jewell and Breaux examined. Against such odds, only a foolish, wealthy, or supremely self-confident challenger would risk running. Deber (1982) thus considers incumbency, not anti-female sentiment, as the major factor explaining why Pennsylvania has sent so few women to Congress and why its state legislature ranks near the bottom (along with Mississippi, Kentucky, and Louisiana) in its proportion of women members.

Pennsylvania has a strong local government tradition; it ranks second only to Illinois in the number of local government units (cities, counties, boroughs.) In many smaller rural or suburban communities, a major locus of citizen involvement has long been the volunteer fire department. This is of course affords an opportunity for public service and civic-mindedness, which should attract women candidates with experience as volunteers. But in Pennsylvania, volunteer fire departments also provide a form of machismo and male bonding that attracts many male veterans of the armed services — and a few firebugs as well.[1] In 1989, the volunteer fire department in Pleasant Hills developed a "Blazes of Glory" girlie calendar, showing sturdy young firemen rescuing fair damsels in distress (and in flimsy lingerie) from the flames. The calendar was a huge financial and media success, and attracted national attention from *People* magazine and the "Donahue" show. Another local volunteer unit made headlines when it fired its ladies' auxiliary.[2] Since local fire halls provide speaking venues and endorsements, women candidates' efforts to build grassroots support may confront obstacles rooted deep in local traditions.

Finally, Pennsylvania has a highly professional state legislature: it is well-paid, meets for most of the year, boasts a large staff, and has a strong committee system. The high pay enjoyed by Pennsylvania state legislators—only New York and California lawmakers are paid more—provides an incentive for politicians to make a career of public service. Proponents of legislative professionalism have argued that it would increase membership diversity and end white-male-lawyer dominance (Bell and Stone 1980). However, as Squire (1992) has recently shown, legislative professionalism is positively related to the proportion of black legislators, but is negatively related to the proportion of women (see also the discussion by Thomas in chapter 8). As the value of public office increases, parties and interest groups seem less willing to accept women in positions of power and expertise.

Political culture, party, incumbency, and legislative professionalism thus combine to produce a relatively small pool of female congressional candidates with skills and electoral experience comparable to male candidates in Pennsylvania. As Darcy, Welch, and Clark (1987) stress, it is these aspects of the political opportunity structure, rather than sexism by voters or male candidates, that limit the number of women running for or winning public office in the Commonwealth.

Nevertheless, in recent years these four elements have shown signs of change. The parties are noticeably weaker at the precinct and county levels, due in part to increasing media and PAC influence and in part to a decline in available state patronage (Margolis and Owen 1984). Party-endorsed candidates in Pittsburgh and elsewhere in the state have lost primaries. Television has increased in importance, and with this, the necessity of raising huge sums of money has emerged; Governor Milton Shapp (1971-1979) and the late Senator H. John Heinz, both millionaires, were two of the wealthy individuals who used their personal fortunes to gain public office in Pennsylvania with little need for traditional party support. And in 1992, incumbency was widely perceived as a handicap rather than an advantage as the term limitation movement gained nationwide attention.

The "eligibility pool" of qualified, experienced women candidates is expanding in Pennsylvania, although more slowly than in states with younger, fast-growing populations and with more women in the labor force. More women are gaining seats on school boards and city councils; even volunteer fire departments are beginning to admit women. But incumbency and the prevailing political culture combined to discourage women from running for state legislative seats or for Congress—until 1992, when anger over the Anita Hill-Clarence Thomas debate catapulted a political amateur into a race for the U.S. Senate.

Backgrounds of the Candidates

Lynn Yeakel came from a political family; her father, Porter Hardy, had served as a Democratic congressman from Virginia for twenty-two years (her father's opposition to the 1964 Civil Rights Act later became an issue Specter tried to use against Yeakel). After college, Yeakel worked in public relations, married, and raised three children. She became an active volunteer and was well-known in the Philadelphia area as the head of Women's Way, a fund-raising umbrella organization that since 1980 had supported a variety of social and advocacy services for women and functioned as a pro-choice alternative to the United Way. Yeakel's success in raising and managing money had won her favorable publicity and numerous civic awards.[3]

It was the Clarence Thomas confirmation hearings that brought Yeakel into politics—specifically, the grilling Anita Hill received from Pennsylvania Republican Arlen Specter. Yeakel's campaign ads showed the all-white-male Senate Judiciary Committee, and asked voters, "Does this make you as mad as it made me?" This anger fueled her campaign.

Like most women (and many men) who decide to run for public office in the state, Yeakel was actively recruited by prominent women in Pennsylvania politics, such as Kathryn Kolbert, a lawyer and director of the Women's Law Project (a Women's Way agency), who argued the *Planned Parenthood v. Casey* case before the U.S. Supreme Court in April 1992. These women wanted *someone* to take on Specter, hoping to scare him a bit and make a point, even if he could not be beaten. Yeakel—an articulate, experienced organizer and fundraiser with ties to a network of corporations and women's groups—was a good prospect. The fact that Yeakel was personally wealthy did not hurt her prospects either, since she was unknown outside Philadelphia and would have to run in her party's primary and against a well-funded incumbent; having money meant that she could focus on campaigning rather than fundraising.

Arlen Specter was born in Russell, Kansas and educated at the University of Oklahoma. As a young prosecutor in Philadelphia he built a reformist reputation pursuing corrupt Teamsters. Specter served on the Warren Commission investigating the assassination of President John F. Kennedy. He then returned to Philadelphia, but his political ambitions were rebuffed by the local Democratic party; he changed his registration to the Republicans *after* winning election as district attorney. Specter subsequently ran (and lost) four elections—for mayor of Philadelphia in 1967, reelection as district attorney in 1973, the Republican nomination for the U.S. Senate in 1976, and the Republican primary for Governor in 1978.

Because Specter had run two statewide campaigns before the 1980 race, his name was well-known, and he won a narrow victory in an open- seat election. He did better against a stronger liberal Democrat, four-term Congressman Bob Edgar, in 1986. Specter himself said he had learned from his many losses, "I don't discourage at all.... I learned character, I learned tenacity, I learned steadfastness" (quoted in Fenno 1991, 2). Despite less than enthusiastic support from his own (more conservative) party leaders, he became a dedicated campaigner devoted to cultivating the grassroots and developing local contacts in each of Pennsylvania's sixty-seven counties.

In the Senate, Specter served on the Appropriations, Veterans' Affairs, and Select Intelligence Committees, as well as the Judiciary Committee whose review of Supreme Court nominees catapulted him into national view.[4] Drawing on his strong Jewish faith, Specter became a staunch supporter of Israel, a spokesman for religious liberty, and the leader of an interfaith Bible-study group meeting weekly in his Senate office. Specter maintained a markedly liberal voting record for a Republican. He voted against the confirmation of Judge Robert Bork to the U.S. Supreme Court, and in 1992, his presidential support score was the lowest of all Republican senators.[5] Specter took such pains to distance himself from George Bush that at one point during the 1992 campaign he was observed running from the room so as not to be photographed with the President.[6] But his Appropriations and Veterans' Affairs Committee assignments placed him in an ideal position to generate federal funds for Pennsylvania: a new jail for Pittsburgh, keeping the Philadelphia Navy Yard open, and bedside phones for veterans' hospitals in the state. Critics called this pork, but others (including Specter) called it the "vitally important and responsible allocation of public funds."[7]

The Primary

Pennsylvania, despite a Democratic edge in voter registration, had not elected a Democrat to the U.S. Senate between 1958 (Joseph Clark) and Harris Wofford's upset victory over Richard Thornburgh in 1991. The state Democratic party has a long history of bruising party primary battles for the Senate, and 1992 was no exception; Yeakel had to face four other contenders, including one (Lieutenant Governor Mark Singel) formally endorsed by the party, before she could confront Arlen Specter. The other candidates were Allegheny County

District Attorney Bob Colville, Philip F. Valenti (a follower of Lyndon H. Larouche Jr.), and Philadelphia family therapist Frederica Mann Friedman.

Singel had run twice previously for statewide office. When Yeakel formally announced her candidacy in December 1992, Singel had already amassed a war chest and collected many significant endorsements. Also, Yeakel faced a challenge in western Pennsylvania, where she was almost completely unknown, from popular Allegheny County District Attorney Bob Colville.[8] But the other primary candidates had their problems as well. Colville had difficulty raising money, had almost no television advertising, and ultimately did not do well even in western Pennsylvania. Singel failed to receive support from his boss, Governor Robert Casey, and faced a lack of name recognition despite his long public career; he was also short of money and had to mortgage his own home in Johnstown to raise funds. Friedman and Valenti had minimal backing, but still had the potential to siphon away votes in a five-person race. Yeakel even initiated a lawsuit to try to keep Friedman off the ballot because of too few signatures on her qualifying petition, which prompted criticism from Singel about Yeakel's lack of support for other women.

Yeakel had several advantages. First, while she was well-known in the state's most populous area (Philadelphia), voters knew little about her positions on most issues, which helped her to focus on the Anita Hill issue. Second, her years of non-profit, social service work gave her a squeaky-clean image, an asset in a year in which the state's usual assortment of political scandals had received the usual overdose of media attention. And third, she was personally wealthy. Wealth does not guarantee success in Pennsylvania politics; the failed Democratic candidate for attorney general in 1992 spent $2.7 million of his family's money.[9] But money helps, particularly with television advertising; candidates who spend less time fundraising have more time to campaign. Yeakel spent $500,000 of her own funds during the primary, and received early support from EMILY's List.

Yeakel's primary ads, prepared by experienced media consultant Neil Oxman, articulated two simple themes: Yeakel's Women's Way experience and the Hill-Thomas hearings. As it did in other states, the replay of the all-white-male Senate Judiciary Committee grilling Anita Hill made many people (especially women) angry at Specter, and implicitly called on voters to reject career politicians.[10] Yeakel also played the typical candidate role, visiting steel plants, ethnic markets, African-American churches, and women's groups, and criticizing Singel for remodeling his office at state expense. But Yeakel's focus on Specter's prosecutorial tactics, even in the Democratic primary, helped her considerably; she became widely perceived as the Democrat most likely to provide a viable challenge to the two-term Republican incumbent. She also benefited by association with Senator Harris Wofford, whose surprise victory in 1991 focused national attention on the health care issue and made even well-known incumbent Republicans appear vulnerable.

In 1986, Specter's formidable fundraising advantage had staved off any primary challenges (Fenno 1992, 151-152). But in 1992, Specter had his hands full with a primary challenge from State Representative Stephen Freind. Freind was the author of the state's Abortion Control Act (upheld by the Supreme Court in *Casey*). A devout Roman Catholic, he had focused on the abortion issue throughout his sixteen years in the state legislature. This did not endear him to his colleagues, many of whom resented his grandstanding and efforts to attach anti-abortion riders to other legislation. But Freind had name recognition[11] and a network of grassroots supporters grounded in the religious right and Pennsylvania's strong anti-abortion movement.[12] He also waged an aggressive campaign, castigating Specter for his pro-choice stance and liberal voting record. Freind criticized Specter's role in the Kennedy assassination investigation and accused him of links to the mob (Specter and his wife had on one occasion been observed dancing at a nightclub owned by an alleged mobster.)

Specter felt he could not ignore such a threat. Party-endorsed Republican gubernatorial candidate Barbara Hafer barely survived a primary challenge from a political unknown, anti-abortion activist and Johnstown housewife Peg Luksik, in 1990. The religious right has been particularly effective in low-turnout elections such as party primaries, and has won many school board and county commissioner elections in central Pennsylvania. Specter cautioned his supporters that the religious right would turn out in force, no matter what the weather, and Freind stated publicly that his chances would be better in a low-turnout election because of his "army" of grassroots supporters.

Freind was never able to raise much money, and his staffers even said they hoped to defeat Specter on the basis of Yeakel's ads, since he could not afford his own. And his remarks at a March public debate about "accepting Jesus Christ as my Lord and Savior" and calling Specter the "Senator from Israel" were interpreted critically by the media as anti-Semitic and the cause of further decline in Freind's support.[13]

As of early April, polls showed Yeakel with only 6 percent of the vote, but moving up fast, to 26 percent by April 20-22.[14] She was undoubtedly helped by the widespread free coverage she received in the national media, which placed her in the company of Dianne

Feinstein, Barbara Boxer, and Carol Moseley-Braun as a Year of the Woman phenomenon. In the April 28 primary, Yeakel received 44 percent of the Democratic vote and carried thirty counties, including Allegheny and Philadelphia. She was preferred among women by 50 to 30 percent over her nearest rival. Although Yeakel led among male voters also (38 percent to 35 percent for Singel), it was women voters who contributed most to her decisive victory.

Specter did well too, defeating Freind by a decisive two to one margin. But his triumph was all but buried in the hyperbolic media reaction to Yeakel's plurality win. "Little short of a political revolution is taking place. Women voters have flocked to her campaign in record numbers," said pollster G. Terry Madonna the day after the primary.[15] Reporter Thomas Turcol wrote that "the men who dominated the state's Democratic party didn't know what hit them."[16] A Montgomery County Democratic chair said that "Given a choice between insider and outsider, male and female, Arlen Specter should be one nervous fellow."[17]

Specter was widely perceived as vulnerable and without a strategy.[18] He could not attack Yeakel without reminding voters of his attack on Anita Hill, but neither could he afford to ignore her. President Bush's declining popularity and the weak economy also boded ill for Republican incumbents. Nevertheless, Specter was a skilled campaigner, with a huge war chest, and a reputation as the hardest working pol in Pennsylvania;[19] he could not be counted out. Yeakel had a hard road ahead.

The Campaign

Yeakel began the general election campaign with favorable media coverage and high expectations. She was female and an outsider in the Year of the Woman and of anti-incumbent sentiment. Further, a statewide poll as of July 7 found that voters favored her on the issues which were most prominent in the campaign: unemployment, health care, corruption, and the need for a change. Early polls showed Yeakel with a strong lead. But in the next few months, this lead declined steadily (see Table 5.1). What went wrong?

Yeakel's Problems

Yeakel's first problem was that she fielded no television advertising until after Labor Day. Although this is the traditional beginning for

TABLE 5.1 Trends in Support for Yeakel and Specter Pennsylvania Senatorial
Campaign, 1992

	June 28-30	Oct. 3-6	Oct. 24-27
Percent for Yeakel	39	43	36
Percent for Specter	37	41	40
Percent undecided	20	20	23
Yeakel (male-female %)	37-50	36-43	34-39
Specter (male-female %)	45-28	48-36	44-37
Undecided (male-female %)	18-22	16-21	22-24
Yeakel (Black-white %)	49-43	56-39	36-37
Specter (Black-white %)	24-38	16-42	35-41
Yeakel			
Protestant	48	42	36
Catholic	42	34	32
Jewish	41	52	45
Specter			
Protestant	37	40	40
Catholic	37	46	47
Jewish	28	33	34
N	624	688	897

Source: Statewide telephone surveys of likely voters, conducted by Millersville State
University/Penn State Harrisburg, G. Terry Madonna and Berwood A. Yost, directors.

Democratic campaigns, the delay was dictated in part by lack of
funds; Yeakel used most of the summer fundraising to match Specter's
war chest. Specter broke with tradition with a well-crafted summer
television campaign designed to tout his own accomplishments and
services to various Pennsylvania interests; many of these ads featured
women describing how Specter had helped them through some
difficulty. His speeches derided Yeakel as a "one-issue" candidate
(i.e., the Anita Hill issue). Yeakel in fact had detailed position papers
on a variety of issues, and stressed job creation and health care reform
in her speeches and interviews. But without television advertising,
her messages reached only the Democratic faithful until late in the
campaign.

Yeakel's second and third mistakes were made in the glare of
publicity: poor performances in public debates. The first forum was a
"Citizens' Jury" sponsored by the League of Women Voters in
Philadelphia, where Yeakel and Specter debated health care, the
economy, and other issues. The citizen jurors gave Yeakel a 5.5 rating
out of a possible 10, to Specter's 7.4,[20] and his own advertising and
media coverage highlighted the differences. The jurors also found
fault with Yeakel's ads. Yeakel came on much stronger in a second

televised debate, handling herself well and attacking Specter as "Senator Flip-Flop" for changing his votes on key issues. But within two days her staff had to issue a retraction; Specter had in fact voted consistently on the education issue in question.[21] From then on, Yeakel was in serious trouble, and Specter supporters derisively waved windshield wipers at her campaign rallies.

Yeakel's fourth problem was that she was unable to maintain her "gender gap" advantage. As many observers have noted, women do not constitute a solid voting bloc; they are divided by party, race, religion, ideology, and many other concerns. Appeals on the basis of gender alone are not enough, especially if your opponent has a good voting record on women's issues. Whenever he was pressed on the Anita Hill issue, Specter stressed his support for family and medical leave, breast cancer research, and abortion rights.[22] In the Pennsylvania race, many women remained undecided until late in the campaign, and Yeakel's gender gap was smaller in November than it had been in July (see Table 5.1).

Specter was able to exploit these divisions by convincing several women's groups (e.g., Business and Professional Women and the American Nurses Association) to support him because of his seniority, his proven political skills, and his voting record on behalf of women's concerns. The choice between Yeakel and Specter was a particularly painful one for many politically active women in the pro-choice camp, who valued Specter's solid pro-choice voting record and were unwilling to punish one of their few Republican supporters in the Senate.[23] After some bloody battles among board members, NARAL-PA and Planned Parenthood remained officially neutral in the race. Yeakel may have gained a few votes from frustrated pro-life voters, who preferred her to Specter because they thought she would be easier to defeat in the future.

Finally, Yeakel was hurt by the increasingly negative media coverage she received. Early on, she was a novelty, with no voting record to defend and a squeaky-clean image. The national media linked her favorably with other female senatorial candidates, but did little investigative reporting on Pennsylvania concerns. After her strong primary showing, state newspapers began to take a closer look (by many reports, at the instigation of the Specter campaign.) Her payment of $17,000 in overdue taxes the day before she announced her candidacy in February was not covered by the press before the primary,[24] but received plenty of attention later in the campaign.

Specter's Strategy

What did Specter do right? For one thing, he spent money early in the campaign. Although Specter's primary election was not close, by the end of June, he had outspent Yeakel by $2.6 million. Specter's early cash reserves allowed him to come out early with television ads highlighting his own accomplishments and his ties with many state interests. Since he started with a huge war chest, he was able to spend less time and effort on fundraising. Yeakel outspent Specter later in the campaign, but by then she was on the defensive against Specter's charges.

Second, Specter pulled off a major coup by enlisting the support of Teresa Heinz, widow of the late and well-regarded Senator H. John Heinz and a respected philanthropist in her own right. In a paid political announcement, Teresa Heinz started by admitting that she disagreed with Specter on the Anita Hill incident. She then stressed his other accomplishments for women and African-Americans, the virtues of his senatorial seniority, and his good working relationship with his fellow Republican colleague John Heinz. Her straightforward and balanced support was highly effective—particularly since the ad was played and replayed ad nauseam on radio and television throughout the state. According to several campaign activists who spoke with me, this was by far the most damaging ad directed against Yeakel.

Third, Specter targeted several traditionally Democratic constituencies: Jews, African-Americans, and labor. Even though he did not carry a majority of any of these groups of voters, he made serious inroads into their support for Yeakel, who received many fewer votes from these groups than did Bill Clinton.

With black voters, Specter stressed the jobs and federal monies he had been able to bring to the state, and he criticized Yeakel for a primary faux pas (she had inadvertently backed two black candidates running against each other in the primary.) His support among blacks thus increased between July and November (see Table 5.1), and he received endorsements from the AME Zion churches in Philadelphia, the major black newspapers in Philadelphia and Pittsburgh, and several Democratic black elected officials.

Specter also received the endorsement of several unions, including the United Mine Workers and the Building Trades Council, based on his record of pro-labor votes and job creation efforts. Some labor unions (United Auto Workers, United Steelworkers) did support Yeakel, but not without grumbling from their locals, and the state's

TABLE 5.2 Percentage Support Among Key Voting Groups Exit Polls, Pennsylvania, 1992 (N=1,606) (in percent)

	Clinton	*Yeakel*	*Specter*
Democrats	76	68	32
Independents	39	51	49
Republicans	15	25	75
Whites	43	47	53
Blacks	84	70	30
Men	43	44	57
Women	48	54	48
Less than High School	53	46	54
Income > $75,000	36	42	58
Union households	56	56	44
Unemployed	65	67	33
Retired	51	42	58
Working Women	48	56	44
Homemaker	42	43	57
Abortion should be legal	55	58	43
Abortion should be illegal	30	31	69
Oppose Thomas confirmation	62	67	33
Important to have woman in Senate	65	76	24

Source: Voter Research and Surveys.

AFL-CIO remained officially neutral. The intensity of grassroots effortsmade by labor on behalf of Harris Wofford in 1991 was not in evidence in 1992, especially in Allegheny and Philadelphia counties. Yeakel initially led among Jewish voters. Her campaign literature stressed her strong pro-Israel position; she insisted that it was one issue on which she and Specter did not differ. But Specter's campaign gave considerable publicity to the fact that the pastor at Yeakel's Presbyterian church had been supportive of pro-Arab groups, and that her church had sponsored discussions of the Palestinian viewpoint on the Middle East. Yeakel insisted that she had not taken part in these discussions, and did not endorse them. For whatever reason, Yeakel's support among Jewish voters fluctuated, while Specter's increased, as did the number of "undecided" Jewish voters (see Table 5.1).

Fourth, Specter did well among men, with a thirteen-point lead over Yeakel (see Table 5.2). Two predominantly male groups are very influential in Pennsylvania politics: veterans and the National Rifle Association. Specter had cultivated veterans' groups for years from his position on the Veterans' Affairs Committee. And although Yeakel criticized Specter for his consistent opposition to any form of gun control, that is not a winning position in rural Pennsylvania, with its many hunters and National Rifle Association members.

Finally, Specter played his incumbency advantages to the hilt. He dispensed federal checks when he visited counties and boroughs, "taking care of what he termed 'Senate business'."[25] Yeakel cited *Congressional Record* evidence that Specter had sent over 40 million pieces of unsolicited, franked mail (worth about $5 million) since 1985. He stressed his experience, seniority, and expertise on issues such as health care. He could (and did) tell reporters and audiences just how many visits he had made to each of Pennsylvania's sixty-seven counties, and what he had done for them in Washington. Specter can recite the whole list of counties by memory, and he revisited each of them (even the Democratic strongholds) on a whirlwind bus tour during the last two weeks of the campaign. Yeakel, by contrast, visited many rural counties for the first time during this campaign, and even mispronounced the name of Juniata County at an address there.

Specter made some mistakes too, such as being in arrears on his electric bill and faxing campaign materials from his Senate office. But his experienced campaign staff, led by highly regarded consultant David Garth, was usually able to recover and issue the appropriate apology or rejoinder. Yeakel's mistakes were more serious, and more difficult to remedy, especially by her less experienced staff. She was criticized throughout the campaign for not paying her city payroll tax until the day before she declared, for doing poorly in the televised debate, for her husband's membership in an all-white country club,[26] for trying to remove Frederica Mann Friedman from the primary ballot, and for her church's discussion of Palestinian perspectives. Any of these in isolation might not have hurt; together, Specter's press staff and ad campaign used these missteps to mold an image of inexperience, poor judgment, and sloppy staff work. The result was a steady decline in Yeakel's standing in the polls, and a difficulty in focusing the campaign agenda on her own policy priorities.

Yeakel, of course, had advantages as well. She spoke to genuinely enthusiastic audiences (especially of women's groups), and was able to use the Hill-Thomas issue effectively to hold public and media attention. She got a boost from Anita Hill herself, who criticized Specter on NBC's "Today" show on October 6, "He is seeking reelection and I am skeptical. I am not convinced that, given the vigor with which he undertook his role during those hearings, that he has truly had a raised awareness of the issue."[27] But when Yeakel returned to the Anita Hill issue, when she was trailing, it only reinforced Specter's picture of her as a one-issue candidate. It is ironic that, although national polls found that Anita Hill's version of events became steadily more credible to respondents between the 1991 hearings and the 1992 election, this shift in public sentiment did not appear to help Yeakel in Pennsylvania.

The poor economy was a major issue in the state, and unemployment increased throughout the campaign. Yeakel criticized both Specter and Bush for failing to create or retain jobs. Yeakel also received the endorsement of several major state newspapers, including the *Philadelphia Inquirer*, *Philadelphia Daily News*, *Pittsburgh Press*, and *Harrisburg Patriot*, as well as national media attention. Clinton and Gore campaigned hard for her (and she for them), as did Harris Wofford, Senator Edward Kennedy, and Democratic National Committee chairman Ronald Brown. Gloria Steinem, Texas Governor Ann Richards, and Maryland Senator Barbara Mikulski also spoke on her behalf. Governor Bob Casey endorsed her, although he was publicly critical of her pro-choice stance.

Despite official party support, there were some troubling Democratic endorsements of Specter. Former State Democratic chairman Larry Yatch criticized Yeakel for implying "Here, I've got breasts, vote for me" (a backhanded endorsement Arlen Specter was moved to repudiate, although he welcomed and publicized Yatch's support.) It is unprecedented in highly partisan Pennsylvania for a state party chair to endorse the opposition's candidate, but the state Democrats have a very poor record of endorsement of female candidates. There was also lingering animosity within the party over the contentious Democratic primary.

Results

Early returns on election night gave Yeakel a slim lead, but Specter eventually triumphed, by 49.3 to 46.7 percent, with anti-abortion Libertarian John Perry at 4 percent. Yeakel made a strong showing for a newcomer facing an incumbent, giving Specter his closest race since 1980, but he still won a convincing victory. He carried fifty-one of Pennsylvania's sixty-seven counties. He did particularly well in the usual Democratic strongholds of Philadelphia and Allegheny Counties, even winning the latter by 15,000 votes despite a five to two edge in Democratic registrations. Yeakel carried suburban Philadelphia, Erie County, and a few counties in central and western Pennsylvania.

Bill Clinton carried Pennsylvania for the Democrats, winning with 46 percent to George Bush's 36 percent and 18 percent for H. Ross Perot. Although Clinton and Gore had campaigned hard for Yeakel, their coattails were not in evidence in a state known for split-ticket votes; Clinton led Yeakel in thirty-three counties, but trailed her in thirty-four. Clinton's largest margins over Yeakel were in Allegheny and Philadelphia counties. This suggests the importance of organized labor, which worked hard for Clinton in those urban areas but did little for Yeakel.

Exit poll results show that the sources of Yeakel's support were very similar to Clinton's. Nevertheless, although Yeakel outpolled Clinton in total votes, she lost; 25 percent of Clinton supporters backed Specter, while fewer Bush supporters backed Yeakel. Table 5.2 shows some of the differences in support for Clinton, Specter, and Yeakel among key electoral groups. The data suggest that Specter was able to siphon away potential Democratic votes from among blacks, retired people, and persons with a high school education or less.

On the other hand, Yeakel did benefit from a gender gap, and if the electorate had been composed entirely of women, she would have won the election. Her gender gap was twice that of Clinton. She attracted many more votes from Republicans (presumably women) than did Clinton, and also did well for a Democrat among the wealthy. Yeakel did better than either Clinton or Specter among Independents (in fact, 40 percent of her supporters backed Perot.) She received strong support from working women and the unemployed, while homemakers went for Specter. Her best numbers came from those who thought Clarence Thomas should not have been confirmed, those who favored more women in the Senate, and those who thought abortion should always be legal. Ironically, Specter, despite his solid pro-choice record, received more support from Pennsylvanians who thought abortion should mostly or always be illegal. But only 12 percent of those polled considered abortion one of the two most important issues in the campaign, and those who thought so tended to support Specter.

While Yeakel did lose votes among some traditionally Democratic groups, she did well (better than either Clinton or Specter) among liberals, Independents, and supporters of abortion rights. But support from these groups was not sufficient to overcome the advantages of incumbency and Specter's years of cultivating the grassroots. Yeakel would have had to run a near-flawless campaign to succeed against an incumbent in a state whose traditions and institutions have not been favorable to women.

Many Yeakel supporters pointed to another reason for Yeakel's defeat: the lengthy Teamsters' strike which shut down Pittsburgh's two city dailies throughout the campaign. Certainly Yeakel did very badly in Allegheny County; since she was not known in western Pennsylvania, the lack of news coverage could have hurt her more than it did Specter, and made her more vulnerable to his negative advertising. But she would have lost the race even if she had carried Allegheny County by the same margin as Clinton. And Mondak's (1993) research suggests that in the Senate campaign, voters were neither less attentive nor less informed due to the strike (unlike House campaigns, for which national media and television did not provide alternative coverage.) Whether her poor showing in the Pittsburgh area was entirely due to the newspaper strike, or to a lack of Jewish or union support, or to a poorly managed local campaign, cannot be determined from the exit poll data. Some of her campaign workers even argued that the lack of newspaper coverage in fact helped Yeakel, by not publicizing her errors and staff problems.

The *Philadelphia Inquirer* reporter who had followed Yeakel's entire campaign concluded that "she could have had it.... A campaign with fewer errors by the candidate—and a better, more honed message—would have sent Republican Specter into retirement."[28] More party support, and an earlier airing of Yeakel's most effective anti-incumbency ad, could have made the difference, since she only needed a few hundred votes more in each of the Commonwealth's sixty-seven counties. A woman with a political base and legislative experience probably would have won—but none of the women in such positions in Pennsylvania were willing to challenge an incumbent senator.

One unanswered question from this election concerns the role of the third candidate, John Perry. His 4 percent of the vote was larger than the difference between Specter and Yeakel. We lack exit poll information to tell us who voted for him, and why. Perry was repudiated by the state's Libertarian party because his pro-life stance was considered contrary to their philosophy of individual liberty, yet he did far better than other Libertarian candidates. He may have attracted some pro-life voters who were not happy with either major party candidate's pro-choice position.

Conclusion

The special circumstances of the Hill-Thomas hearings catapulted a relatively unknown feminist and community activist into a very close Senate election campaign against a powerful incumbent with a good record on women's issues. Lynn Yeakel had less political experience than the other three people who beat senatorial incumbents in the general election, but she still came very close. In the end, the advantages of incumbency triumphed in Pennsylvania as in other states. No female challenger defeated an elected male senatorial incumbent in the general elections of 1992;[29] no one without previous political experience was elected to the Senate even in a year of term limits and anti-incumbency sentiment.

Specter had spent years building a political base in every corner of the state, and successfully cultivated traditionally Democratic groups. But Yeakel did far better than many (including members of her own state party) ever expected. She and her staff made their share of mistakes and strategic miscalculations, but doing as well as they did was a tribute to much hard work, sophisticated fundraising, enthusiastic grassroots support, and Yeakel's own style and savvy. Many in Pennsylvania expect her to seek state or national office in the future.

Aside from her gender, would Yeakel's success in 1992 have made much difference for Pennsylvania? Specter had the lowest presidential support score (for George Bush) of any Republican senator. His rankings from national liberal and conservative groups were much closer to those of Democrats than to Republicans.[30] He was a staunch supporter of labor, abortion rights, Head Start funding, and family leave. But Specter did vote with the solid Republican bloc for the filibuster that killed President Clinton's economic stimulus package in April 1993, even though this bill contained $400 million for Pennsylvania. Another liberal Democratic vote could have helped end the filibuster and pass Clinton's agenda in the Senate.

Specter's victory over an attractive and well-funded (albeit inexperienced) candidate will not make it any easier for women in Pennsylvania to challenge incumbents. And major reforms diminishing incumbents' advantages (term limits, public funding of campaigns) are highly unlikely in a strong-party state lacking initiative or referenda provisions.[31] It will be many, many years before Pennsylvania women can anticipate equitable legislative representation in either Harrisburg or Washington.

Nevertheless, politicians like Arlen Specter may well find it advantageous to pay more attention to women's interests if they wish to maintain their grip on power. The number of women in party, public, and appointive office is increasing—even in Pennsylvania. The surprise election in 1992 of Democrat Marjorie Margolies-Mezvinsky to the U.S. House of Representatives is one such indicator of change in Pennsylvania politics. Margolies-Mezvinsky, 50, has been a local and network TV reporter in Philadelphia, Washington, and New York City, and was (in 1970) the first single American to adopt a foreign child.[32] While this background places Margolies-Mezvinsky solidly in the ranks of new-style career women now being elected to Congress, she also exemplifies more traditional patterns: she is the mother of eleven children and the wife of a former Iowa Congressman and Pennsylvania State Democratic chairman (Ed Mezvinsky), and first ran for elective office in middle age. She also won in a race for an open seat, but by only 1,000 votes in an overwhelmingly Republican district (Montgomery County.) It remains to be seen whether Margolies-Mezvinsky will be able to build a solid constituency base for reelection as an incumbent. But she can expect powerful assistance from senior members of Pennsylvania's congressional delegation, who have already eased her way onto key committees.[33]

The most important result of Yeakel's loss (and Margolies-Mezvinsky's narrow win) may lie in the willingness of women to run. Yeakel was personally wealthy, campaigned hard, spent a lot of her own money, obtained crucial early support from EMILY's List, attracted national press attention—and still lost. The stranglehold of white-male incumbents on Pennsylvania politics will continue to discourage women from seeking legislative office, at least until the next redistricting opens up a few seats. Nevertheless, the eligibility pool of women in county, local, and state offices has been growing. Eventually, a woman from Pennsylvania will be elected to the U.S. Senate. But don't hold your breath.

Notes

My thanks to my tireless research assistant, Cheryl Gaston, and to G. Terry Madonna for providing me with the primary poll results. Thanks also to Terry Madonna, Nathan Gorenstein, Jeff Mondak, and the editors for helpful comments on an earlier draft.

1. *Pittsburgh Post-Gazette*, February 1, 1993, p. A1.

2. These patterns may now be changing as rising equipment and insurance costs force volunteer departments to modernize, merge, and search harder for volunteers. Under current state law, department bylaws must now permit admission of women and minorities before a unit can qualify for state loans to buy equipment, and Pennsylvania is now above the national average in its percentage of women volunteer firefighters (see *Pittsburgh Post-Gazette*, February 1, 1993, p. A7). However, one department (Belle Vernon) is still before the Commonwealth's Human Relations Commission because of its persistent refusal to admit women.

3. *Philadelphia Inquirer*, April 29, 1992, p. A1.

4. See Fenno (1991) for a detailed account of Specter's Senate record and his earlier campaigns.

5. *Congressional Quarterly Weekly Report*, December 19, 1992, 3844.

6. *New York Times*, October 15, 1992, p. A22.

7. *Philadelphia Inquirer Magazine*, September 27, 1992, pp. 3, 14-19.

8.   In fact, the *Pittsburgh Post-Gazette* buried the announcement of Yeakel's candidacy at the end of a longer article featuring a picture of the Democratic challenger to Attorney General Ernie Preate Jr., a Republican (see *Pittsburgh Post-Gazette*, February 7, 1992, p. B6).

9. *Pittsburgh Post-Gazette*, February 4, 1993, p. A6.

10. *Philadelphia Inquirer*, April 29, 1992, p. A1.

11.   To know him was not to love him, however; polls conducted by Millersville State University/Penn State Harrisburg found that while most Republican voters (61 percent) had heard of Freind, many more held unfavorable than favorable views (35 to 18 percent, with 47 percent undecided).   Specter, by contrast, had a 58 to 30 percent favorable/unfavorable ratio.

12.   According to the 1992 exit poll conducted by Voter Research and Surveys, 27 percent of Pennsylvania voters thought that abortion should always be legal, 35 percent believed that it should be mostly legal, 24 percent thought that it should be mostly illegal, and 10 percent thought that abortion should always be illegal.

13. *Philadelphia Inquirer Magazine*, September 27, 1992, p. 18.

14.   Statewide telephone survey of likely voters, April 20-22, 1992, conducted by Millersville State University/Penn State Harrisburg, G. Terry Madonna and Berwood A. Yost, directors.   Results of the poll were published in the *Madonna Report*, April 24, 1992.

15. Quoted in *Philadelphia Inquirer*, April 29, 1992, p. A1.

16. *Philadelphia Inquirer*, April 29, 1992, p. A13.

17. Quoted in *Philadelphia Inquirer*, April 29, 1992, p. A1.

18. *Newsweek*, April 27, 1992, p. 31.

19. *Philadelphia Inquirer Magazine*, September 27, 1992, pp. 3, 14-19.

20. *Philadelphia Inquirer*, October 2, 1992, p. A9.

21. *Philadelphia Inquirer*, October 6, 1992, p. B1.

22. *Apprise: Central Pennsylvania's Regional Magazine*, October 1992, pp. 50-54.

23. *Philadelphia Inquirer*, August 9, 1992, p. C7.

24. *Apprise*, October 1992, pp. 50-54.

25. *Philadelphia Inquirer Magazine*, September 27, 1992, pp. 3, 14-19; *Philadelphia Inquirer*, October 27, 1992, p. A5.

26.   Yeakel's husband, an avid golfer, was an active member of the suburban Waynesborough Country Club.   Yeakel stressed that the club allowed and actively sought minority members, although it had no African-American members in 1992; Specter claimed this was evidence of exclusion.

27. Quoted in *Philadelphia Inquirer*, October 7, 1992, p. B3.

28. *Philadelphia Inquirer*, November 8, 1992, p. B6.
29. *New York Times*, November 4, 1992, p. A15.
30. *Congressional Quarterly Weekly Report*, May 2, 1992, 1203.
31. All fourteen states passing term-limitations laws in 1992 did so by means of initiatives (see *Congressional Quarterly Weekly Report*, November 7, 1992, 3596-3599). Initiatives are not permitted under Pennsylvania law.
32. *Pittsburgh Post-Gazette*, February 1, 1993, p. C1.
33. Ibid.

References

Apprise: Central Pennsylvania's Regional Magazine. October 1992, pp. 50-54.

Bell, Charles G., and Charles M. Price. 1980. *California Government Today: The Politics of Reform*. Homewood, IL: Dorsey.

Breckinridge, Sophonisba P. 1933. *Women in the Twentieth Century*. New York: McGraw Hill.

Center for the American Woman and Politics. 1993. "Women in Elective Office," yearly fact sheet. Rutgers, NJ: Eagleton Institute of Politics, Rutgers University.

Congressional Quarterly Weekly Report. November 7, 1992. 3596-3599.

— — —. December 19, 1992. 3854-3915.

Darcy, Robert, Susan Welch, and Janet Clark. 1987. *Women, Elections, and Representation*. White Plains, NY: Longman, Inc.

Deber, Raisa B. 1982. "The Fault, Dear Brutus: Women as Congressional Candidates in Pennsylvania." *Journal of Politics* 44: 463-479.

Fenno, Richard. 1991. *Learning to Legislate: The Senate Career of Arlen Specter*. Washington, DC: CQ Press.

Hill, David. 1981. "Political Culture and Female Political Representation." *Journal of Politics* 43: 159-168.

Huckshorn, Robert, and Robert Spencer. 1971. *The Politics of Defeat: Campaigning for Congress*. Boston: University of Massachusetts Press.

Jewell, Malcolm, and David Breaux. 1988. "The Effect of Incumbency on State Legislative Elections." *Legislative Studies Quarterly* 13: 495-513.

Kincaid, Diane D. 1973. "Over His Dead Body: A Positive Perspective on Widows in the U.S. Congress." *Western Political Quarterly* 31: 96-104.

Madonna Report, April 24, 1992.

Margolis, Michael, and Raymond Owen. 1984. "From Organization to Personalism: The Transmogrification of the Local Political Party." *Polity* 17: 313-328.

Mondak, Jeffrey. 1993. "Nothing to Read: News and Information Acquisition in the American Electorate." Presented at the annual meeting of the Midwest Political Science Association, Chicago.

Newsweek. April 27, 1992, p. 31.

New York Times. October 15, 1992, p. A22.

— — —. November 4, 1992, p. A15.

New York Times Book Review. October 25, 1992, pp. 1, 33.

Philadelphia Inquirer. 1992. Articles as noted in text.

Philadelphia Inquirer Magazine. September 27, 1992, pp. 3, 14-19.

Pittsburgh Post-Gazette. 1992-93. Articles as noted in text.

Squire, Peverill. 1992. "Legislative Professionalism and Membership Diversity in State Legislatures." *Legislative Studies Quarterly* 17: 69-79.

6

When Women Run Against Women: Double Standards and Vitriol in the New York Primary

Craig A. Rimmerman

It's a terrible disappointment because New York is a state that was ready to and would elect a woman to the United States Senate. It's a great missed opportunity."
—Harriet Woods, President, National Women's Political Caucus

Harriet Wood's observation echoed the frustration of many national women's leaders upon learning that Robert Abrams had defeated Geraldine Ferraro, Elizabeth Holtzman, and Al Sharpton to win the September 16, 1992 New York Democratic Senate primary. For women, this was a particularly bitter loss. The race began with Geraldine Ferraro as the clear frontrunner and a sense that this election might best be characterized as an "embarrassment of riches" since both Ferraro and Elizabeth Holtzman were strong candidates for the nomination.

In addition, there were a number of national trends at work that led many observers to conclude that 1992 was indeed the "Year of the Woman." As Clyde Wilcox points out in Chapter 1, "Women's gains in Congress were unprecedented." Carol Moseley-Braun of Illinois, Patty Murray of Washington, and California's Dianne Feinstein and

Barbara Boxer all prevailed in their general elections. Two major events during the Bush presidency helped to galvanize women: the Supreme Court's 1989 *Webster v. Reproductive Health Services* decision, which reflected a dramatic shift in the federal government's view of abortion rights, and "Bush's nomination of Clarence Thomas to the Supreme Court in 1991, featuring Anita Hill's stunning charges of sexual harassment, aired during nationally televised Senate Judiciary Hearings."[1] Party leaders also encouraged women to run and introduced them to interest groups and potential campaign contributors (see Chapter 1). The active role played by party elites undoubtedly contributed to the ability of women to run strong campaigns nationally. Finally, the 1992 electoral landscape was characterized by a volatile electorate committed to change, "the latest political buzz word for voters and candidates alike."[2]

This chapter evaluates the 1992 New York Senate race with special attention to the Democratic primary. The race is of particular importance because it raises interesting questions regarding our expectations concerning women candidates, especially when they run against one another. The primary campaign itself was particularly divisive and characterized by negative campaigning. In the primary aftermath, some analysts speculated that the negative nature of the race, characterized by one woman attacking another, undermined the more fundamental goal of gains for women at the highest levels of national politics. To what extent is such a claim justified?

In answering this question, the analysis begins with a discussion of each of the primary candidates' electoral strategies and the issues raised in the primary campaign. The results of the primary are then presented, followed by a discussion of possible explanations for Robert Abrams's primary victory and its implications for women's groups. Finally, the chapter concludes with a brief analysis of the general election and the factors that allowed Alfonse D'Amato to retain his Senate seat.

The Primary: Issues and Candidate Electoral Strategies

The women who ran for the United States Senate in 1992 generally came from one of two different backgrounds. They had either served in the House of Representatives, like Barbara Boxer, or had held executive office in the statehouse or in the state's largest cities, like Dianne Feinstein. Others, such as Patty Murray and Lynn Yeakel, were not expected to run for the Senate but were motivated to do so by the Hill-Thomas hearings (see Chapter 1). Ferraro and Holtzman are examples of the first kind of senatorial candidate, since both served previously in the House and appeared to be waiting to run for the Senate at what they perceived to be the most opportune time.

Geraldine Ferraro's decision to seek the Democratic nomination came after considerable research and reflection. She conducted statewide public opinion polls, consulted with close political friends and advisors, and her family. This was all necessary given the critical scrutiny she experienced as Walter Mondale's running-mate in the 1984 presidential election, when questions were raised regarding her finances and her husband's possible Mafia ties.

Despite this potentially negative baggage, Ferraro emerged as the early frontrunner due to several factors. Her celebrity status, name recognition, political skills, and personal style contributed to her fast start. According to one account of the campaign:

> *As the first woman to run on a major party's national ticket (losing with Walter F. Mondale in 1984), Ferraro gained widespread support from women's groups, despite Abrams's and Holtzman's own feminist credentials. As a campaigner, Ferraro has outshone the intense, distant Holtzman and the earnest but plodding Abrams.*[3]

Ferraro's lead was whittled considerably after the *Village Voice* published an article entitled "Ferraro and the Mob," which described "links between her businessman husband and other family members to alleged members of criminal organizations."[4] Both Holtzman and Abrams argued persuasively that in light of these renewed charges, Ferraro was the weakest Democrat to challenge the incumbent, Alfonse D'Amato, who faced ethics problems of his own.

For New York City Comptroller Elizabeth Holtzman, the 1992 bid for Alfonse D'Amato's Senate seat would potentially allow her to vindicate her loss to D'Amato in the 1980 senatorial election. The 1980 election featured a three-way race among Holtzman, D'Amato, and Senator Jacob Javits, who ran as the Liberal party candidate. Javits pulled enough votes away from Holtzman that D'Amato was elected to the Senate in a close race. It was a bitter loss for both Holtzman and the Democratic party, for Holtzman was regarded as a rising star in Congress, largely because of her performance as a member of the House Judiciary Committee during the Watergate hearings.

The 1992 race posed a different set of challenges for Ferraro, Holtzman, national women's groups, and their female supporters. A May 1992 article in *Time* magazine captured the essence of the challenges facing women in the 1992 New York Senate primary well:

The four-way race for New York's Democratic Senate nomination poses a different challenge: Which of two strong female candidates should women support? Both Geraldine Ferraro... and Elizabeth Holtzman are veteran politicians who need no introduction to voters. Yet their rivalry has stirred deep divisions among progressive women who seemingly cannot stomach the thought of two women competing for the same office. Holtzman finds the quandary absurd, particularly since she and Ferraro stand far apart on certain issues. Ferraro, for example, backs the death penalty, while Holtzman opposes it. "Women are capable of making a distinction between two women, and have been from time immemorial," she says. Ferraro quite agrees. "Tell those women to start acting like grownups," she says. "The men can always figure out whom to vote for."[5]

The rivalry between the two women also caused problems for national women's groups who desperately wanted a Democratic woman to challenge D'Amato in the general election. EMILY's List endorsed Ferraro, much to the displeasure of the Holtzman camp, which argued that the organization was "playing politics instead of playing its conscience," because Ferraro's consulting and polling staff had ties to EMILY's List.[6] Ellen Malcolm, EMILY's List's president, responded to such charges by saying that her organization decided to throw its full weight behind one of the candidates to help guarantee that one would ultimately win the nomination. Ferraro and Holtzman both received the endorsement of the Women's Campaign Fund, while the National Women's Political Caucus remained neutral throughout the primary.

Trailing badly in the polls throughout the summer, Holtzman took the lead in attacking Ferraro's ethics in an effort to chip away at her thirty-point lead in the polls. Following particularly damaging articles in late August in *New York Newsday* and the *Village Voice* concerning Ferraro's alleged ties to organized crime, Holtzman and Abrams embraced campaign strategies designed to wound the frontrunner. The *Village Voice* article, published some three weeks before the primary election, was particularly damaging. Authors Wayne Barrett and William Bastone offered this conclusion:

After a two-month investigation, we have concluded that Geraldine Ferraro is the candidate with the most extensive intertwining of unsavory relationships that either of us has seen in two and a half decades of city investigative reporting. This story documents twenty-four mob associations of Ferraro's or her husband's, John Zaccaro, some familiar and some unknown, stretching from her political to her business to her personal life.[7]

Ferraro's response to these charges was similar to her response when they first surfaced during the 1984 presidential election. She denied them categorically and suggested that such charges were a smear on her Italian-American heritage.

But for her Democratic primary opponents, these charges allowed them to raise the legitimate question of whether Ferraro was the best candidate to take on Al D'Amato in the general election. Both Holtzman and Abrams suggested that she was unfit to be a senator. Holtzman ran a particularly negative television commercial, asking Ferraro to "come clean" or else be defeated by D'Amato in the general election.[8] In response, Ferraro ran ads that compared the smears against herself with those levied against Anita Hill. She hoped that these ads would allow her to win the support of women who might view her as an unfair victim of an orchestrated smear campaign.

Ferraro received unexpected support from New York Governor Mario Cuomo, who had refused to endorse any of the four Democratic candidates. Cuomo attacked the *Village Voice* article as "innuendo" and claimed that Ferraro had been "smeared solely on the basis of her surname." In an interview on WCBS radio, he lamented that the story had driven the campaign "into the gutter."[9] By implication, then, he criticized Holtzman and Abrams for attempting to capitalize politically on the ethics charges.

As we will see, State Attorney General Abrams was in the best position to capitalize on Ferraro's ethics problems, much to the chagrin of local and national feminist leaders. Throughout the campaign, Abrams attempted to cast himself as the true liberal in the New York Senate primary, by emphasizing his opposition to the death penalty, support for deep cuts in military spending, and his commitment to a national health insurance plan financed by a new payroll tax on employers.[10] Abrams did not air any ads until the last two weeks of the primary campaign, preferring to allow Holtzman to take the lead in relentlessly attacking Ferraro's alleged connection to organized crime.[11] Ferraro issued her own ad, however, that attacked Abrams for improper fundraising practices, an ad that became a part of D'Amato's general election strategy.[12] But Ferraro did not have the money needed to run television commercials in the campaign's final days, which undoubtedly contributed to her defeat in a close election.[13]

Al Sharpton's primary strategy was to remain above the fray and to reach out beyond black voters for electoral support. Sharpton's own reputation had been seriously damaged by his role in the 1987 Tawana Brawley case. The case also led to the first of several conflicts between Sharpton and Abrams. The two clashed over the case of Tawana Brawley, a black teenager who claimed that "she had been raped by a group of white men. A grand jury supervised by Abrams's office found her story without substance, and Abrams criticized Sharpton and Brawley's other advisers." Abrams later prosecuted Sharpton on charges of charity fraud in an unrelated case. Sharpton was acquitted of this charge, but he served a short jail term for state tax evasion.[14]

Analysis of the Primary Results

Perhaps in response to the negative nature of the primary campaign, voter turnout in the Senate primary was just under 30 percent of the state's registered Democrats.[15] In the final tally, Abrams received 37 percent of the vote, while Ferraro received 36 percent; Sharpton garnered 15 percent, and Holtzman received 13 percent. In accomplishing his narrow win, Abrams built a coalition of defectors from Ferraro and Holtzman.[16] Abrams defeated Ferraro in New York City by roughly 23,000 votes, and bested her in the suburbs by 11,000 votes, but lost to her upstate by about 23,000 votes.[17]

The biggest surprise of the election was Holtzman's dismal fourth place finish behind Sharpton. For Holtzman, her disappointing finish was a public rebuke of her primary campaign strategy. The exit polls indicate that Holtzman and Sharpton each received an equal share of the women's vote, while Ferraro drew the votes of four in ten women, and Abrams won the support of three in ten women. Sharpton received two-thirds of the black vote, and Ferraro was the only other primary candidate to garner more than 10 percent. Abrams finished a disappointing third in the black vote, a result that suggested he would need to shore up support in the black community for the general election. Not surprisingly, Abrams did well among Jewish voters, a group that accounted for roughly one in four primary voters. His strong showing among Jews enabled him to eke out a primary victory. As expected, Ferraro did well among Italian voters, garnering two-thirds of their support.

Interestingly, Ferraro actually received the support of more voters who identified themselves as liberal (36 percent for Ferraro, 34 percent for Abrams, 16 percent for Sharpton, and 14 percent for Holtzman) suggesting that Abrams's efforts to paint himself as the most liberal of the four candidates were not nearly as successful as he and his advisors would have liked. Finally, of the four candidates, Abrams ran the strongest among the wealthiest of voters, garnering the support of four in ten voters who had family incomes between $50,000 and $75,000 and gaining the support of five in ten voters who had incomes over $75,000.[18]

In the aftermath of the hard-fought primary, political strategists tried to ascertain why Ferraro lost her double-digit lead. Not surprisingly, analysts focused on the role that Holtzman played in costing Ferraro the nomination and women a chance to elect one of their own to represent New York in the United States Senate. One analyst called the campaign "extraordinarily rancorous," and claimed that "it left two landmarks on New York's political landscape — Ms. Ferraro and one of her opponents, Elizabeth Holtzman — badly bruised and pondering their futures after what many feminists had hoped would be a year of triumph for women turned instead into a harsh and unforgiving fight between them."[19]

Ferraro and her supporters were particularly distressed by a series of Holtzman commercials "which stressed the long time it took Ferraro and her real-estate broker husband to oust a kiddie-porn firm from a building they owned."[20] Did Holtzman ruin her political career by running these commercials? Some feminists believe so. Letty Pogrebin, a prominent feminist who has supported Holtzman in the past, was particularly critical: "In my view and the view of many other people with whom I have spoken, I will never support her for anything again. Her turn would have come. It was clear she never could have won this race. It was hubris that kept her in."[21] Reflecting on her overwhelming and disappointing defeat several months later, Holtzman blamed the larger society for her loss. She claimed that those who disagreed with her campaign strategy are "simply not ready to accept a woman who campaigns like a man. Being on the cutting edge sometimes means you will be misunderstood. It comes with the territory."[22]

Holtzman's analysis received support in the broader feminist community. Betty Friedan, for one, rejects the notion that Holtzman paved the way for Ferraro's defeat:

> What is this, for God's sakes? Why should Holtzman be blamed for Geraldine Ferraro's defeat? How dare they try to blame Liz Holtzman for the question marks about Geraldine Ferraro. Blame the people who put forward a candidate about whom they knew these questions existed.[23]

Others concluded that Holtzman's tough approach was entirely justified given that male candidates have embraced the same kind of strategy with great success and without criticism in the past. One New York political advisor said, "She tried to deliver a death blow and that is an option that any politician has at their disposal, though many people have taken it as some kind of betrayal of feminist ideology."[24]

It is interesting to note that when Holtzman beat Bess Myerson and captured the 1980 Democratic senatorial nomination in a four-candidate race, there was virtually no criticism of her strategy at that time. One reason is that D'Amato's successful and nasty Republican primary campaign against Jacob Javits received most of the attention.

Those who wish to blame Holtzman for Ferraro's defeat must also confront the fact that the four primary candidates agreed on most of the major issues of the day. All four were in favor of abortion rights and other issues of importance to women. All four also pledged to work on behalf of women's issues if they were elected to office. This may help to explain why the race was so close at the end.

The Abrams candidacy was undoubtedly helped in the end by the decision to run television commercials only in the two weeks prior to the primary election. Ferraro, by contrast, had run out of television money and could not respond to the Holtzman and Abrams attacks through television. She had to rely on television news coverage, press reports, and personal campaigning to deliver her response to the voters.

The end result was a low voter turnout and a very close primary election. In trying to account for Abrams's narrow victory and the low voter turnout, Tracy A. Essoglou, a member of the Women's Action Coalition pointed to "the ugliness of the battle that the general public really responded to."[25] Essoglou claims that Abrams was the primary beneficiary of the attacks on Ferraro because "when both Abrams and Holtzman started challenging Ferraro, rather than believing her and standing with her, some went with Abrams, who was just as much a part of the mud-slinging."[26]

In the end, the Democrats were in disarray coming out of the primary. Ferraro refused to concede or to endorse Abrams. Holtzman had to respond to charges that she cost the Democrats an opportunity to elect a woman to the Senate from New York and attempt to explain her own embarrassing electoral performance. Al Sharpton had to decide whether to endorse his rival Robert Abrams. As we will see, the primary beneficiary of this disarray was Alfonse D'Amato, who was poised to capitalize on his opponent's missteps and to aggressively wage a fight to retain his seat in the United States Senate.

The General Election

Robert Abrams entered the general election with several key disadvantages. Abrams began the post-primary season with some

$750,000 in general election funds compared to D'Amato's campaign war chest of $4 million. The fact that the September 15 primary was held so close to the November 3 general election meant that Abrams had little chance to plot a coherent campaign strategy. In addition, his slim primary victory meant that the results would not be made official until all absentee ballots were counted and certified on September 30.[27] Finally, Ferraro refused to concede defeat for several days, and only gave Abrams a tepid endorsement late in the general election campaign.

Polls taken just before the Tuesday primary revealed that Abrams had a slight lead over D'Amato in head-to-head matchups. These polling results confirmed what the D'Amato camp had known all along—D'Amato would be in a much tighter race than his easy 1986 re-election defeat of Democratic challenger Mark Green. With this in mind, D'Amato went on the attack immediately by arguing that Abrams "is cut from the same, dangerous mold as every other hopelessly liberal tax-and-spend addict."[28] The notion that Abrams was "hopelessly liberal" was featured prominently in D'Amato's first television advertisements. In addition, D'Amato received the endorsements of former New York Mayor Edward I. Koch and HUD Secretary Jack Kemp. Their endorsements were also part of D'Amato's early television advertising blitz and helped him woo the support of conservative Democrats, which he needed to gain if he was to maintain his Senate seat.

This aggressive D'Amato strategy had the effect of putting Abrams on the defensive from the start. After the divisive, hard- fought primary, Abrams had little time to plot a well conceived general election strategy. Instead of responding to D'Amato's attacks directly, Abrams told cheering supporters at his primary victory celebration that he wanted "to go to Washington to shake things up. Al D'Amato's been in Washington shaking them down."[29] The reference was unmistakably to D'Amato's own ethics problems. D'Amato responded by charging that Abrams owed Geraldine Ferraro an apology for mudslinging during the primary campaign that impugned her Italian heritage and linked her husband to mob figures. In addition, he warned, "If he continues those kind of personal attacks... then I can assure you I'm not going to allow that kind of manure at me by Bob Abrams without responding."[30]

Despite all of this, some polls indicated that Abrams was slightly ahead of D'Amato as the campaign headed into mid-October. But then Abrams made an October 11 statement that became the turning point of the entire campaign. At an evening campaign rally for students in Binghamton, New York, Abrams was antagonized by a handful of D'Amato supporters who heckled him and honked their car horns. Abrams responded in frustration by denouncing D'Amato for sending the hecklers and calling the Senator "a fascist."[31] D'Amato immediately denounced Abrams's remark at a Columbus Day parade the next day, and "seemed to be gulping back sobs as he spoke of the hurt that being called a fascist had caused him."[32] His response received considerable press and television coverage. In addition, D'Amato capitalized on Abrams's remark by running a commercial "showing Mussolini on a balcony haranguing a crowd."[33] The commercial's purpose was to remind voters of the unfortunate comparison intimated by the Abrams claim. Abrams's remark unwittingly allowed the D'Amato camp to link Abrams's primary campaign attacks on Ferraro to a broader disdain for Italian-Americans, a group that D'Amato was clearly courting for much needed support in the general election campaign.

Finally, D'Amato distanced himself as much as possible from George Bush's policies and the Bush re-election campaign. Instead, much to the disgust of Abrams's supporters, D'Amato tied himself closely to the Clinton campaign by citing specific policy areas where they agreed. This campaign strategy led Robert Guskind to conclude in the *National Journal* that "possibly no other Republican has tried to put more distance between himself and the President than Senator Alfonse M. D'Amato."[34] On election day, Bill Clinton carried New York by a margin of 50 to 34 to 16 percent, vindicating D'Amato's campaign strategy.

Polls up until election day showed a very tight race between Abrams and D'Amato. In the end, D'Amato prevailed 49 percent to 48 percent. Exit polls reveal that women did not abandon Abrams despite his treatment of Ferraro in the primary. He received 53 percent of the women's vote and 44 percent of the men's vote, a significant gender gap. D'Amato, on the other hand, was more popular with men, garnering the support of 56 percent of the men voting and 47 percent of the women's vote.

In the aftermath of D'Amato's stunning victory, the prevailing sentiment was that the Democrats blew a golden opportunity to defeat an incumbent senator who had been wounded by a wide array of ethics charges. Michael Tomasky nicely summarized this perspective: "This was probably the best chance ever to beat D'Amato, and Abrams would have been a good senator, but he ran one of the worst campaigns you'll ever see."[35]

Conclusion

For Democratic women both in New York and nationwide, the general election results were particularly distressing. Al D'Amato was re-elected to the Senate, and Geraldine Ferraro and Elizabeth Holtzman were confronted with charges that their political careers had been destroyed by the vitriolic primary campaign. Some feminist leaders even argued that women's gains nationwide were somehow diminished by the nastiness of the New York race.

This perspective seems short-sighted and unfair for several reasons. If the New York race is any indication, women are being held to a higher standard than men who campaign for higher office. Liz Holtzman merely engaged in an electoral strategy that she believed would allow her to win the New York primary. It was the same kind of campaign strategy used by many men in the past, who received little or no criticism for their efforts.

Some feminist leaders have accurately pointed out that the press expects much more from women candidates and their campaigns than it has typically expected from men. Ellen Malcolm lamented this development in a *New York Times* editorial: "Time and time again, I am told by someone in great confidential detail why a particular candidate cannot win. Men's campaigns are criticized, too, but not with the same level of minutiae as the women's."[36]

The success of women candidates in the 1992 elections and the high visibility of women's political action committees, such as EMILY's List, indicate that more women will be competitive candidates in future national elections. What this means in practice is that we can expect to see a repeat of the New York primary in which one woman candidate attacked the frontrunner, who happened to be a woman, in order to win the nomination. The problem of negative campaigning deserves considerable scrutiny by both parties. But such scrutiny should not be gender-specific, as we saw during much of the New York primary campaign.

From the vantage point of women, it is indeed regrettable that neither Geraldine Ferraro nor Elizabeth Holtzman secured the Democratic nomination to face Al D'Amato. But their failure to win the nomination does not mean that women's gains nationwide should be diminished. If anything, the results of the 1992 elections should inspire more women to recognize that barriers to women's candidacies are slowly being eliminated, to run for higher office, and to win election to positions of policymaking power that were once the exclusive province of men.

Notes

1. *Congressional Quarterly Weekly Report,* October 17, 1992a, 3265.
2. *Time,* May 4, 1992, p. 34.
3. *Congressional Quarterly Weekly Report,* September 5, 1992, 2638.
4. *Congressional Quarterly Weekly Report,* September 19, 1992, 2844.
5. *Time,* May 4, 1992, p. 34.
6. *National Journal,* June 13, 1992, 1403.
7. *Village Voice,* August 25, 1992, p. 12.
8. *Economist,* September 5, 1992, p. 26.
9. *Village Voice,* September 8, 1992, p. 14.
10. *New York Times,* September 17, 1992, p. A1.
11. *National Journal,* October 31, 1992, 2481.
12. *National Journal,* October 31, 1992, 2482.
13. *Congressional Quarterly Weekly Report,* October 17, 1992b, 3272-3273.
14. *New York Newsday,* September 17, 1992a, p. 3.
15. *New York Times,* September 17, 1992, p. A1.
16. *New York Times,* September 17, 1992, p. B4.
17. *New York Newsday,* September 17, 1992a, p. 3.
18. *New York Times,* September 17, 1992, p. B4.
19. *New York Times,* September 17, 1992, p. A1.
20. *New York Newsday,* September 21, 1992, p. 20.
21. *New York Times,* September 17, 1992, p. B5.
22. *New York Times,* March 7, 1993, p. 37.
23. *New York Times,* September 17, 1992, p. B5.
24. *New York Times,* September 16, 1992, p. B6.
25. Ibid.
26. Ibid.
27. *Roll Call,* September 21, 1992, p. 1.
28. Gannett News Service, September 16, 1992, p. 1.
29. Ibid.
30. *New York Newsday,* September 17, 1992b, p. 21.
31. *New Yorker,* November 2, 1992, p. 47.
32. Ibid.
33. Ibid.
34. *National Journal,* October 31, 1992, p. 2480.
35. *Village Voice,* November 17, 1992, p. 16.
36. *New York Times,* August 5, 1992, p. A23.

References

Congressional Quarterly Weekly Report. September 5, 1992. 2638.
— — —. September 19, 1992. 2844.
— — —. October 17, 1992a. 3265.
— — —. October 17, 1992b. 3272-3273.
Economist. September 5, 1992, p. 26.
Gannett News Service. September 16, 1992, pp. 1-2.
National Journal. June 13, 1992. 1403.
— — —. October 31, 1992. 2477-2482.
New York Newsday. September 17, 1992a, p. 3.
— — —. September 17, 1992b, p. 21.
— — —. September 21, 1992, p. 20.
New York Times. 1992-93. Articles as noted in text.
New Yorker. November 2, 1992, pp. 46-50.
Roll Call. September 21, 1992, pp. 1-2.
Time. May 4, 1992, p. 34.
Village Voice. August 25, 1992, p. 11.
— — —. September 8, 1992, p. 14.
— — —. November 17, 1992, p. 16.

7

Women and the 1992
House Elections

Carole Chaney
and Barbara Sinclair

To the extent that 1992 can be considered the Year of the Woman, House elections contributed greatly. In the primaries, 106 women won major party nominations for the House of Representatives—a large increase from the previous high of sixty-nine in 1990.[1]   In California alone, nineteen women won the Democratic or Republican nomination; Florida nominated ten women and New York nine. In the general elections, forty-seven women won House seats; twenty-three incumbents were reelected and twenty-four new women were chosen. Thus in the 103rd Congress (1993-1994), women constitute 10.8 percent of the membership of the House—up from the previous high of 6.4 percent in the 102nd Congress (1992-1993).   California is represented by seven women in the House (as well as by two in the Senate); Florida and New York each sent five women to the House.

The female House members of the 103rd Congress are a diverse group ethnically and geographically.   Eight are African-Americans, three are Latinas—one a Puerto Rican— and one is Asian-American. Collectively they represent twenty-seven states and come from every region of the country. In partisan terms, they are less diverse; thirty-five of the forty-seven are Democrats, only twelve are Republicans.

Although women are still far from parity in the House, 1992 was an indisputably good year. What accounts for women's success? Are unique events such as the Hill-Thomas hearings most responsible, or do more systemic factors offer a better explanation? The answer is important because it has implications for women's progress in the future. Will 1992 be remembered as an aberrant year or as particularly good but part of an ongoing trend?

To answer these ultimate questions, we need to answer the following proximate questions: What factors determine election outcomes in House races? Can these factors explain women's lack of success in the past? Can they explain their greater success in recent years and especially in 1992?

The extensive body of research on House elections shows that outcomes are largely determined by the partisan make-up of the district, the quality of the candidates,[2] and the resources, especially money, the candidates command (see Jacobson 1992). Party identification still serves as an important voting cue; districts in which Democratic identifiers significantly outnumber Republican identifiers are likely to elect a Democrat to the House and vice versa.

Quality candidates are well-known and well-regarded in the district, have political skills, and thus are more likely to win. Incumbents are especially likely to be well-known and are usually well-liked. Non-incumbent candidates who have held other elective office may be known in the district, and are more likely than those without such experience to possess skills necessary for making themselves well-known and well-liked.

Candidates amply endowed with the resources needed to run a good campaign are more likely to win than those who lack those resources. The primary resource is, of course, money and it is of special importance to a candidate who is not already familiar to voters before the campaign. Through media advertising and direct mail, an obscure candidate can become well-known, but this costs a great deal of money.

These three factors are interrelated. Those nominations that have little value because the partisan balance is highly adverse are more likely to be won by novices because quality candidates do not run. Quality candidates are most likely to run in districts with a partisan balance favorable to them. Competition for the party nomination is likely to be especially fierce in districts with a favorable partisan balance, and, in the primary as in the general election, the best known, most highly regarded candidate is likely to prevail. Money goes to those candidates who are perceived to have a good chance of winning. Thus, quality candidates can usually raise more money than those without electoral experience. This is especially true if they are running in favorable districts.

Incumbents are so difficult to beat because usually all three factors work in their favor and against the challenger. The majority of incumbents represent districts favorable to their party, so the challenger is at an immediate disadvantage. Incumbents are generally well-known and well-liked and can raise large amounts of money. Since defeating the incumbent seems improbable, quality candidates are unlikely to run, leaving the field to neophytes. Even a quality challenger is likely to have trouble raising money in what political elites perceive as a hopeless race.

Can these factors explain how women have fared in House elections in the past and in 1992? To answer that question, we first need to consider how those factors might affect women specifically. Are women now and have they been in the past quality candidates? Are women able to raise needed campaign funds and were they able to in the past? Now and in the past, did women run in districts with favorable or unfavorable partisan balances?

The question about candidate quality is a question about perceptions as well as about reality. Given notions of appropriate gender roles prevalent in our society when many of today's voters were growing up, some voters may believe that women ipso facto are not good candidates. Certainly one would not be surprised if such prejudice had existed two decades ago. And if voters are or were prejudiced, might those political elites who control campaign funds also believe that women do not make good candidates? It is also, however, a question about whether women with the objective characteristics that define a quality candidate exist in large numbers—about the eligibility pool—and about whether they choose to run.

Are Voters Biased?

Are people unwilling to vote for women candidates for Congress simply because they are women? Evidence suggests that voter bias against female candidates is not as consequential in the 1990s as it was in the 1970s. In fact, in light of contemporary public disenchantment with Congress as an institution and growing mistrust of members of Congress, who are currently disproportionately male, women House candidates may have benefited in 1992 from their status as "outsiders."

In 1970, 1975, and 1984, the Gallup Poll asked the following question, "If your party nominated a woman to run for Congress in your district, would you vote for her if she were qualified for the job?" In 1970, 13 percent of respondents said they would not vote for a qualified woman candidate. In 1975, that number was down to 9 percent and by 1984 the percentage had fallen to 6 percent.[3] There was a sharp decline in voter bias over this period, but women candidates were still disadvantaged as recently as 1984.[4]

However, research has shown that this bias against women candidates competes with other voter cues such as party identification, incumbency status, and candidate name recognition. An analysis of the relative importance of these cues suggests that the sex of the candidate is the least important when compared to the other vote determinants (Darcy, Welch, and Clark 1987).

Further evidence that voter discrimination is waning comes from a study which examined the results of five races in 1982 that involved women candidates (two for governor and three for U.S. Senate). The authors concluded that sex was not a major determinant of the vote for either male or female voters and that all voters tended to rely primarily on party identification cues when casting their votes (Zipp and Plutzer 1985). One subgroup in the study, female Independents, did tend to vote for women candidates whom they perceived were supportive of issues of concern to women. This finding suggests that women candidates who identify themselves with women's issues may have an increasing advantage over male candidates in light of declining partisanship in the electorate (Abramson and Aldrich 1990) and the fact that, in absolute numbers, more voters are women. This study also showed that strong female candidates were just as effective as strong male candidates at attracting crossover votes of both men and women, further indicating that, as early as 1982, women were not significantly disadvantaged by voter discrimination.

The findings from the study cited above are supported by a 1987 study which found no significant differences between voter reactions to Democratic male and female congressional candidates. The only significant relationship between sex and voter preference that was found revealed that Republican women were rated significantly (albeit slightly) more favorably than Republican male congressional candidates (Darcy, Welch, and Clark 1987). Thus, it appears that women congressional candidates were not discriminated against by voters throughout the 1980s.

In 1992, female candidates may actually have been more favorably perceived by the electorate than male candidates. Strong anti-"politics-as-usual" sentiment seems to have increased the attractiveness of women candidates, who are still not perceived as standard-issue politicians. Similarly, there was also a perception following the Hill-Thomas hearings of a need for greater female representation in the legislature. In a poll taken in July 1992, registered voters were asked to respond to the following statement, "In a race between a man and a woman who had equal qualifications and skills, I would vote for the woman, because this country needs more women in high public office"; 57 percent of women and 45 percent of men agreed with the statement, 34 percent of women and 48 percent of men disagreed, and 9 percent of women and 7 percent of men were not sure.[5] A survey conducted by *Life* magazine asked, "If women ran America, would America be a better place?" While almost 60 percent responded that there would be no difference, about one out of three stated that America would be a better place with women in charge.[6] And a *U.S. News and World Report* survey taken in April 1992 sampled 1,000 adults and found that 61 percent believed that if more women held office, the country would be governed better; 12 percent said worse and 14 percent suggested there would be no difference (13 percent didn't know or refused to answer) (Center for the American Woman and Politics (CAWP) 1992). Public attitudes towards women running for office in 1992 were decidedly favorable.

The results of the 1992 elections suggest that voter prejudice against women candidates is an artifact of a not-too-distant past. On the other hand, the short-term factors that appeared to favor women candidates in 1992, such as the perception that women were "outsiders", may diminish as more and more women join the legislature and become "insiders."

Campaign Finance

Another reason commonly advanced for the dearth of women in public office has been their inability to raise campaign funds as effectively as their male counterparts. Bella Abzug, a former member of Congress contends that, "Women lose because they don't have enough support; they don't have enough support because they don't have enough money to conduct effective campaigns; they have trouble raising money because people think they're losers" (Abzug and Kelber 1984). She refers to this as the "Catch-22" of women's politics, and some figures appear to support her contention. For example, in 1982, the Women's Campaign Fund released figures that showed that the average male challenger spent $170,000 on his campaign as compared to $133,000 for the average female challenger (Abzug and Kelber 1984). However, reliance upon averages can be deceiving, for they tell us nothing about how much a particular candidate needs to spend in a particular district to affect the outcome of the race. In addition, the figures used to suggest that women are at a financial disadvantage often do not take into account the nature of the candidacies involved, i.e., they average campaign receipts for incumbents, challengers, and for open seat candidates. When political scientists looked at the question of gender discrimination in campaign funding, they controlled for these important differences and came to very different conclusions.

An analysis of campaign receipts and gender in congressional elections from 1972-1982 revealed that, although, on average, women raised less money than men, when one controls for the type of race, there is no significant difference between male and female candidates. That is, incumbents, whether male or female, generally raise a great deal more money than their challengers. The fundraising success of candidates for open seats (those without an incumbent running) outpaces that of challengers and depends on the match between the candidate's partisanship and that of the district, not on gender. In some cases, women were even more adept at fundraising than similarly situated male competitors. The author also found a trend toward parity in average amounts raised starting in 1976 and continuing through 1982, a year in which women raised 90 percent of what men did (Burrell 1985). A study of the 1980 congressional elections similarly concluded that, while women are overrepresented in the group that tends to receive less funding (non-incumbents), there is no evidence that gender, per se, affects the ability of candidates to raise money (Uhlaner and Schlozman 1986).

Figures from the 1992 House elections reveal that, overall, 48 percent of the 108 women candidates raised more money than their opponents. That the two successful female challengers raised less than their opponents attests to the fact that variables such as the partisanship of the district can be more influential than money in particular House races.[7] Further evidence of the parity that women have achieved is found in Federal Election Commission data which shows that in 1992 women were slightly overrepresented among the top fifty money raisers for House seats (CAWP 1993, 23).[8]

Table 7.1 shows how women candidates fared in fundraising when compared with all candidates in 1992.

Clearly, the primary determinant of fundraising success was whether the candidate was an incumbent or an open seat candidate, on the one hand, or a challenger on the other; the former generally raised much more money than the latter. Overall, women were certainly not noticeably less successful than the average candidate. Democratic women incumbents did raise less than the average Democratic incumbent, but Republican women incumbents raised more than their average male counterparts. The three women incumbents who lost were all Democrats, but a lack of funds was not responsible; two of the three raised almost twice as much as their opponents, the third raised over $800,000, 91 percent of what her opponent raised.

TABLE 7.1 House Campaign Funding in 1992
(Median Receipts as of November 23, 1992)

	All Candidates	Women Candidates
Incumbents		
Democrats	$479,980	$387,280
Republicans	$468,268	$581,793
Challengers		
Democrats	$ 62,764	$ 99,666
Republicans	$ 83,182	$ 79,749
Open Seats		
Democrats	$395,276	$540,959
Republicans	$416,244	$396,058

Source: Center for the American Woman and Politics, Eagleton Institute of Politics, Rutgers University, 1993, "Women Congressional Candidates: 1992 Campaign Receipts," *News & Notes* 9, no. 1: 23. Compiled from Federal Election Commission data.

Among both challengers and open seat candidates, Democratic women raised significantly more than the average, while Republican women raised slightly less. The fundraising success of Democratic women running in open seats is especially notable; open seats offer the best prospects for significant gains in female representation and, as we will see, that is where women made their biggest gains in 1992.

While scientific studies have not shown gender to be a significant determinant of fundraising ability, the fact remains that women do not share the advantage of incumbency equally with men. Hence, as a group they have been at an absolute disadvantage vis-a-vis male candidates. Perhaps because of this, efforts to overcome this absolute disadvantage have been underway since the 1980s. These efforts have favorably influenced the amount of money available for all female candidates in 1992.

When the Equal Rights Amendment failed in the early 1980s, many women's rights organizations refocused their energies and resources on getting women elected to public office (Carroll 1985). Both Patricia Ireland of the National Organization for Women and Emily Malcolm of EMILY's List attribute the successful showing of female House candidates in 1992 to long-term organizing, fundraising, and recruiting of female candidates.[9]

In 1983, there were sixteen women's political action committees (PACs) established nationwide (Kleeman 1983). By 1992, there were forty-two PACs which either gave money predominantly to women candidates or had a predominantly female donor base (CAWP 1993, 10). One notable PAC established in the 1980s is EMILY's List, a very important player in the House elections of 1992, which is discussed in more detail in Chapter 10.

In 1992, EMILY's List supported fifty-five women candidates—eight running for the Senate and forty-seven for House seats. All of the nineteen successful Democratic female candidates for open seats were funded by EMILY's List as were eleven unsuccessful open seat candidates. This translates into a 63 percent success rate for EMILY's List candidates for open seats, slightly better than the overall success rate for open seat female candidates (56 percent). In addition, EMILY's List provided support to fourteen unsuccessful female challengers and three female incumbents (two were reelected).

EMILY's List was only one of forty-two PACs devoted to raising money for female candidates in 1992, albeit the most powerful. The total amount of financial support for female congressional candidates from these PACs in 1992 was $11.5 million (CAWP 1993, 10).[10] This is a 400 percent increase over the $2.7 million raised by women's PACs for women candidates in 1990, which in turn was a 150 percent increase over the $1.1 million raised for women candidates in 1988.

As in the case of voter discrimination, it appears that talk about women candidates' inability to raise money for campaigning can be relegated to the history books. In light of present trends, one would expect that as the number of female incumbents increases, the absolute financing gap remaining between male and female candidates should disappear.

The Eligibility Pool

If women do not face discrimination from the voters or a disadvantage in campaign funding, are the women who run less likely to be quality candidates? Candidates who are well-known and highly regarded are considered quality candidates. Since ascertaining whether candidates have these attributes, especially for past elections, is difficult or impossible, political scientists frequently use previous elective experience as a surrogate measure (see Jacobson 1992). A candidate who has won a political office in the past is likely to be better known and more politically skillful than one without that experience.

Service in the House carries considerable power and prestige. Competition for a winnable seat is usually intense and quality candidates have the advantage. The eligibility pool for the House can be defined as those people with previous elective experience. To be sure, there are other routes to becoming well-known and well-regarded—non-elective political experience, for example, or celebrity in another field. Yet these are exceptions. If there are few women in lower elective office, there are unlikely to be many viable women House candidates.

In fact, before the 1970s, not many women held elective office. In 1970, only 4 percent of state legislators were female (CAWP 1993); in 1975, women made up only 4 percent of mayors and city councils (Clark 1991, 67). By 1985, the latter figure had increased to 14 percent and, by 1991, women held 18 percent of state legislative seats (Clark 1991, 67). Although women are still far outnumbered, their presence in the eligibility pool has greatly expanded.

Since 1980, non-incumbent women who have won major party nominations have been at least as likely as their male counterparts and often more so to have held elective office; for men, the mean with such experience for the six elections from 1980 through 1990 is about 25 percent; for women, about 32 percent (28 percent if the atypically high 1982 election is excluded.) For women, these percentages are, however, based on very small numbers. The average number of experienced non-incumbent women candidates in the elections from 1980 through 1990 was only about twelve, compared with about eighty-eight experienced male candidates per election. In 1992, the number of such women candidates was almost two and a half times the average for the previous six elections.[11]

Two-thirds of the women who won major party nominations in 1992 had run for office before and more than half of the total and about 37 percent of the non-incumbents had held a previous elective office.[12]

The winners were still more likely to have held elective office; eighteen of the twenty-four women elected to the House for the first time had previously won an elective office, most often state legislative office. With 75 percent having previous service in elective office, women elected in 1992 were actually slightly more experienced than the men in their class, 71 percent of whom had previously won elective office. Furthermore, the winners without elective experience were far from being political neophytes: Jennifer Dunn (R-WA) had served as chair of her state Republican party for twelve years; Lynn Schenk (D-CA) had been in Governor Jerry Brown's cabinet; Blanche Lambert (D-AR) worked on Capitol Hill as a congressional aide.

TABLE 7.2 Women House Candidates, Running and Winning by Candidate Type and Party

Candidate Characteristics	Total running	Number who won	% who won
Incumbents	26	23	88
Open Seat Candidates	39	22	56
Challengers	42	2	5
Democrats	70	35	50
Republicans	36	12	33
Democratic Open Seat Candidates	26	19	73
Republican Open Seat Candidates	13	3	23

Source: Center for the American Woman and Politics, 1992, *News & Notes* 8, no. 3: 4-17. *Congressional Quarterly Weekly Report*, November 7, 1992, 3570-3579, 3600-3607.

True novices seldom win election to the House. The growth in the pool of electorally experienced women was therefore a critically important precondition to the increase in women elected to the House. The potential for future increases is a function of the continued growth of that pool.

The Structure of Competition

An election is a contest between two (or more) candidates; the characteristics and resources of both candidates make a difference as does the character of the terrain on which the battle is waged. Theory backed up by extensive empirical data leads us to expect a specific pattern of outcomes depending upon the characteristics of the candidates and of the district. Incumbents tend to be strongly advantaged in all three of the factors that determine who wins and are most likely to win the election. Candidates running for open seats (races without an incumbent) should have the next highest rate of success, with its level being a function of the district's partisan complexion. Challengers, those candidates running against incumbents, should have the lowest success rate — they are facing the most formidable type of opponent and, in good part because of that, are less likely than candidates running in open seats to have previously held electoral office and to be able to raise significant campaign funds.

As Table 7.2 shows, these general patterns hold for women House candidates as well.

Most female incumbents who chose to run again in 1992 were reelected; only three of twenty-six were defeated. Liz Patterson (D-SC) and Joan Kelly Horn (D-MO) represented districts marginal for their party and Mary Rose Oakar (D-OH) had been implicated in both the House bank and post office scandals. (One other woman lost in the primary.) On the other end of the spectrum, women who challenged incumbents did not fare well in the general election; only two of forty-two were successful. Both — Pat Danner (D-MO) and Carolyn Maloney (D-NY) — prevailed in marginal or Democratic-leaning districts. (Two women defeated incumbents in primaries: Blanche Lambert defeated a twelve-term Democrat beset with check problems in Arkansas; in New York, Nydia Velazquez beat a nine-term Anglo Democrat in a newly-redrawn Latino-majority district.)

Women running for open seats did well; over half won their races. In four open seat contests, both major party nominees were women. If we exclude women who lost to other female candidates, women won 63 percent of the thirty-five open seats they contested.

Table 7.2 shows that Democratic women were considerably more successful than Republican women; Democrats outnumbered Republicans by about two to one among general election candidates but by about three to one among winners. The differential is not a result of a greater proportion of Republican than Democratic women running against incumbents — that is, in the least winnable races — 39 percent of Democratic candidates and 38 percent of Republican candidates were challengers. Nor were a greater proportion of Democratic women incumbents; 24 percent of Democratic and 25 percent of Republican candidates were incumbents. Republican women incumbents fared a little better than Democratic women incumbents at the ballot box in November; 100 percent were returned

compared to 82 percent of Democrats. On the other hand, while no
Republican challengers were elected, two Democratic challengers won.
As Table 7.2 shows, Democratic women were much more likely to win
their open seat races than were Republican women. This differential is
largely a function of the partisan character of the districts in which
Democrats and Republicans won open seat nominations. In 1992, both
Democratic and Republican women tended to win their party's
nomination in districts favorable to Democrats. Well before the
election, *Congressional Quarterly*, on the basis of registration figures,
voting history, and demographic characteristics, rated twenty-seven
open districts as safe for one party or the other.[13] Women won the
Democratic nomination in six of the twenty-three safe Democratic
districts, thus assuring themselves of a House seat; no Republican
women won nomination in the four safe Republican districts.   Six
women did win the valueless Republican nomination in safe
Democratic districts, while only one Democratic woman won in a safe
Republican district.

TABLE 7.3 Women Candidates, Running and Winning in Open Seats by Partisan
Character of the District and Party

		Democrats		*Republicans*	
	Success				
Partisan Character of the District	*Rate (%)*	*Ran*	*Won*	*Ran*	*Won*
Safe for party	100	6	6	0	0
Leans to or party favored	73	7	6	4	2
Competitive	63	6	4	2	1
Leans to or other party favored	43	6	3	1	0
Safe for other party	0	1	0	6	0
Totals		26	19	13	3

Source: "Safe for party districts" are those listed in *Congressional Quarterly Weekly Report*,
September 19, 1992, 2841. "Leans to or party favored" and "competitive" districts are taken from
Congressional Quarterly Weekly Report, October 24, 1992, 3358-3361.

Table 7.3 shows that the probability of a party's candidate winning
a given open seat depends heavily on the district's partisan
complexion.

To be sure, in 1992, Democratic women did better than Republican
women at every level of competitiveness. But far more important in
explaining the difference in overall success rates is the character of the
open districts in which Democratic and Republican women won
nomination. Seventy-three percent of the open seat nominations that
Democratic women won were in districts that either favored their

party or were toss-ups, compared to only 46 percent for Republican women.

The large increase in women elected to the House came in open seats. The great majority of the new women are Democrats, largely because they won nominations in districts favorable to their party.

The unusually large number of open seats in 1992 clearly contributed to women's success. Redistricting and the House bank scandal combined to boost both retirements and primary losses. On election day, ninety-one districts were open. In comparison, the average number of open seats in House elections from 1970 through 1990 was only about forty-five.[14] Clearly 1992 offered an unusually favorable opportunity for increasing the proportion of women in the House.

Surprisingly, the proportion of female major party nominees who won in 1992 was not extraordinarily high by the standards of recent history. Between 1970 and 1992, the percentage who won has varied between a high of 48 and a low of 33, averaging 40 percent.

TABLE 7.4 Women Candidates, Running and Winning, 1970-1992

Election	Major Party Nominees	Winners	% Who Won
1970	25	12	48
1972	32	14	44
1974	44	18	41
1976	54	18	33
1978	46	16	35
1980	52	19	37
1982	55	21	38
1984	65	22	34
1986	64	23	36
1988	56	25	45
1990	69	28	41
1992	106	47	44

Source: Center for the American Woman and Politics, 1992, *News & Notes* 8, no. 3: 19.

At 44 percent, the 1992 figure is one of the higher success rates, but it is certainly within the historic range. The maintenance of a relatively high success rate in the 1990s even as the number of female major party nominees increased greatly is, however, important. In the 1970s, as the number of female major party nominees increased, their success rate decreased.

The relatively narrow range in which the success rate varies suggests that a major predictor of the number of women winning election to the House is the number winning major party nominations. Barbara Burrell has shown that the same is true in open seat primaries; women candidates were as likely as male candidates to win their party's nomination (Burrell 1992, 493-508). Thus the more women who run, the more who will win.

Does this mean that the determinants of House outcomes discussed earlier—candidate quality, resources, and the partisan character of the district—are not important after all? To the contrary, it indicates that potential female candidates with electoral experience and the ability to raise money are, like their male counterparts, strategic politicians who run when and where their chances of winning are good (see Jacobson and Kernell 1983). So many more women ran in 1992 because, given the large number of open seats as well as the anti-incumbent mood, that year offered quality candidates a better than usual chance to win.

Conclusion

In the earlier chapters in this volume, several scholars reported that women chose to run for the Senate in response to short-term political events, specifically the Anita Hill-Clarence Thomas hearings and the *Webster* decision. These factors may have stimulated some women to run for the House who would not have done so otherwise and almost certainly stimulated giving by women to women's campaign funds. In addition, gridlock in Washington and the House bank scandal engendered broad-based dissatisfaction with government. This may have helped women candidates, who are more likely to be perceived as outsiders.

Yet the evidence overwhelmingly points to more systemic factors as the primary determinants of women's success in the 1992 House elections. As more women have sought and won elective office at the state and local level, the pool of potential quality candidates has expanded. Acting as we would expect experienced strategic politicians to behave, a large number of these well-prepared women ran for their party's nomination in a year that promised an unusually high probability of success. Democratic women in particular ran in districts favorable to their party. As quality candidates, many women won their party's nomination and many of these went on to win in the general election as well. To a large extent, they won because they were good candidates who took advantage of their opportunities—a favorable year and a favorable district.

The combination of factors that produced such a large number of open seats in 1992 and thus made it such a favorable year for non-incumbent quality candidates to run is not likely to be repeated soon. Thus, we are not likely to see the same magnitude of increase in female representation in the next few years. Yet the opportunities for more modest progress certainly exist. Barriers to increased female representation such as voter discrimination, campaign financing difficulties, and low representation in the eligibility pool have fallen over the past two decades, leveling the playing field on which men and women compete in primaries and general elections. Burrell's study strongly suggests that, were more quality women candidates to seek their party's nomination in open districts, more would win both the nomination and the general election (1992, 493-507). With the pool of potential quality female candidates increasing and other barriers to female representation falling, we can expect steady if not spectacular gains in the coming years.

Notes

1. Excluded from these figures is the District of Columbia's non-voting delegate seat which is currently held by Eleanor Holmes Norton. Her opponent in 1992 was also a woman.

2. A "quality" candidate is difficult to define in an objective manner with the information that is usually available. For this reason, political scientists usually define quality candidates as those who have previously held elective office. As discussed later, this is the definition we will use here.

3. In all three surveys, 3 percent of those surveyed expressed no opinion. In 1970, 84 percent said they would vote for a qualified woman candidate. In 1975, 88 percent said they would vote for a qualified woman candidate, and in 1984, 91 percent said they would vote for a qualified woman candidate.

4. It is important to note that survey questions such as this tend to underestimate prejudice against women candidates. Some respondents may be reluctant to admit bias against women.

5. Yankelovich for CNN-Time, in *National Journal*, August 15, 1992, 1920.

6. *Life*, June 1992, p. 46.

7. Patricia Danner (D-MO) raised 95 percent of what her opponent raised, but Carolyn Maloney (D-NY) raised only 14 percent of what her opponent raised.

8. Fourteen percent of the top fifty money raisers for House seats were women, while women candidates for the House constituted 13 percent of the major party nominees.

9. *Los Angeles Times*, November 8, 1992, p. M3; *Washington Post*, November 4, 1992, p. A30.

10. This amount reflects dollar amounts provided from thirty-five of the forty-two PACs which responded to a survey by the Center for the American Woman and Politics. The figures include direct cash contributions, in-kind contributions, and bundled gifts.

11. These data were gathered from the *Congressional Quarterly Weekly Report* and *National Journal* and may not be complete, thus the figures should be considered approximate. Our thanks to Mary Bendyna, Thomas Brandt, and Katherine Naff for gathering the data.

12. National Women's Political Caucus survey reported in the *Riverside* (CA) *Press-Enterprise*, October 24, 1992, p. 15.

13. *Congressional Quarterly Weekly Report*, September 19, 1992, 2841.

14. *Congressional Quarterly Weekly Report*, November 7, 1992, Supplement to No. 44, 23.

References

Abramson, Paul R., and John H. Aldrich. 1982. "The Decline of Electoral Participation in America." *American Political Science Review* 76: 502-521.

Abzug, Bella, and Mim Kelber. 1984. *Gender Gap*. Boston: Houghton Mifflin Co.

Burrell, Barbara. 1985. "Women's and Men's Campaigns for the U.S. House of Representatives, 1972-1982: A Finance Gap?" *American Politics Quarterly* 13: 251-272.

— — —. 1992. "Women Candidates in Open Seat Primaries for the U.S. House: 1968-1990." *Legislative Studies Quarterly* 17: 493-508.

Carroll, Susan J. 1985. *Women as Candidates in American Politics*. Bloomington, IN: Indiana University Press.

Center for the American Woman and Politics, Eagleton Institute of Politics, Rutgers University. 1991. "Women's PACs in 1990: Continuing to Make A Difference." *News and Notes* 7, no. 1: 10.

— — —. 1992. "U.S. News and World Report Survey." 8, no. 3: 3.

— — —. 1993. "Women Congressional Candidates: 1992 Campaign Receipts." 9, no. 1: 10.

— — —. 1993. "Women's PACs Dramatically Increase their Support in 1992." 9, no. 1: 23.

Clark, Janet. 1991. "Getting There: Women in Political Office." *Annals of the American Academy of Political and Social Scientists* 515: 63-76.

Congressional Quarterly Weekly Report. September 19, 1992. 2841.

— — —. October 24, 1992. 3358-3361.

— — —. November 7, 1992. 3570-3579, 3600-3607.

— — —. November 7, 1992. Supplement to No. 44. 23.

Darcy, Robert., Susan Welch, and Janet Clark. 1987. *Women, Elections and Representation*. White Plains, NY: Longman, Inc.

Jacobson, Gary. 1992. *The Politics of Congressional Elections*, 3rd ed. New York: Harper Collins Publishers, Inc.

— — —. and Samuel Kernell. 1983. *Strategy and Choice in Congressional Elections*. New Haven: Yale University Press.

Kleeman, Katherine E. 1983. *Women's PACs*. New Brunswick, NJ: Eagleton Institute of Politics.

Life. June 1992, p. 46.

Los Angeles Times. November 8, 1992, p. M3.

National Journal. August 15, 1992. 1920.

Riverside (CA) *Press-Enterprise.* October 24, 1992, p. 15.

Uhlaner, Carole, and Kay Schlozman. 1986. "Candidate Gender and Congressional Campaign Receipts." *Journal of Politics* 48 (February): 30-50.

Washington Post. November 4, 1992, p. A30.

Zipp, John F., and Eric Plutzer. 1985. "Gender Differences in Voting for Female Candidates: Evidence from the 1982 Election." *Public Opinion Quarterly* 49: 179-197.

8

Women in State Legislatures: One Step at a Time

Sue Thomas

Was 1992 the "Year of the Woman" for candidates for state legislative seats? Women did make meaningful gains: 2,373 women ran for statehouse seats in 1992, a 15 percent increase over 1990, and 1,516 women won state legislative seats, representing 20.4 percent of these offices. In 1990, 1,368 women held state legislative office, which represented 18.4 percent of all seats (Center for the American Woman and Politics (CAWP) 1992; 1993). Nevertheless, because women achieved incremental rather than dramatic progress at this level, the media, who used the "Year of the Woman" as shorthand for large increases in the number of women running for and winning seats in the U.S. Congress, did not apply the term to state legislatures.

However, this does not mean that 1992 was not an important year for women who sought to enter statehouses. Not only did a record number of women seek and win state legislative seats across the nation, but thirty states bested their previous highest numbers of women candidates for state legislative positions (CAWP 1992). After the balloting, one-fifth of legislative seats across the fifty states are held by women, meaning that more women than ever before are a part of key decisions in their states.

As was the case in the U.S. House and Senate elections, Democratic women running for statehouses made much larger advances than those competing under the Republican banner—a 20 percent increase for Democratic women, but only 8 percent for Republicans. Fully 60.8 percent of women state legislators in 1993 are Democrats compared to

38.5 percent who are Republicans and 0.7 percent who are nonpartisans or Independents. As has been the case in the past, more women serve in lower houses than upper ones: 336 women hold seats in state senates (17 percent of the total), and 1,180 hold seats in lower chambers (22 percent of the total).[1]

Diversity in Representation

Although women represent 20 percent of state legislators nationwide, female representatives are more common in some states than in others. As Table 8.1 shows, the ten states with the highest percentages of female state legislators are Washington, Arizona, Colorado, Vermont, New Hampshire, Maine, Idaho, Kansas, Minnesota, and Wisconsin. The states with the lowest proportions are Kentucky, Alabama, Louisiana, Oklahoma, Arkansas, Pennsylvania, Mississippi, Virginia, Tennessee, and New Jersey (CAWP 1993). There is a wide range across these states, with nearly 40 percent of seats in Washington held by women but only 4 percent of seats in Kentucky.

TABLE 8.1 Women in State Legislatures in 1993 (in percent)

	Women Legislators		% of Total Legislators
	1,516		20.4
Party Breakdowns			
	Total Legislators	Senators	Representatives
Democrats	60.8	61.6	60.5
Republicans	38.5	35.1	39.5
Nonpartisans	.7	3.0	———
Independents	.1	.3	———
The ten states with the highest percentages of women state legislators:			
Washington	39.5	Maine	31.2
Arizona	35.6	Idaho	30.5
Colorado	34.0	Kansas	28.5
Vermont	33.9	Minnesota	27.4
New Hampshire	33.5	Wisconsin	27.3
The ten states with the lowest percentages of women state legislators:			
Kentucky	4.3	Pennsylvania	9.9
Alabama	5.7	Mississippi	10.9
Louisiana	6.9	Virginia	11.4
Oklahoma	9.4	Tennessee	12.1
Arkansas	9.6	New Jersey	12.5

Source: All of the information presented here was supplied by the Center for the American Woman and Politics, Eagleton Institute, Rutgers University, New Brunswick, NJ.

Interestingly, these lists of states with the highest and lowest proportions of women in their legislatures are not very different from those emerging from recent election cycles.[2] It is natural, therefore, to wonder which factors are conducive to women's participation and success, and which ones have the opposite effect. Scholars working in this field have explored several sets of explanations that could reasonably explain differences in women's representation in the states, including voters' propensity to choose or avoid women candidates, how variations in competition levels for seats affect women, the inclination of party elites to support or steer clear of female candidates, women's difficulty or success raising money, and whether variations in political culture (the set of values and historical experiences that shape the conduct of a political grouping) affect women's presence. Perhaps surprisingly, none of these factors is particularly useful in explaining the variation among the states. In addition, the size of legislative districts, their level of urbanization, whether legislatures meet part-time or full-time, and the level of compensation offered do little to explain inter-state differences (Darcy, Welch, and Clark 1987).

With little research validation for any of these explanations, we are left to speculate about what does account for women's greater levels of success in some states than others. It is possible that once women achieve a toe-hold in a state, other women are encouraged to run in large numbers, or that women's groups in that state may work particularly hard at recruitment and support of candidacies (Rule's 1993 discussion of these effects is especially helpful). Since legislative party caucuses are major fundraising arenas for candidates, this explanation is entirely plausible (see Salmore and Salmore 1993). It is also possible that, with different types of measurement or the addition of extra election cycles, some of the factors mentioned above might prove to be more significant than previously discovered. Whatever the case, this area is ripe for additional investigation.

Gains at the State Level—From 1969 to 1992

Lost in the media concentration on women's gains at the federal level are two key questions about female state-level representation: why have women penetrated the glass ceiling in statehouses more quickly and with greater effect than they have at the congressional level, and why didn't women make the kinds of dramatic gains in representation in 1992 that their congressional counterparts achieved? The answers to these questions are interrelated.

The percentage of state legislative seats held by women is currently nearly double the number they hold in Congress, and women have been able to achieve steady progress in gaining statehouse seats over the last twenty years, whereas the percentage of women in Congress barely budged until this election year. In 1969, women were 4 percent of the nation's state legislators; in 1981, they were 12.1 percent; and in 1991, they were 18.3 percent (see Chapter 1 for a more complete listing). In contrast, in 1975, women were only 4 percent of Congress and had only reached 6 percent before the 1992 elections. As the director of the Center for the American Woman and Politics at Rutgers University notes, "In contests for state legislative seats, women also made important advances—here following a precedent for progress which has now sustained itself for two decades. The emerging picture of the state legislatures for 1993 reveals that women's forward movement continues at its long-established pace" (Mandel 1992).

What factors, then, account for women's greater share of state legislative than congressional seats and their more modest gains at the state level? Three interrelated explanations are relevant and explored in more depth below. First, over-time changes in the attractiveness of state legislatures relative to Congress and the effects of these shifting patterns of seat turnover have had a considerable impact on women's levels of representation. Similarly, the electoral systems used to select representatives on each level are associated with women's greater share of statehouse than congressional seats. The final contributory factor to women's differential rates of gain in Congress and the states in 1992 is attributable to the base from which women at each level were building.

The Shifting Power of the States

That women's representation in state legislatures grew steadily from 1969 onward whereas female representation in Congress was (and still is) quite limited is related directly to differential opportunities for access. Women (and other newcomers) made relatively rapid progress in state legislatures in the late 1970s and early 1980s in part because a greater number of seats were available through turnover (Rosenthal 1990). It was not unusual in the 1960s and 1970s to find about 30 percent of state legislative seats turning over every two years (Gray and Eisinger 1991; Benjamin and Malbin 1992), and a substantial number of seats came open in each election. In contrast, at the federal level, turnover has been lower due largely to extraordinarily high incumbency re-election rates and, although this was not the pattern in 1992, the fact that most incumbents choose to run again (Jacobson 1992).

Much of the difference in attractiveness of the two positions relates to the scope of power accorded to each. Members of Congress have the ability to involve themselves in a vast array of local, national, and international issues, but state legislators have a much narrower set of issues to which to devote their attention. Furthermore, in many states, membership in the legislature is a part-time job. These legislatures meet for short periods of time, and members' primary occupations and interests lie elsewhere. This means that governors are the key players in statehouse politics in many states, and legislators know it. Until recently, legislative and regulatory power had become ever more concentrated at the federal level and decision-making leeway enjoyed by the states diminished over time (see Rosenthal 1990).

Over the last fifteen to twenty years, state legislative office in many states has become more attractive. First, in the 1970s, state legislatures collectively undertook reforms intended to make them more effective and consequential. These efforts resulted in a professionalization (some call it congressionalization) along the lines of the U.S. Congress and included increased staffing, strengthening of committee systems, increased lobbying activity, and more frequent and longer lasting sessions (Rosenthal 1990; Salmore and Salmore 1993). Moreover, the scope and level of responsibility accorded to state legislatures has expanded as programs have shifted from the federal to the state governments.

The increased attractiveness of state legislative seats has gradually transformed the nature of state legislative elections into one that resembles its federal counterpart. According to Benjamin and Malbin (1992), in 1988, for example, only 16 percent of state legislators were newcomers, the lowest level ever. Also, as Salmore and Salmore (1993, 64) report:

In the 1960s and 1970s, typically fewer than a fifth of all legislative incumbents were defeated. In the 1980s, this number rarely approached a tenth and was frequently close to zero. Nor do large number of incumbents have close races. Half or more of all legislators in a sizable number of states run unopposed.

The changes in the professionalism of state legislatures that altered levels of electoral competition and decreased access for newcomers has had a substantial effect on women's representation within them. In the 1970s, aspirants could stake their claims more easily than today.

Nevertheless, women continued to make progress in statehouses even as opportunities for access became more scarce, because as women's presence increased, they had a power base from which to recruit other female candidates and the money necessary to offer support. In addition to direct encouragement, the presence of female state legislators may very well have been a psychological boost to those women considering candidacies and one factor in the decision to commit to a race.

Despite the recent trend toward state legislative professionalism, it is unlikely that statehouse seats will become as coveted and as difficult to obtain as congressional seats. First, resources necessary for high-powered campaigns are more limited at this level and the advantages of incumbency are fewer. In addition, even if state legislative jobs are, on the whole, more attractive than previously, there is still the lure of higher office or more lucrative positions elsewhere to create vacancies that can be translated into opportunities for women. Finally, the enactment of term limits in more than a dozen states across the nation (in both the elections of 1990 and 1992) means that opportunities (at least in some places) will be greater than ever. [3]

Electoral Variation

Another explanation for the greater success of women in state legislative races than in federal races concerns the type of district from which one is elected. A substantial amount of research on the effects of running in multi-member versus single-member districts concludes that women have a greater chance of winning in multi-member districts (more than one representative per district is chosen) than they have otherwise (Welch and Studlar 1990; Herrick and Welch 1991; Matland and Brown 1992). Although the number of seats in which multi-member elections still take place are declining, according to Gray and Eisinger (1991), "As of 1985, about 25 percent of house members and 8 percent of senate members are chosen from multi-member districts." All congressional seats, on the other hand, are of the single-member variety.

What would make this type of election more advantageous for women? Darcy, Welch, and Clark (1987) speculate that those responsible for creating slates of candidates may feel pressure to be representative when multiple seats within a district are available. Decision-makers may also be interested in adding women to slates to make those slates distinctive and noteworthy. When multiple seats are available, voters too may be more willing to make their districts "look like America," as President Clinton is fond of saying. Finally, say Darcy, Welch, and Clark, women themselves may be more comfortable stepping forward as candidates in situations where there is no one single opponent and where they can promote themselves rather than attack another candidate.

The gradual movement away from multi-member to single-member districts (the congressional model) over the last two to three decades meant that the electoral structures that assisted women in building their numbers in the 1970s and 1980s eroded. That they did not storm the barricades of statehouses nor enjoy exceptional increases in representation in 1992 can, therefore, also be linked to this trend.

How Strong the Foundation?

One last explanation for why women's progress in 1992 was not as great on the state level as for federal office concerns the base from which women on each level were working. In other words, it is much easier to rack up large percentage gains when starting from a small base rather than a relatively large one. Since the percentage (and the absolute number) of women in the 102nd Congress was so small (5.8 percent or thirty-one women out of 535 representatives and senators) a substantial increase was neither unreasonable nor difficult to achieve—especially given the favorable circumstances surrounding redistricting, retirements, and scandals. In contrast, women at the state level had made enough progress winning seats that striking gains of the sort exhibited by Congress would have required nearly wholesale retirements or defeats of incumbent men. Hence, while 1992 may not have been the year of the state legislative woman, it certainly was an important election for both maintaining previous gains and extending them. When the gains women made in state legislatures in 1992 are put in context of their previous successes and current circumstances, it is easy to see why the media attention in this election cycle went to women candidates and winners in the U.S. House of Representatives and the U.S. Senate.

It is likely that the proportion of women in statehouses will continue to increase steadily. The growing term limitation movement could create large numbers of open legislative seats in many states in the near future. Such open seats would increase opportunities for women to run for state legislative seats, and encourage women who now hold such seats to run for Congress. Yet in states that currently have large numbers of women in their state legislatures, term limits may result in women replacing women.

While it is possible that a dramatic increase in female representation in state legislatures in a single election cycle will occur, this is fairly unlikely. The federal Year of the Woman phenomenon transpired because opportunities were uncharacteristically abundant. As Carole Chaney and Barbara Sinclair note in Chapter 7, women won in the House because of the large numbers of open seats and because a ready pool of qualified women was ready to run top-notch campaigns. A similar potent combination of factors is less likely at the state level because the fifty states have different electoral systems, and because scandals and other factors that might limit the viability of incumbents are not likely to affect legislators equally in all (or even most) states across the nation.

Women in Office: Change or Continuity?

Ultimately, the most important question about the gains of women officeholders is not how dramatic or quick the rise in proportion, but why their presence matters. As is illuminated more fully in the final chapter of this book, we may have in mind several types of answers to this question. First, it is appropriate to question the legitimacy of a democratic system of government that precludes or inhibits certain groups from the halls of deliberation. Forgoing the diversity of the citizen pool also raises questions about the efficacy of the decisions made by representative bodies. Another reason having women in legislatures matters concerns the symbolic benefits to society of having a wide variety of people among the political elite. When this occurs, both adults and children may see their options in an expansive light.

A final reason, and one that is often associated with the question of increasing the number of women in political office, is the possibility of expanded governmental agendas and new governmental policies. There has been widespread discussion in the political, journalistic, and scholarly communities about whether bringing women into political office will make a policy difference (see Kirkpatrick 1974; Diamond 1977; Frankovic 1977; Gehlen 1977; Leader 1977; Johnson and Carroll 1978; Welch 1985; Norris 1986; Thomas 1990; Dodson and Carroll 1991; Thomas and Welch 1991; Thomas forthcoming). New evidence on this last point suggests an affirmative answer for women at the state level. This is particularly consequential since a great deal of the policy that affects our day-to-day lives, such as comparable worth, insurance equity, and child and elder care, are decided on the state level. Thus, the remainder of this chapter explores how women's presence in state legislative office affects public policies.

Women's Policy Priorities

One way to judge the kind of difference women make in governmental decision-making concerns the policies on which they place priority. I recently completed research on this question in twelve states across the nation including Arizona, California, Georgia, Illinois, Iowa, Mississippi, Nebraska, North Carolina, Pennsylvania, South Dakota, Vermont, and Washington. The states were chosen to represent the range of regions, political cultures, and proportions of women in the legislature.[5] Data were gathered using a mail survey of female and male state legislators in each of the twelve states and in-person interviews with women legislators in six of the states: California, Georgia, Mississippi, Nebraska, Pennsylvania, and Washington. All women of the lower chambers in each state were surveyed along with a sample of male legislators in each state. In all, 226 women and 375 men were surveyed and the final response rate stood at 54 percent. (For a fuller discussion of the research design and response rates per state and for women and men separately, see Thomas forthcoming).

TABLE 8.2 Gender Differences on Indirect Indicators of Priorities (by percentages)

	Male	*Female*
Perceptions of Constituency:		
Elderly	70	72
Business	53	47
Labor	31	38
Women	33*	57*
Party	21*	28*
Racial Minorities	30	38
Pride in Accomplishments (first choice):		
Public Interest	15	12
Business	23	12
Ed./Medical/Welfare	23	28
Crime	5	5
Budget	9	6
Women/Children	11	16
Pride in Accomplishments (second choice):		
Public Interest	22	19
Business	26*	10*
Ed./Medical/Welfare	20	20
Crime	3	3
Budget	8*	3
Women/Children	6*	30*

* Gender difference significant at the .05 level.   N=322

Several types of questions were asked of the legislators that illuminate how women and men in statehouses think about priorities and what actions they take to define and implement them. The first two questions deal indirectly with policy priorities and the last is a direct indicator.

When asked which interests are most important for them to represent, the respondents provided a variety of answers including the elderly, business, labor, women, their party, and racial minorities.[6] Only in two areas were there significant differences between women and men, however. The first concerned the respondents' political party. As Table 8.2 shows, 28 percent of the women considered this interest very important while 21 percent of the men agreed with that formulation. One explanation for this finding is that women feel more tied to their party than do men because the party provides them with the contacts that are so necessary for successful candidacies of their own. Traditionally, men have had larger outside networks from which to draw support than have women (Costantini 1990).

The biggest gender gap, however, concerns the importance of representing women. Fully 57 percent of women state legislators considered representing women very important while only 33 percent of men responded similarly. It is clear that women state legislators feel a special affinity for the status of women in society and consider representing those interests as important.

Respondents were also asked to identify one or two of the accomplishments of which they are most proud. Women were more proud than men of bill passage on issues regarding women and those relating to children and families. In contrast, men were significantly more likely to feel pride in their legislation relating to business and to budget and tax issues.

That female legislators consider representing the interests of women very important and take pride in accomplishments in this area suggests that they accord special attention to such issues when developing legislative priorities. To test this proposition, the twelve-state mail survey asked respondents to list their top five legislative priorities in the last complete legislative session.[7] Follow-up questions were asked in the personal interviews.

The data in Table 8.3 show that women's lists of priority bills contain more legislation pertaining to children (topics such as child care, family leave, and early childhood education) than the list of men. Women introduce an average of .35 more bills on children than men. This means that an increase of ten women legislators would result in introductions of three or four more children's bills each session (see

TABLE 8.3   Average   Number   of   Bill   Introductions   and   Passages
by Men and Women

	Male	Female
Total Bill Introductions	17.5	13.6
Total Bill Passage (through legislature)	8.4	6.6
Types of Priority Bill Introductions:		
Women	.03*	.11*
Children/Families	.20*	.55*
Business	1.1+	.68+
Passage of Priority Bills (through legislature)	2.2	2.3
Passage of Priority Bills (governor's signature)	1.8	2.1
Passage Rate of Bills Dealing with Women, Children & Families (through legislature)	11.1*	27.1*
Passage Rate of Bills Dealing with Women, Children & Families (governor's signature)	8.0*	25.6*

* Statistically significant at the .05 level.
+ Significant at the .10 level.

Coding: For total bill introduction, legislators could enter an unlimited number; total bill passage was some portion of total bill introductions. For priority bills, legislators were held to their top five, so the range was from zero to five. Passage of priority bills also ranged from zero to five. The passage rate of bills dealing with women and with children and families is the total number of such bills introduced divided by the total number of those bills that were passed.

Kathlene, Clarke, and Fox 1991 for similar patterns in the Colorado legislature). These distinctive interests also hold in multivariate analysis.[8] Consider this comment from an in-person interview with a Western legislator:

Women's legislative priorities are similar to men's, but women are more attuned to issues that are family oriented. Men do some also though men are interested in teen pregnancy and family violence, but almost all women have something in all categories [of bills of interest to women] and will support your bills of this kind with no question.

Another area of interest to women in statehouses is women's issues—those ranging broadly from comparable worth to domestic violence.[9] Women are slightly more likely than men to make them a high priority. Although the data do not indicate a very large difference between women and men, the personal interviews suggested that female legislators are more committed to women's issues than are men. Consider these comments explaining why women's legislative priorities are distinctive:

"Women are different in some capacity. Women have perspective men don't have. I am introducing legislation to help women. Women must protect women. That's what I do" (a Southern legislator).

"Women in general tend to focus on women's issues. You seldom see men work on displaced homemakers' issues, etc." (a Southern legislator).

"Most of the women are or have been married and have kids. Since they had that experience, those issues are very important to them. They see it as their responsibility" (a Western legislator).

"Women lean more toward compassion issues and education. Men lean toward farming, fishing and retirement issues. Also there is a totally different approach. Women are more family oriented; men are more economics" (a Southern legislator).

"Women tend to look at more issues of women and children. This is not to say others aren't addressed, but they [women] carry more legislation more quickly and put in more energy and effort. Women are lead people on this type of stuff" (a Southern legislator).

While I cannot quote all the women I interviewed on the differences in priorities between women and men in statehouses, I can say that almost all mentioned some differences along the lines suggested above.[10]

One final way to examine the types of priorities to which women legislators are committed is to devise a composite indicator. I calculated a figure in which all of the priority bills of legislators that dealt with women and with children and families were combined. Forty-two percent of women had at least one priority bill dealing with issues of women or of children and families compared with only 16 percent of men. These differences are statistically significant.[11]

In contrast to the types of bills that women consider high priority, men, more often than women, place priority on bills dealing with business. In fact, men introduce an average of .42 more bills on business than do women. Looked at another way, men in all twelve states, introduce higher numbers of business bills than do women in their states.

It would be a mistake to interpret the findings discussed above as meaning that women only care about bills dealing with women and with children and the family, and that men only care about bills dealing with business. That is most certainly not what is going on. Women and men are both interested in and introduce legislation concerning the full range of issues before legislatures. However, even allowing for wide-ranging interests by both sexes, we do find some important patterns. Women do give more time, energy, and effort to bills dealing with women's issues and with children's and family issues, and men commit more effort to business issues. The areas of expertise of women and men are not polarized, but they are distinctive.

Success in Passing Policy Priorities

A list of the priority bills of legislators is a key to understanding their values and how those values translate into legislative action. However, the mere introduction of bills tells us nothing about whether legislators were successful in seeing those bills through the process. If women are to have an effect on legislative agendas, they must not only introduce distinctive legislation, they must pass it.

As Table 8.3 indicates, when comparing the success rates of women and men on their entire lists of policy priorities, there is substantial equality.[12] Women passed an average of 2.3 of their top five priorities while men average about 2.2. This translates to women legislators passing 46 percent of their top five priority bills compared to men's passage rate of 44 percent. Perhaps more interesting are the success rates related to priority bills dealing with the distinctive priorities of the sexes. The ratio of introduction to passage of bills relating to women's issues and children's and family issues is higher for women than men (27.1 for women compared to 11.1 for men). Similar patterns are evident with respect to obtaining gubernatorial signature. Women legislators' average ratio of introduction to signature of these types of bills is 25.6 compared to men's average of only 8.0.[13]

Augmenting the conclusions drawn from data analysis is a comment from the in-person interviews. A staff member in a Western legislature who works on women's issues noted: "Women absolutely make a policy difference. They are more sensible, more practical, and more comprehensive. The are more willing to fight for women's and children's policies. They don't give up as easily."

Does Proportionality Matter?

In addition to investigating priorities of representatives as a group, it is instructive to explore the conditions under which their distinctive contributions are most likely to be pursued. At issue here is whether women introduce women's and children's and family legislation as well as successfully see it through the process in places where there are the greatest proportions of female representatives. A corollary question concerns whether those legislatures with the highest percentages of women are also those in which the highest general level of such legislation (introduced by women or men) is passed. In other words, are legislatures that are closest to gender balance ones in which men and women see such issues as important and legitimate?

Data from the twelve-state mail survey are useful for testing these questions. With respect to the first question, the legislatures were divided into three categories of proportionality. Mississippi and Pennsylvania comprise the low category because they had less than 10 percent female representation. In the middle category are states with from 10 to 20 percent women legislators, including California, Georgia, Illinois, Iowa, Nebraska, North Carolina, and South Dakota. Finally, Arizona, Vermont, and Washington, states with at least 30 percent women legislators comprise the high category.[13]

The results of the analysis reveal that women in states with higher proportions of female membership tend to introduce more priority legislation dealing with women and with children and families than the men in their states and are more successful in passage of these bills. In states such as Arizona, Vermont, and Washington, the women introduced and passed more of their priority legislation on these issues than did men. Conversely, in Pennsylvania and Mississippi, no such pattern is manifested (see also Berkman and O'Connor 1993 for a similar analysis regarding abortion policy, and Saint-Germain 1989 for a longitudinal analysis of Arizona). When asked to discuss whether variation in the proportion of women in the legislature was relevant to pursuit of policy priorities, women across the states had this to say:

"Fewer women would mean no comparable worth, no abortion initiatives and no state ERA. Compare our state to states with few women legislators. There are altogether different attitudes and legislation" (a Western legislator).

"With twenty-one women we can't make a difference. We need much more to have a real impact" (a Southern legislator).

"Absolutely, our issues get attention and supporters out there and the supporters are more outspoken about their position if women [legislators] are in the lead.... Numbers also mean power or a potent voting bloc. Numbers are one of the reasons we have been as effective as we have been" (a Western legislator).

A Midwestern legislator who spoke of what she called quality of life issues such as the environment and water—issues that were more long-term and children's issues said: "If there were 2 percent women in the legislature, you might not see some issues get raised. If there were 50 percent women, there would be an emphasis on issues that women are likely to champion."

And a Southern legislator observed: "Women protect women—with more women, things would be better. The numbers here are too small to make a big difference."

The presence of a formal women's legislative caucus is also highly salient to how much legislation on women's issues and on children's and family issues is passed in a given legislative session. The top five states in the overall passage of such legislation are, in order, California, Iowa, Illinois, Washington, and North Carolina. Except for Washington, these are the only states of all twelve that have formal legislative caucuses. Further, Washington is the state with the highest percentage of women in the lower house. This suggests that support, either in the form of the presence of a formal women's caucus or relatively high percentages of women, is important for the passage, on a general basis, of legislation dealing with women and with children and the family. The in-person interviews support this conclusion. As one Western legislator stated, "The caucus can be a power bloc; it can make an impact." The same legislator also said: "Women would vote together three-quarters of time if you got rid of party. They think first about the issue, not the politics."

Conclusion

For women in state legislatures, there has been no single Year of the Woman—1992 or otherwise. Instead, women have made steady and continuous progress in increasing their share of statehouse seats. Perhaps Ruth Mandel, director of the Center for the American Woman and Politics, put it best: "Inch by inch, election year by election year, these women in the states move us toward parity for women and men in politics" (Mandel 1992).

Along with increases in numbers comes increased attention to constituencies and issues that were heretofore considered marginal such as child care and comparable worth. Women not only inhabit state legislative seats in greater numbers than before, they make a distinctive contribution to the governmental process.

Notes

1. For an interesting comparison of female winners and losers of state legislative races in 1992, see Kathlene and Lenart 1993.

2. Indeed, the top six states in the list were among the top ten states in 1974. See Rule 1993 for a listing of women in state legislatures in 1974 and 1984. For a discussion of women's representation in Wisconsin, see Duerst-Lahti 1993.

3. It is true that some states' citizens voted for term limits for congressional seats, however, the constitutionality of these decisions is in

doubt, and it may be a very long time before any limits of this kind are put in force.

4. Political culture is a concept used by political scientists to explain how states differ in terms of predominant political, social, and cultural influences. The study was designed to incorporate all three major political cultures because the women and men surveyed in the states may feel differently about the political world or may have a different impact on the system depending on which culture they inhabit. Daniel Elazar identified three major cultures: traditionalistic, moralistic, and individualistic. For a fuller description, see Elazar 1984.

5. Some of this material appeared in two recent articles. See Thomas and Welch 1991 and Thomas 1991.

6. From their responses, eight categories of bill type were constructed for analysis. These categories included women's issues; child and family issues; issues of education and medical care; welfare; criminal justice; energy and environment; state budget and governmental efficiency; and business and transportation.

7. Women in eight of the twelve states introduce more legislation dealing with children and the family than do their male counterparts.

8. I chose, as the definition of women's issues, those issues that embrace both feminist and traditional concerns of women for several reasons. The first is that traditional women's issues such as the Equal Rights Amendment and reproductive rights are not necessarily the only ones that can be labeled women's issues. Yet, these are the measures usually used in studies of women elites and whether they are supportive women's issues. It may be a better measure to use issues that remove the bias of only those who refer to themselves as feminists. Indeed, it is perhaps the more mainstream issues that provide an indication of policy responsiveness to the general population rather than a small, specific one.

9. Out of the twelve states in the study, women in eight of them have a higher average priority level on bills dealing with children and families than do men. Further, women in seven of the twelve states have a higher average of policy priority on bills pertaining to women's issues than do men.

10. Examining the first priority state legislators list among their five is also interesting. Women have an average of .05 more bills dealing with women or with children and families among their single top priority than do men. This finding is statistically significant at the .10 level. Additionally, women legislators in seven out of twelve states conform to this pattern.

11. Women in seven of the twelve states had higher passage rates of priority bills than did the men in those states. Women and men are substantially equal in obtaining their governor's signature on bills, and, therefore, seeing them become law.

12. Once again, the overall priority passage ratio is higher for women than men in nine out of the twelve states.

13. The reader may wonder why so many states fall into the middle category while only two or three states comprise the high and low categories. The reason is simply that so few states fall significantly above and below the average, there was little to choose from. The problem was compounded by the need to have regional balance and diversity in political culture in each category. In short, the problem here is the same one faced by all studies of women officeholders. We simply do not have the range and diversity that would be ideal.

References

Benjamin, Gerald, and Michael J. Malbin, eds. 1992. *Limiting Legislative Terms.* Washington, DC: Congressional Quarterly.

Berkman, Michael B., and Robert E. O'Connor. 1993. "Do Women Legislators Matter? Female Legislators and State Abortion Policy." *American Politic Quarterly* 21: 102-124.

Center for the American Woman and Politics, Eagleton Institute of Politics, Rutgers University. 1992. "Fact Sheet: Women Moving into State Legislatures 1974-1993."

— — —. 1993. "Fact Sheet: Women Who Will Serve in State Legislatures 1993."

Costantini, Edmond. 1990. "Political Women and Political Ambition: Closing the Gender Gap." *American Journal of Political Science* 34: 741-770.

Darcy, Robert, Susan Welch, and Janet Clark. 1987. *Women, Elections, and Representation.* White Plains, NY: Longman, Inc.

Diamond, Irene. 1977. *Sex Roles in the State House.* New Haven: Yale University Press.

Dodson, Debra L., and Susan J. Carroll. 1991. *Reshaping the Agenda: Women in State Legislatures.* New Brunswick, NJ: Center for the American Woman and Politics.

Duerst-Lahti, Georgia. 1993. "Year of the Woman, Decade of Women: Wisconsin Legislative Elections." Presented at the annual meeting of the Midwest Political Science Association, Chicago.

Elazar, Daniel J. 1984. *American Federalism: A View From the States,* 3rd ed. New York: Harper & Row.

Frankovic, Kathleen A. 1977. "Sex and Voting in the U.S. House of Representatives 1961-1975." *American Politics Quarterly* 5: 315-331.

Gehlen, Freida. 1977. "Women Members of Congress: A Distinctive Role." In Marianne Githens and Jewell Prestage, eds. *A Portrait of Marginality: The Political Behavior of the American Woman.* New York: McKay.

Gray, Virginia, and Peter Eisinger. 1991. *American States and Cities*. New York: Harper Collins Publishers, Inc.

Herrick, Rebekah, and Susan Welch. 1991. "The Impact of At-Large Elections on the Representation of Black and White Women." In Lucius J. Barker, ed. *Ethnic Politics and Civil Liberties*. New Brunswick, NJ: Transaction Publishers.

Jacobson, Gary. 1992. *The Politics of Congressional Elections*, 3rd ed. New York: Harper Collins Publishers, Inc.

Johnson, Marilyn, and Susan J. Carroll, with Kathy Stanwyck and Lynn Korenblit. 1978. *Profile of Women Holding Office II*. New Brunswick, NJ: Center for the American Woman and Politics.

Kathlene, Lyn, Susan E. Clarke, and Barbara A. Fox. 1991. "Ways Women Politicians Are Making A Difference." In Debra L. Dodson, ed., *Gender and Policymaking: Studies of Women in Office*. New Brunswick, NJ: Center for the American Woman and Politics.

Kathlene, Lyn, and Silvo Lenart. 1993. "Who Are the Women Candidates? A Typology of Women Candidates in the 1992 Congressional and State Level Races." Presented at the annual meeting of the Midwest Political Science Association, Chicago.

Kirkpatrick, Jeane. 1974. *Political Woman*. New York: Basic Books.

Leader, Shelah G. 1977. "The Policy Impact of Elected Women Officials." In Joseph Cooper and Louis Maisel, eds. *The Impact of the Electoral Process*. Beverly Hills: Sage.

Mandel, Ruth. November 17, 1992. "Solid Gains for Women in the State Legislatures." Press Release. New Brunswick, NJ: Center for the American Woman and Politics.

Matland, Richard E., and Deborah Dwight Brown. 1992. "District Magnitude's Effect on Female Representation in U.S. State Legislatures." *Legislative Studies Quarterly* 17: 469-492.

Norris, Pippa. 1986. "Women in Congress: A Policy Difference?" *Politics* 6: 34-40.

Rosenthal, Alan. 1990. *Governors and Legislatures: Contending Powers*. Washington, DC: CQ Press.

Rule, Wilma. 1993. "Why Are More Women State Legislators?" In Lois Lovelace Duke, ed. *Women in Politics: Outsiders or Insiders?* Englewood Cliffs, NJ: Prentice Hall.

Saint-Germain, Michelle A. 1989. "Does Their Difference Make A Difference? The Impact of Women on Public Policy in the Arizona Legislature." *Social Science Quarterly* 70: 956-968.

Salmore, Stephen A., and Barbara G. Salmore. 1993. "Transformation of State Electoral Politics." In Carl E. Van Horn, ed. *The State of the States*, 2nd ed. Washington, DC: Congressional Quarterly.

Thomas, Sue. 1990. "Voting Patterns in the California Assembly: The Role of Gender." *Women & Politics* 9: 43-56.

— — —. 1991. "The Impact of Women on State Legislative Policies." *Journal of Politics* 53: 958-976.

— — —. Forthcoming. *How Women Legislate.* New York: Oxford University Press.

— — —, and Susan Welch. 1991. "The Impact of Gender On Activities and Priorities of State Legislators." *Western Political Quarterly* 44: 445-456.

Welch, Susan. 1985. "Are Women More Liberal Than Men in the U.S. Congress?" *Legislative Studies Quarterly* 10: 125-134.

— — —, and Donley Studlar. 1990. "Multimember Districts and the Representation of Women: Evidence from Britain and the United States." *Journal of Politics* 52: 391-412.

9

Political Parties
and the Year of the Woman

Robert Biersack
and Paul S. Herrnson

Even before the political pundits began to anticipate a "Year of the Woman" in 1992, the Democratic and Republican parties were hard at work attempting to increase the number of women in Congress. Early in the election cycle, the parties were seeking ambitious and skilled women to run for Congress, and encouraging their candidacies. For those women who won their party's nomination, party committees provided training, services, assistance, and money. Party leaders introduced women candidates to individuals and institutions that might contribute to their campaigns.

The national political parties have had a mixed record in providing access to the political system for women, minorities, and disadvantaged groups. During some periods of American history, they have excluded these groups from the political process. In more recent periods, they have recruited women and minorities, and helped them organize, build electoral coalitions, and put some of their members in state and local offices and Congress.

This chapter discusses the activities by the parties that helped elect women to the U.S. House of Representatives and Senate in 1992. The first set of activities, which are often referred to as candidate recruitment, are concerned with increasing the number of women in the field of candidates who run for Congress. The second set of activities focused on helping women amass the money and other resources needed to conduct a viable campaign.

After reviewing the efforts parties made on behalf of female candidates in the 1992 House elections, we conclude that the parties played a significant but not determining role in the election of women in 1992. Our analysis and conclusions for the role of parties in helping elect women to the Senate are more tentative because of the smaller number of campaigns and the tremendous diversity across states. While the parties clearly made a difference in the outcomes of some women's races for both the House and Senate, the talents and efforts of the candidates themselves were more important in enabling women to claim seats in the 103rd Congress.

Parties and Underrepresented Groups

Political parties and other political institutions can treat women and other underrepresented, unempowered groups in a variety of ways. They can seek to exclude them from the political process by erecting barriers to their participation. Threats of violence are the most extreme type of barrier, followed by laws that deny individuals the right to participate in the process. Less extreme barriers include holding meetings at inconvenient times and locations, or exhibiting behavior designed to make women or minorities feel ill at ease. Parties and other political institutions have discouraged women and minorities from participating in politics using a variety of these techniques during various periods in American history (see e.g., Darcy, Welch, and Clark 1987).

Parties can also treat women and other underrepresented groups neutrally by neither discouraging nor encouraging their participation. "Neutral" treatment seems the most likely course of action in an individualistic capitalist democracy like the United States. The underlying theory, based on such notions as the free market of ideas, is that the best individuals and ideas will ultimately prevail under conditions of free competition.

Finally, parties can consciously court underrepresented groups in order to win their loyalties and votes. Such behavior is motivated by the desire to win elections and is exemplified by the outreach of the old-fashioned political machineIIIs. Party organizations, like the Tammany Society of New York and the Daley machine of Chicago, were famous for providing economic assistance, jobs, and other social services to newly-arrived immigrants and ethnic groups. All that was asked of most members of these groups was that they vote for the machine's candidates; others were occasionally asked to lend a hand in turning out the vote in their neighborhood. Many of the more successful machines improved their support among the racial, religious, and ethnic communities by giving them the opportunity to vote for "one of their own" in an election. By personalizing, demystifying, and increasing the relevance of politics in their constituents' eyes, party organizations were able to attract the support of new constituencies that otherwise might have been left out of the political process (Merton 1957; Royko 1971; Rakove 1975; Riordan 1985).

Modern party leaders, like the old-style political bosses, recognize that once previously disenfranchised groups have exercised their right to vote in significant numbers, the exigencies of winning elections compel the parties to take steps to gain their loyalties. The number of jobs and other patronage benefits that modern political leaders can distribute, however, is minuscule compared to that of their forerunners. Parties therefore use different techniques to attract the votes of these groups. First, they have substituted highly visible, symbolic appointments for the scores of jobs given out by the parties of yesteryear. In addition, modern parties try to attract the support of previously disenfranchised groups by addressing their policy concerns. Another important technique the parties can use to win the support of unempowered groups is to give them formal representation in party conventions and committees, as the Democrats have done since 1972. Finally, parties can recruit group members to run for office under the party label and provide them with the campaign resources needed to win.

The 1992 election cycle provides examples of all four activities. Prior to the election, former Representative Lynn Martin was appointed secretary of labor by Republican President George Bush. The Democrats sponsored family leave legislation, championed a woman's right to choose whether to have an abortion, and continued to reserve national committee and convention delegate positions for women. Moreover, both parties undertook special efforts to recruit women to run for Congress.

A Year of Special Opportunities

Nineteen ninety-two was an especially opportune year for the parties to pursue a gender-based election strategy. Women had met a threshold of participation to make them a vital bloc of voters to be aggressively pursued by both parties. They had achieved parity with men in voter turnout a few election cycles earlier (Conway 1991), and their larger numbers meant that a majority of voters in 1992 would be women. Public opinion polls had shown that the vast majority of Americans were willing to support qualified female congressional candidacies (see e.g., Darcy, Welch, and Clark 1987)

A significant number of women held positions in politics that could enable them to take advantage of the call for change. Prior to the election, women accounted for roughly 18 percent of all state legislators and had made substantial inroads into city and county offices. Women also occupied key decision-making positions in a number of national party committees, including such elected posts, as the secretary of the Democratic National Committee, and staff positions, such as PAC directors of the two parties' congressional campaign committees. They comprised 56 percent of the staff of the Democratic Congressional Campaign Committee and 44 percent of the staff of its Republican counterpart. Women held positions at all levels of the party organizations' hierarchies.

Women had also made substantial inroads into positions of economic and social influence. One example of this advancement that is directly related to their future political prospects is the increase in the number of women in the legal profession. Women comprised only 3 percent of all lawyers in 1970 and 13 percent in 1984, but by the mid-1980s they accounted for 35 percent to 40 percent of all first-year law students.[1] The growth in the number of women in the legal profession is important because these young women lawyers comprise a potential pool of candidates and contributors to campaigns.

Despite women's progress, most voters generally perceived them to be outsiders in the political process. Anita Hill's testimony before the all-white, all-male Senate Judiciary Committee dramatized this point in a way few voters could miss. This was a very important consideration in an anti-Washington, anti-incumbent election year. Prior to the 1992 election cycle, House and Senate incumbents had been tainted by institutional scandals, the perceived failures of divided government, and the economic problems that faced our nation. The electoral security of a large number of House members was further called into question by redistricting.

Moreover, a major theme of the 1992 election was change, and women politicians were widely identified as change agents. The results of an NBC News/*Wall Street Journal* poll taken in October 1992, showed that 53 percent of all registered voters believed that female candidates were more likely to create political change than men; only 14 percent felt that male candidates were more likely to bring about change. Public outcry for change appeared to manifest itself in a demand for the election of more non-traditional, "outsider" candidates. By virtue of their sex, women were easily identified as members of this group. The winds of change were blowing and women were positioned to be carried into office by a "favored tack."

Leaders in both political parties recognized the opportunities the 1992 elections offered to women and to themselves, but neither party was in the position to give every female candidate for the House or Senate the resources needed to get elected. First, parties have finite resources and play a limited role in America's election system. Party organizations cannot award nominations as they do in other western democracies. Nor are they able, or expected, to be the dominant force in congressional campaigns. American political institutions, election laws, political culture, history, and the parties themselves have contributed to the development of a largely candidate-centered election system (Epstein 1986).

Second, the parties' congressional campaign committees are controlled by current members of Congress. They tend to run the committees like boards of directors, and their concerns for their own and their colleagues' reelections are preeminent. Incumbent concerns are particularly influential in affecting how the Democratic Congressional Campaign Committee (DCCC) distributes its resources (Herrnson 1989; Jacobson 1992), and this has the potential to skew resources away from members of underrepresented groups.

Third, the parties' ability to give candidates election resources is limited by the Federal Election Campaign Act of 1974 and its amendments (FECA). The FECA allows the national, congressional, and state party organizations to give a maximum contribution of $5,000 to general election candidates for the House. Another $5,000 could be given for the primary election, but parties rarely make contributions before the primary, for they are reluctant to involve themselves in intra-party competition.[2] The parties' national and senatorial campaign committees can give a combined total of $17,500 to Senate candidates; state party organizations can give another $5,000. The expenditures that national party organizations and state party committees can make in coordination with their congressional candidates' campaigns are also limited.[3] Originally set at $10,000 per committee, the limits for coordinated expenditures for House candidates reached $27,620 each per national and state committee in 1992 after being adjusted for inflation.[4] The limits for coordinated expenditures in Senate elections vary by state population and are also indexed to inflation. In 1992, they ranged from $55,240 per committee in less populous states like Alaska, to $1,227,322 in each of the two California races. The state and national parties have separate spending authority, making actual possible expenditures $55,240 in House campaigns and between $110,480 and $2,454,644 in Senate races.

In addition to these direct cash contributions, parties can help candidates raise money from other sources. Party leaders can introduce candidates to individuals or institutional actors who may contribute to the candidate's campaign. Party committees frequently introduce their candidates to PAC officials in official or unofficial gatherings, and provide advice and other assistance in fundraising.

Candidate Recruitment and Nominations

In 1992, electing women challengers and open-seat contestants to Congress became a major goal of both parties. As they have routinely done during the last decade, congressional leaders and congressional campaign committee staffers met with state and local party leaders to identify talented individuals and convince them to run. They used polls, the promise of party support, and the persuasive talents of party leaders, their colleagues, and even the President to convince highly qualified individuals to run. They also held candidate training schools and sought to familiarize potential candidates with life on Capitol Hill (see e.g., Herrnson 1988).

During the 1992 election cycle, a greater share of party recruitment activity was directed toward women than in previous years. Recent increases in the number of women officeholders at the state and local levels made women a more important element in the pool of potential congressional candidates than they had been in the past. The conditions that led the press to proclaim 1992 the Year of the Woman also encouraged the parties to pay greater attention to female politicians. DCCC staff stated that committee chairman Vic Fazio and other Democratic House members made special efforts to seek out qualified female House candidates. Staffers at the National Republican Congressional Committee (NRCC) credited Representative Mickey Edwards with taking the lion's share of the responsibility for recruiting Republican women.

Yet there are limits to that which national, state, and even local party leaders can do to encourage male and female candidates to run for the House or Senate. In the first place, the decision to run for Congress is an intensely personal one, and family, friends, and confidants typically have a greater impact on a prospective candidate than do national party leaders (Herrnson 1988; Maisel et al. 1990).

TABLE 9.1 Women as a Percentage of All Major Party, Primary Election House Candidates, 1986-1992

	1986	1988	1990	1992
Democratic Women	9%	9%	10%	16%
Democratic Men	91%	91%	90%	84%
(N of Democrats)	845	744	702	1,041
Republican Women	9%	8%	8%	10%
Republican Men	91%	92%	92%	90%
(N of Republicans)	599	624	668	974

Source: Federal Election Commission data.

Second, experienced politicians, who form the group of potential candidates party leadersare most interested in recruiting, make their decisions strategically (Jacobson and Kernell 1983). They consider their prospects for victory carefully and also weigh the impact that defeat could have on their political careers (Rohde 1979). As a result, those individuals whom party leaders may consider to be the most desirable candidates may choose not to run.

Moreover, when more than one individual expresses interest in entering a congressional primary for the same seat, party leaders cannot prevent the primary from being contested. Occasionally a party will attempt to discourage someone from challenging their preferred candidate. This "negative" recruitment however, can cause deep divisions within a party. Democratic party leaders have traditionally been hesitant to discourage potential candidates or take sides in congressional primaries. The Republicans, who have been more active in this regard, have reduced their negative recruitment activities during the last few election cycles.

In 1992, the parties did not attempt to clear the field of primary competition for women. Neither party tried to discourage men from running against women or women from running against each other. The Republican party, which has in the past given some primary candidates assistance over others, shied away from getting involved in nomination races because of the record numbers of highly qualified GOP candidates and the uncertainties imposed by redistricting. Because it could not predict exactly where district boundaries would be drawn in a number of states, the NRCC was not prepared to actively discourage GOP primary contestants, including those challenging women, to withdraw from the candidate pool.

Women made up about 11 percent of the total field of House candidates in 1992, reaching double digits for the first time. Their

TABLE 9.2 Women as a Percentage of Major Party Senate Candidates, 1986-1992

	1986	1988	1990	1992
Democratic Women	8%	5%	9%	20%
Democratic Men	92%	95%	91%	80%
(N of Democrats)	127	79	82	121
Republican Women	9%	7%	15%	6%
Republican Men	91%	93%	85%	94%
(N of Republicans)	92	79	69	124

Source: Federal Election Commission data.

greatest gains took place in the Democratic party, although the GOP experienced a slight increase as well (see Table 9.1). With record numbers of women running for office, women's gains might have been greater had it not been for the record number of men who also believed that 1992 would be a promising year for non-incumbents. The unprecedented number of open seats, incumbent vulnerabilities that resulted from redistricting, and an electorate that seemed to pine for change, caused politicians of both sexes and both parties to take their chances on a race for Congress.

Although Senate elections are significantly different from those for the House, female and male candidates for the upper chamber also responded to the opportunities brought on by the mood of the nation.

As usual, most of the Senate candidates who ran for election in 1992 enjoyed greater stature than candidates for the House. Senate candidates' need to raise enormous sums of money forced them to start fundraising early, making their intentions to run readily apparent. In spite of the financial obstacles, the percentage of female candidates contesting senatorial primaries was higher than in any election held during at least the last ten years. The Democratic Senatorial Campaign Committee (DSCC) had substantial success in fielding female candidates; sixteen chose to run. The Republicans, on the other hand, had only limited success. The GOP fielded only four female Senate candidates, and the National Republican Senatorial Committee (NRSC) was unable to convince any of its female House members to give up their House seats in order to mount a bid for the Senate. Many members of the GOP found this disappointing in light of the competitive but unsuccessful senatorial campaigns waged by former Republican House members Lynn Martin, Patricia Saiki, and Claudine Schneider in 1990.

The number of women seeking Senate seats has fluctuated over time, a function of the states holding elections and the political conditions of each election year (see Table 9.2). With a small number of high profile races contested each year, a few incumbent retirements or other unusual circumstances can lead to substantial changes in the number and types of candidates running for the nomination. These factors encouraged many Republican women to run in 1990 and may have discouraged some from running in 1992. The defeats of Martin, Saiki, Schneider, and Christine Todd Whitman of New Jersey might have made Republican women reluctant to seek a Senate seat.

Although an abundance of women chose to run for their party's nomination for the House or the Senate, the parties could not guarantee them an easy path to victory. Fully 64 percent of all Democratic women who won their party's nomination for the House had to defeat a primary opponent in order to win their party's nomination, compared to 48 percent of their male counterparts. The figures for Republicans are similar, with 60 percent of successful women facing primary opposition, compared to only 46 percent of Republican men. This disparity is partly explained by the greater number of incumbents who are men and unlikely to face a primary challenge.

Things were nearly identical in the Senate. Nearly every successful woman in a 1992 Senate campaign faced serious primary opposition. In fact, several of the nine non-incumbent Democratic women on the November ballot were not initially expected to be their party's standardbearer. Moreover, primary competition clearly harmed at least one woman's chances of getting elected to the Senate. The Democratic primary in New York pitted frontrunner Geraldine Ferraro against New York City Comptroller Elizabeth Holtzman, New York State Attorney General Robert Abrams, and the Reverend Al Sharpton (see Chapter 6 for details). Holtzman's relentless attacks on Ferraro's integrity destroyed the candidacies of both women and played a key role in enabling Abrams to capture the nomination, although he was too scarred by the divisive primary to defeat incumbent Alfonse D'Amato.

At the end of the primary election period, it was clear that substantial progress was made by women in both parties. The number of female Republican House nominees doubled between 1988 and 1992, and the number of Democratic nominees grew by a factor of three (see Figure 9.1). This outcome was the result of the increase in the number of women candidates who ran for Congress, not an increase in their success in winning primaries. The overall number of women House primary election candidates more than doubled from 107 in 1990 to 224 in 1992, and the proportion of those women who won primaries remained nearly steady, at 47 percent.[5]

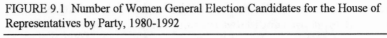

FIGURE 9.1 Number of Women General Election Candidates for the House of
Representatives by Party, 1980-1992

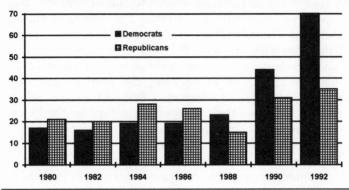

Source: Federal Election Commission data

Nevertheless, it is important to place these advances within their
proper context. Among the Democrats, there were five men for every
one woman who won the right to run under the party label.   The
figures are even more stark for the Republicans. Republican male
House candidates outnumbered their female counterparts by a ratio of
ten to one.

Women made substantially more progress in securing their places
on the ballot for the Senate.   Eleven of the sixty-seven major party
general election candidates for the Senate were women. Of these, ten
were Democrats and one was a Republican. One (Democrat Barbara
Mikulski of Maryland) was an incumbent, six Democrats and the lone
Republican (Charlene Haar) were challengers, and three Democrats
were competing for open seats.   Carol Moseley-Braun, an open-seat
candidate, actually began her bid for office as a challenger, defeating
incumbent Alan Dixon in the Illinois Democratic primary.

Campaign Finance

The House

Although the ability of political parties to help their general election
candidates is limited by the Federal Election Campaign Act, party
financial support can be considerable.   In a House race, if a party's

TABLE 9.3   Average National Party Financial Support of House Candidates, 1991-1992

| | Contributions | | Coordinated Expenditures | |
	Men	Women	Men	Women
Democrats				
Incumbents	$1,778	$1,742	$7,362	$7,017
Challengers	$1,840	$2,623	$17,310	$13,572
Open Seats	$2,094	$2,894	$12,847	$12,891
Republicans				
Incumbents	$4,578	$3,568	$26,565	$34,286
Challengers	$3,902	$5,342	$24,001	$27,120
Open Seats	$5,602	$6,943	$27,696	$33,256

Source: Federal Election Commission data.

congressional campaign committee, the national committee (the Democratic National Committee (DNC) or Republican National Committee (RNC)), and the state party organization were to make the maximum contribution for the general election, and the state and national committees also made the maximum expenditure on behalf of the candidate, the nominal value of party support would be $70,480. These "coordinated expenditures" include direct mail, polls, media advertising, hiring consultants, etc. The party is permitted to make these expenditures in coordination with the candidate. The actual value of party support would be higher because the parties' ability to produce or purchase blocs of campaign services allows them to contribute them to candidates at below market rates. With the typical non-incumbent candidate in a close race spending about $500,000 in 1992, this could amount to a substantial proportion of a competitive campaign.

The data in Table 9.3 show that both parties appear to have contributed more money to non-incumbent women candidates than to men, and the Republicans made higher coordinated expenditures on behalf of their women candidates as well. Democratic women in open-seat races received more coordinated expenditures than men, but Democratic women challengers received less funding than men. On average, Republicans received more party support than Democrats, and they appear to have favored women to a greater extent as well.

The contribution and expenditure differences in Table 9.3 may be due to factors other than gender. The financial support that parties direct to candidates, especially non-incumbents, is believed to be largely a function of two basic factors: the quality of the candidate and expectations about the closeness of the election. These two factors, combined with the amount of financial resources used by both candidates in the race are very strong predictors of the percentage of the vote a candidate will receive.

Candidate quality is largely determined by political experience. People who have held public office before, especially state legislators, typically have the political skills necessary to run an effective campaign. They also enjoy some level of recognition among voters. In 1992, 37.5 percent of all female and 35.4 percent of all male non-incumbent general election candidates had the requisite political experience to be classified as "highly qualified."

Expectations about the outcome of the election are usually based on knowledge of the partisan tendencies of voters in the district, as well as whether or not an incumbent is seeking reelection. Incumbents have many advantages in campaigns, and House members have been successful in seeking reelection at least 95 percent of the time in recent years. In addition, the partisan composition of congressional districts are often tilted toward one party or the other. When that party also has an incumbent member seeking reelection, those two factors make a formidable obstacle to potential challengers.

We might expect, then, that party financial support of candidates would be determined by the quality of the candidate involved, the status of the candidate (incumbent, challenger, or open seat) and the closeness of the two party vote in the district. Differences in the closeness of the race or the quality of the candidates may mask the true effect of gender on party financial support (Jacobson 1987). The difference between the two parties that appears in Table 9.3, for example, may be the result of these other factors, and not simply the gender of the candidates.

To see if there are gender differences in party support for candidates with similar political experience who are running in similar types of races, we must hold constant candidate quality and the closeness of the district. Although party committees generally seek to concentrate their funds on quality candidates in close races, we might expect that women would receive more money than men in 1992, since being a woman was widely recognized as shorthand for being an agent of change, and change was what the electorate wanted.

The results of our regression analysis are presented in Table 9.4. These data suggest that the national party organizations did not give special consideration to women in 1992, but their gender did not hurt their ability to get party financial support. After controlling for the effects of candidate experience and marginality of the district, there

TABLE 9.4 Predictors of Party Financial Support, House Non-Incumbent Candidates

	Estimate	Standard Error
Republicans		
Gender	$3,247	$3,713
Open Seat	$2,981	$2,629
Quality	$14,984 **	$2,532
Marginal Race	$25,920 **	$2,284
** coefficient more than three times its standard error.		
$R^2 = .47$		
Democrats		
Gender	-$5,594	$2,912
Open Seat	-$2,590	$2,932
Quality	$4,775	$2,814
Marginal Race	$9,817 *	$3,325
* coefficient more than twice its standard error.		
$R^2 = .05$		

The entries in this table represent unstandardized regression coefficients and their standard errors. The coefficients are interpreted as the net impact of the variable on party financial support. For example, the table shows that Republican women received on average $3,247 more than Republican men with the same levels of experience who ran in the same kind of races. Republican candidates who ran in marginal races received $25,920 more than those who ran less competitive campaigns.

Quality is measured by past electoral experience. Marginal races are cases where the candidate received between 43 percent and 57 percent of the general election vote.

Source: Federal Election Commission data.

was no significant difference in party financial support between men and women of either party. Candidate quality and closeness of the election were, however, very important predictors of party financial support for both Democrats and Republicans. Candidates in both parties involved in close races received more party money than those whose victory or defeat seemed certain: Republicans channeled $25,920 more in party money to a non-incumbent candidate in a close election, and for Democrats the figure was $9,817. Both parties also directed more monies to candidates with prior experience in elected office. Republicans directed an additional $14,984 to these quality candidates, while Democrats provided an additional $4,775. Once candidate quality, the closeness of the election, and whether the seat was open are controlled, however, men and women received a similar amount of party money.

These findings are consistent with many other studies of financial support for women candidates, nearly all of which suggest that women face no inherent fundraising disadvantage. Although the data in Table 9.3 show an apparent advantage for Republican women over their male counterparts, this advantage existed because the Republican women candidates were more experienced and also ran in districts that were expected to have close races. When the effect of those two factors is removed, there is no significant difference between men and women in terms of party financing for either party. It is clear from the table, however, that the Republican party was very careful in targeting financial support only to those who would most benefit, while the Democrats made some contributions and expenditures in races that were not as closely contested.

It may seem surprising that in an election when polls showed some advantage for women candidates, the party committees did not give those candidates special support. Perhaps the electoral advantage was directly responsible for this—that is, perhaps women candidates received an electoral boost from their gender, which in turn made their electoral prospects relatively safe and led to less party money. Yet our analysis suggests that women did not receive a higher percentage of the general election vote in the House than men who were running in similar types of districts and who had similar backgrounds.

The Senate

Even in the largest states (where elections are generally quite costly), parties can have an important financial impact on Senate campaigns by both direct and indirect means. In California, Democrats Barbara Boxer and Dianne Feinstein spent $10 million and $8 million, respectively, and the Democratic party committees spent an additional $1.6 and $1.3 million on their behalf. The party's direct investment in Feinstein's and Boxer's races amounted to 14 percent of all funds spent directly on their campaigns. The DNC sent an additional $1.8 million to the California State Democratic Committee to spend on their entire ticket in California. Finally, the California State Democratic Committee spent $10 million of their own money on all races in California. Some of this "soft money" probably helped Feinstein and Boxer as well.

An overview of all of the 1992 Senate races involving women candidates reveals that each non-incumbent female candidate received the maximum contribution from her party's senatorial campaign committee (see Table 9.5). Although the $17,500 limit on contributions from national party committees is considerably more than the maximum legal contribution limit for House candidates, it represents a very small portion of even the smallest Senate campaign. Since each senatorial campaign committee was concerned with only thirty-five

TABLE 9.5   Party Support of Women Senate Candidates, 1991-1992

Candidate	Party Contributions	Coordinated Expenditures	% of Coordinated Expenditures Limit
Boxer D-CA Opn	$24,958	$1,736,124	71%
Feinstein D-CA Chl	$17,500	$1,491,863	61%
Moseley-Braun D-IL Opn	$19,600	$442,735	47%
Lloyd-Jones D-IA Chl	$17,750	$35,755	16%
Mikulski D-MD Inc	$2,500	$13,018	3%
Murray D-WA Opn	$17,500	$378,956	93%
O'Dell D-KS Chl	$17,500	$37,591	19%
Rothman-Serot D-MO Chl	$22,783	$304,487	72%
Sargent D-AZ Chl	$17,500	$22,799	8%
Yeakel D-PA Chl	$19,500	$842,037	83%
Haar R-SD Chl	$27,498	$110,480	100%

Source: Federal Election Commission data.

races, they could readily give this sum to each of their nominees. Some candidates received additional party contributions from state party committees as well, so their total exceeds the $17,500 national limit.

The table also shows that parties can make substantial coordinated expenditures. It is here that the party committees must make hard choices about allocating limited resources. Not all candidates receive the maximum amount of possible support, and the differences are largely dependent on the probability of success for the candidate. Democratic challengers Jean Lloyd-Jones of Iowa, Gloria O'Dell of Kansas, and Claire Sargent of Arizona were given little chance to defeat incumbent Senators Charles Grassley, Robert Dole, and John McCain. As a result, the three women received only 16 percent, 19 percent, and 8 percent, respectively, of the maximum possible expenditures by the DSCC. While the sole Republican nominee, Charlene Haar in South Dakota, was also considered unlikely to unseat Senator Thomas Daschle, she received the maximum expenditure of $110,480 from the NRSC. The low limit imposed in this small state made it easier for the NRSC to provide the maximum in what appeared to be a hopeless cause. Although it was unlikely that Haar would defeat Daschle, this strong support sends a message to women who may be considering a run for the Senate that if they are prepared to make the entrepreneurial decision to run for high office, and if they win their party's nomination, the party will support them with the resources most important to modern campaigns.

Even in states where the races were likely to be much closer, expectations about the electoral outcome were important to the parties' decision-making. Throughout the fall it appeared likely that Dianne Feinstein would easily defeat appointed Senator John Seymour in one California race, while Barbara Boxer's lead over Republican Bruce Herschensohn was more tenuous. In this case, the DSCC chose to provide more support to Boxer, who was thought to have the greatest need. In Missouri, on the other hand, most polling suggested that Democrat Geri Rothman-Serot was in an uphill battle with incumbent Kit Bond. As a result, she received less support (measured as a percentage of the maximum possible) than several other candidates. In the end, she lost a closer race than expected, leaving many to wonder whether a larger party effort at the end of the campaign might have helped her win.

Another Democratic candidate, Carol Moseley-Braun, enjoyed very large leads in the polls throughout the fall, and was given a relatively small proportion of the maximum party expenditures. Elsewhere, Patty Murray in Washington and Lynn Yeakel in Pennsylvania were thought to be in very close races, and both benefited from party expenditures that approached the legal limit for their respective states. We have argued that the overriding desire on the part of the parties to win elections should result in financial support for women at least on a par with support for men. In fact, the staff of the party Senate campaign committees remarked that the unique character of the 1992 election suggested that women might make more promising candidates than men. One might expect women to receive greater support than men in similar positions.

Because of the small number of Senate campaigns, it is not possible to perform a statistical analysis such as the one in Table 9.4. One less formal test of this proposition is to compare the experience of the women Senate candidates with men in similar circumstances. Table 9.6 shows party support of Democratic men who received more than 40 percent of the general election vote and were not incumbents. Once again, the amount of party support is largely a function of the likely outcome of the race, with competitive challengers in Wisconsin, Oregon, and New York receiving at least 80 percent of their state limit, while the Democratic nominee in Indiana received about half the maximum coordinated expenditure and only 41 percent of the general election vote. It is interesting to note, however, that Feinstein, Moseley-Braun, and Rothman-Serot received a smaller percentage of the limit than their male colleagues who ran in close races.

TABLE 9.6 Party Coordinated Expenditures for Senate Non-Incumbent Candidates by Electoral Margin and Gender

	General Vote %	Party Spending	% of Spending Limit
More than 40 percent in the General Election			
Women			
Rothman-Serot D-MO Chl	46%	$304,487	72%
Yeakel D-PA Chl	49%	$842,037	83%
Boxer D-CA Open	50%	$1,736,124	71%
Moseley-Braun D-IL Open	55%	$442,735	47%
Murray D-WA Open	55%	$378,956	93%
Feinstein D-CA Chl	55%	$1,491,863	61%
Men			
Hogsett D-IN Chl	41%	$238,918	52%
Owens D-UT Open	42%	$110,000	88%
Stallings D-ID Open	43%	$105,235	95%
Rauh D-NH Open	47%	$105,000	95%
AuCoin D-OR Chl	48%	$195,493	81%
Abrams D-NY Chl	49%	$1,492,781	99%
Feingold D-WI Chl	53%	$353,210	88%
Campbell D-CO Open	55%	$244,499	89%
Dorgan D-ND Open	60%	$49,815	45%
Forty percent or less in the General Election			
Women			
Lloyd-Jones D-IA Chl	28%	$26,221	11%
Sargent D-AZ Chl	32%	$22,799	8%
O'Dell D-KS Chl	32%	$37,591	19%
Haar R-SD Chl	33%	$110,480	100%
Men			
Reed R-HI Chl	27%	$0	0%
Keyes R-MD Chl	29%	$0	0%
Grant R-FL Chl	34%	$3,326	0%
Sellers R-AL Chl	34%	$0	0%
Williams R-KY Chl	36%	$1,000	0%
Lewis D-OK Chl	38%	$86,299	34%
Smith D-AK Chl	39%	$106,393	96%
Johnson R-CT Chl	39%	$279,182	100%
Huckabee R-AR Chl	40%	$192,898	100%
Sydness R-ND Open	40%	$0	0%

Source: Federal Election Commission data.

Conclusion

The impact of political parties on the success of women candidates in the 1992 congressional campaigns is not measured simply by a count of new women members following the November election, or by the amount of financial support received by women candidates during the fall campaign. Rather, the most important contributions made by parties were usually made before the actual contests, in the evolutionary process that leads women and men to seek a seat in Congress. Parties were part of a political environment in which more and more women were able to develop the skills and gain the experience that would be needed when the opportunity to move to Congress arose. Party officials encouraged those experienced women to run for office in 1992, and helped them by providing financial resources and helping them raise additional funds.

The evidence presented here shows that parties did not single out women for either special support or unusual opposition. In making the choice to emphasize candidate experience and the marginality of the congressional seat, and not to give special support to women candidates, the parties may have missed an opportunity to take advantage of a unique set of circumstances.

The parties continued to adhere to a seat maximizing strategy rather than adopt a strategy that would have focused mainly on women as agents of change. Had both parties, and especially the Democrats, focused more resources on women, more women might have been elected, but other marginal seats ultimately won by men would have been placed at risk. The value of a congressional seat for all Democratic candidates lies in part in the party's ability to maintain a working majority. Electing a larger number of women at the expense of the size of that majority was too great a risk for party leaders in 1992.

In conclusion, 1992 was a good year for women candidates, especially those in the Democratic party. Many talented women ran for the House and Senate, many won their parties' primary, and many were elected to Congress. Their victories, as important as they are for contemporary congressional politics, are equally important for future elections. Nineteen ninety-two demonstrated that women had established equal footing with men in the eyes of the party committees that dole out campaign resources. The message to the increasing number of women participating in state and local politics is that their road to Congress is not blocked by arbitrary bias by the political parties that organize elections, and this message should result in greater future gender balance at the highest levels of American politics.

Notes

1. Darcy, Welch, and Clark (1987) report a strong relationship between the number of female lawyers and state legislators, leading one to expect women to make greater strides in the political arena soon.

2. If the winning candidate is in debt after the primary election, the parties sometimes make contributions to help the candidates retire that debt. These contributions count against the limit for the primary election.

3. Unlike the independent expenditures of PACs, party coordinated expenditures are made in cooperation with candidate campaign committees, giving both the party and the candidate a measure of control over them.

4. Coordinated expenditure limits for states with only one House member are $55,240 per committee.

5. Men, in contrast, won major party nominations in 1992 only 41 percent of the time, in part because of the increase in the number of men who chose to run.

References

Conway, M. Margaret. 1991. *Political Participation in the United States.* Washington, DC: CQ Press.

Darcy, Robert, Susan Welch, and Janet Clark. 1987. *Women, Elections, and Representation.* White Plains, NY: Longman, Inc.

Epstein, Leon D. 1986. *Political Parties in the American Mold.* Madison, WI: University of Wisconsin Press.

Herrnson, Paul S. 1988. *Party Campaigning in the 1980s.* Cambridge: Harvard University Press.

— — —. 1989. "National Party Decision Making, Strategies, and Resource Distribution in Congressional Elections." *Western Political Quarterly* 42: 301-323.

Jacobson, Gary. 1987. *The Politics of Congressional Elections.* Boston: Little Brown.

— — —. 1992. "Party Organizations and the Postreform Congress." In Roger H. Davidson, ed. *The Postreform Congress.* New York: St. Martin's Press.

— — —, and Samuel Kernell. 1983. *Strategy and Choice in Congressional Elections.* New Haven: Yale University Press.

Maisel, L. Sandy, Lynda L. Fowler, Ruth S. Jones, and Walter J. Stone. 1990. "The Naming of Candidates: Recruitment or Emergence." In Maisel, ed. *The Parties Respond: Changes in the American Party System.* Boulder, CO: Westview Press.

Merton, Robert K. 1957. *Social Theory and Social Structure.* Glencoe, IL: Free Press.

Rakove, Milton. 1975. *Don't Make No Waves, Don't Back No Losers.* Bloomington, IN: Indiana University Press.

Riordan, William. 1985. *Plunkitt of Tammany Hall.* New York: Dutton.

Rohde, David W. 1979. "Risk-Bearing and Progressive Ambition: The Case of the United States House of Representatives." *American Journal of Political Science* 23: 1-26.

Royko, Mike. 1971. *Boss: Richard J. Daley of Chicago.* New York: Dutton.

10

Women's PACs in the Year of the Woman

Candice J. Nelson

When people call 1992 the "Year of the Woman," they are usually referring to the successful campaigns waged by women candidates during the spring, summer, and autumn of 1992. For women's PACs, however, the "year" began thirteen months before the November elections. In early October 1991, the Senate Judiciary Committee held hearings on Judge Clarence Thomas's nomination to the Supreme Court. In three days of hearings, University of Oklahoma law professor Anita Hill accused Thomas of sexually harassing her when she worked for him at the Department of Education and the Equal Employment Opportunity Commission, and Thomas refuted the charges. The Hill-Thomas hearings, conducted by an all-male Judiciary Committee, dramatically increased the ability of women's PACs to raise money for women candidates. While the factors discussed elsewhere in this book were all in place to make 1992 the Year of the Woman, women office-seekers still needed significant financial support to become credible candidates. The Hill-Thomas hearings became a rallying point around which campaign contributions could be mobilized, enabling women's PACs to raise money in record numbers.

Definition

Women's PACs are generally considered to be committees whose primary purpose is to elect women to political office. Some women's PACs contribute only to women candidates, others contribute to both women and men. It is important to note that this definition excludes some PACs that support feminist positions, and includes others whose directors may not accept the label of "women's PAC."

For many, but not all, a pro-choice position on the abortion issue is the primary criterion for support from the PAC. Yet the National Abortion Rights Action League (NARAL) is not generally considered a women's PAC, because its primary goal is not to elect women to office, but to enact pro-choice legislation in Congress. Other PACs, such as EMILY's List and WISH List, seek to elect pro-choice women to Congress and are therefore considered women's PACs.

In contrast, the American Nurses Association is a professional association which has a PAC. Because the ANA's PAC gives special consideration to women and minority candidates, and 98 percent of its contributors are women, it is generally included in any listing of women's PACs, even though the PAC director does not think of the group as a women's PAC. [1]

Significance of Women's PACs

Women's PACs were important to the campaigns of women candidates in 1992 in several ways. They helped encourage women to run, helped train women in campaign tactics and strategy, provided vital early money to help start their campaigns, and helped provide a network of supportive organizations that could sustain a campaign during the final weeks.

Women's PACs are involved in recruiting candidates to run for office. Susan Roberts found that recruitment is "in many respects, a two-tiered system, with the smaller PACs recruiting women for local and state offices who will in turn be recruited by the larger PACs for the U.S. Congress" (Roberts 1993). The Women's Campaign Fund works with candidates it has supported for state and local offices to help them identify available resources if they decide to run for Congress. [2] EMILY's List publishes a pamphlet which discusses the issues potential women candidates should consider prior to deciding to seek office. [3]

Once women have decided to run for office, women's PACs help train them to be effective campaigners. Both the Women's Campaign

Fund and EMILY's List hold training sessions for candidates. Following the 1992 elections, EMILY's List expanded its research and training operations in order to enhance its ability to train women candidates to run effective campaigns.[4] The WISH List,[5] a PAC which contributes to pro-choice Republican women, held its first training session in the spring of 1993.

Women's PACs also provide women candidates with vital early money to help them start their campaigns. EMILY's List, the largest women's PAC in 1992, is an acronym for "Early Money is Like Yeast," a metaphor which suggests that early money grows (like yeast) because it enables candidates to raise additional money later in the campaign. Because women candidates have a difficult time establishing their credibility, early seed money is crucial to their campaigns.

The most daunting task for candidates running as challengers and, to a lesser extent, for open seats, is to raise enough money to become competitive (Magleby and Nelson 1990). This task is all the more difficult for women candidates because they often lack the political and financial networks from which campaign contributions can be drawn. Commenting on her contributors' resources several years after her first election to the House of Representatives, Congresswoman Pat Schroeder said, "My friends give $15, not $1,000." (Mandel 1981, 191). Almost a decade later, resources for women candidates had not changed a great deal. A study prepared for EMILY's List following the 1988 election drew the following conclusion:

Isolated and "outside" traditional networks of support, [women candidates] received their early support and encouragement from women and women's groups, who saw them as winners. "It was the women's networks," one candidate remembered, "that gave me the support and the guts to get out there after people had been encouraging me to do it, to go put myself on the line and do it."[6]

For many women candidates, early money is essential to the success of their campaigns. As the political director of a women's PAC put it, "A $10,000 contribution makes a difference when a candidate is only getting a few $25 checks."[7] Early money enables candidates to do the things necessary to establish credibility: hire a pollster, develop a campaign plan, and be prepared for challenges to her credibility when they occur. In the words of one campaign manager, "[Women] need to raise money earlier to get out a media message earlier to build up those positives earlier so when you get to the fall campaign, your negatives won't have as much impact on you."[8]

Julie Tippens, the political director of the Women's Campaign Fund, believes that early support from the WCF and other women's PACs meant some women candidates were successful in 1992 who otherwise would not have been.[9] Early PAC money gives a sense of legitimacy to a campaign, and it shows that organizations apart from the candidate's immediate supporters are paying attention. The first campaign contribution received by Jane Harmon, a congressional candidate in the 36th district in California, was from the Women's Campaign Fund, and it showed, in Ms. Tippens's words, that the "campaign was real."[10]

EMILY's List provided early support to candidates in 1992. Their first contribution to Patty Murray, running for the Senate in Washington, was made in April. After Carol Moseley-Braun won her primary in March, showing that women candidates for the Senate could be successful, EMILY's List decided to support Lynn Yeakel in her quest for the Democratic Senate nomination in Pennsylvania.[11] One race EMILY's List did not enter early was Carol Moseley-Braun's Senate primary contest. The PAC did not feel that the early stages of the Moseley-Braun campaign had been well-run. For example, Moseley-Braun had raised only $85,000 at the end of 1991.[12]

While early campaign contributions from women's PACs were very helpful to women candidates in 1992, other PACs, particularly labor PACs, also provided early seed money to women candidates. Almost half of the PAC contributions both Carol Moseley-Braun and Barbara Boxer received in the first half of 1992 came from labor PACs.[13]

Some PACs, such as the Women's Campaign Fund, help candidates solicit contributions from other PACs. The WCF schedules candidates to meet PACs in Washington, helps candidates prepare for their meetings with PACs, follows up with other PACs to see what other information the PACs need from the candidates, and lobbies other PACs to support candidates endorsed by the WCF.[14] Women's PACs can therefore serve as important cue-givers to other sources of institutional money. Indeed, EMILY's List helped encourage labor PACs to support women Senate candidates in the 1992 elections.

Women's PACs are significant for another reason. Like other like-minded PACs, women's PACs share information through informal information networks. For example, a group of women's PACs, including EMILY's List, the National Organization for Women, and the National Women's Political Caucus, met once a month during the 1992 election cycle to share information about campaigns.[15] While the PACs did not always agree about which candidates to support, they did share mutual information about candidates and campaigns.

Similar networking occurred at the state level in 1992. In California, about twenty-five women's PACs participated in the Summit, an umbrella group of women's PACs that included both state and local PACs in California and national PACs, such as EMILY's List, the Women's Campaign Fund, and the National Women's Political Caucus, that were active in California races.[16] In Missouri, the Missouri Women's Action Fund shared information with the National Abortion Rights Action League, including responses to NARAL's questionnaire to candidates, as well as sharing information with national PACs such as the National Women's Political Caucus, the WCF, and EMILY's List. The Action Fund also cosponsored a fundraising event with the NWPC, in order to raise money for the Fund.[17]

History and Growth

The first women's PAC was the Women's Campaign Fund, formed in 1974. In the 1975-1976 election cycle, there were four women's PACs (Roberts 1992); in the 1991-1992 election cycle, there were forty-nine women's PACs registered with the Federal Election Commission, of which twenty-nine were active in the 1992 election.[18] The receipts and disbursements of women's PACs active in the 1991-1992 election cycle are presented in Appendix 10.

Table 10.1 illustrates the change in receipts and disbursements for women's PACs active in both the 1990 and 1992 election cycles. Of the seventeen active PACs, all but three had an increase in both receipts and disbursements. Among the most interesting increases are those of the Women's Campaign Fund and EMILY's List. WCF receipts increased from a quarter of a million dollars in 1990 to almost $2 million in 1992, while EMILY's List receipts increased from just under $1 million in 1990 to over $4 million in 1992. The story of these two PACs, as well as WISH List, a women's PAC formed in 1992, are illustrative of the effect of the Year of the Woman on women's PACs.

The Women's Campaign Fund

As the oldest women's PAC, the Women's Campaign Fund was poised to take advantage of the Year of the Woman, yet even the WCF staff was surprised by the group's success in 1992. Julie Tippens, the political director of the WCF, summed up the 1992 election cycle as "basically double of everything compared to 1990—twice as much

TABLE 10.1 FEC Receipts and Disbursements, 1990-1992 (in dollars)

Committee Name	Receipts			Disbursements		
	1992	1990	Change	1992	1990	Change
American Nurses Association	334,657	301,469	11%	335,868	330,230	2%
EMILY's List	4,257,404	973,124	337%	3,543,032	799,563	343%
Hollywood Women's Political Committee	1,036,580	735,461	41%	988,111	750,399	32%
Los Angeles Women's Campaign Fund	6,280	24,689	-74%	6,839	24,758	-72%
Marin Women's PAC	15,970	1,203	1,227%	20,243	5,088	297%
Minnesota Women's Campaign Fund	246,976	172,293	43%	243,378	200,044	21%
Missouri Women's Action Fund	29,711	27,364	8%	34,128	24,679	38%
National Organization for Women PAC	707,675	270,995	161%	690,885	256,160	169%
National Women's Political Caucus Campaign Support Committee	76,079	31,268	143%	78,037	30,339	157%
National Women's Political Caucus Victory Fund	204,778	76,744	166%	198,200	74,727	165%
Women for:	176,030	246,492	-28%	181,300	240,548	-24%
Women in Psychology for Legislative Action	33,729	28,018	20%	32,062	26,820	19%
Women's Alliance for Israel	251,683	251,119	0%	264,312	222,239	19%
Women's Campaign Fund	1,957,561	1,143,732	71%	1,921,567	1,154,370	66%
Women's Political Committee	71,678	48,759	47%	70,319	59,755	17%
Women's Political Fund	1,400	2,460	-41%	1,175	1,753	-32%
Women's Pro-Israel National PAC	345,226	240,246	43%	328,741	268,995	22%

Source: Federal Election Commission, Receipts and Disbursements, 1991-1992, (FEC409), January 3, 1993.

cash to candidates as in 1990, twice as much in technical services, twice as many candidates supported."[19] She estimated that the Women's Campaign Fund gave about $650,000 in direct contributions to candidates and about the same amount in technical services. In the 1990 election cycle, the Women's Campaign Fund supported 113 candidates, while in 1992, it supported 242 candidates.[20] While most of the group's support went to challengers and open seat candidates, Ms. Tippens said that most women incumbents also received some money from the WCF, and two incumbents, Rosa DeLauro (D-Connecticut) and Joan Kelly Horne (D-Missouri) each received the maximum $10,000 from the PAC.[21]

Perhaps the first indication that 1992 would not be a normal fundraising year for the Women's Campaign Fund was seen immediately following the Hill-Thomas hearings, when the WCF mailed a fundraising solicitation piece, unrelated to the hearings, which received a higher than expected response.[22] The number of contributors to the Women's Campaign Fund almost doubled between 1990 and 1992, from 10,000 in 1990 to 18,000 in 1992. Average contributions to the Fund in 1992 also exceeded normal expectations for direct mail fundraising. While the average contribution from a direct mail solicitation is about $35, the average response to a direct mail appeal from the Fund in 1992 was between $50 and $75.[23]

While the Women's Campaign Fund had twice as much money in 1992 as in the previous election cycle, it also had almost four times as many candidates to support. Consequently, marginal candidates, who in past election cycles might have received support from the Fund, did not receive support in 1992. Moreover, women candidates could not assume that they would receive support simply because they were women. With more candidates asking for support, those women running the strongest campaigns were most likely to receive support.[24]

EMILY's List

EMILY's List was founded in 1985 by Ellen Malcolm, heiress to an IBM fortune. EMILY's List was first active in the 1986 election cycle, raising $350,000 to support the successful Senate race of Barbara Mikulski in Maryland and the unsuccessful Senate race of Harriet Woods in Missouri. In 1988, EMILY's List raised $600,000 for nine House candidates. In special elections in 1989 and 1990, the group helped Jill Long capture a congressional seat in Indiana and helped Patsy Mink win a House seat in Hawaii.

In 1990, EMILY's List supported nine House candidates, two gubernatorial candidates, and one Senate candidate. In 1992, the list grew to forty-four candidates—eight Senate candidates and thirty-six House candidates. Total spending by the PAC (including contributions and overhead costs) increased as well, from just under $800,000 in 1990 to $3.7 million dollars in 1992. The growth of EMILY's List between 1990 and 1992 illustrates the scope of the financing of women's political campaigns in the Year of the Woman.

EMILY's List made $365,000 in direct contributions to candidates in 1992, but this total greatly underestimates the importance of the PAC to women candidates. Members of the PAC pledge to contribute directly to endorsed candidates, and EMILY's List frequently collects these monies, "bundles" them together, and presents them to the candidates. This bundling of money was far more important than the direct contributions of the PAC. Federal law requires that the PAC disclose the bundling of all contributions over $200: in 1992, the PAC reported approximately $880,000 in bundled gifts of this amount. Yet most of the money bundled by the PAC was in contributions of smaller amounts, and these smaller contributions were not reported to the Federal Election Commission. PAC spokespersons claim to have contributed or bundled fully $6.2 million during the 1992 election cycle, although it is impossible to verify the figure.

The growth of EMILY's List from 1990 to 1992 is the result of the confluence of political events and political talent. At the end of September 1991, just before the Hill-Thomas hearings, the *Los Angeles Times* ran a story on EMILY's List and its president, Ellen Malcolm. The results of the *Los Angeles Times* story were two-fold. First, EMILY's List received 400 inquiries from potential members, and second, a producer at "60 Minutes," the CBS newsmagazine show, saw the *Times* story and became interested in doing a piece on the PAC for the program.[25] Between the Hill-Thomas hearings in October and the airing of the "60 Minutes" segment on EMILY's List in March, the group's membership doubled, from 3,000 members to 6,000 members. Immediately following the "60 Minutes" story, EMILY's List sent out 150,000 pieces of direct mail, to take advantage of the publicity generated by the segment. Membership again doubled between March and the Democratic convention, climbing from 6,000 to 12,000 members.[26] Another quarter of a million direct mail pieces were sent following the Democratic convention, and EMILY's List added another 12,000 members between the convention and the November elections.[27]

The publicity for EMILY's List from both free media and well-timed and well-targeted direct mail contributed to the increase in membership. In addition, EMILY's List benefited from voter dissatisfaction with current officeholders, a record number of open seats as a result of redistricting and retirements, and the presence of women candidates who had held elective office or who had professional experience and who were seen as credible candidates.

In September 1991, EMILY's List, the National Women's Political Caucus, and the Women's Campaign Fund commissioned a survey to evaluate the prospects of women candidates. The survey found that, despite the fact that women candidates better represented the issue positions of respondents than did male candidates, both men and, to a lesser extent, women, thought that women candidates could not win.[28] Carol Moseley-Braun's victory over incumbent Senator Alan Dixon in the Illinois primary in March showed that women candidates could win, and thus bolstered the fundraising success of EMILY's List and other women's PACs. Lynne Yeakel's victory in the Senate primary in Pennsylvania in April further underscored the notion that women could win, as did Barbara Boxer's and Diane Feinstein's victories in the California Senate primaries in June.

There was one other event during the 1992 election cycle that established EMILY's List as a serious political player in the PAC community. The New York Senate race featured two prominent women candidates, Geraldine Ferraro, former member of Congress and the first female major party vice-presidential nominee, and Elizabeth Holtzman, also a former member of Congress. Initially, EMILY's List did not intend to involve itself in the primary. However, during the fall of 1991, it became clear to Ellen Malcolm and the steering committee of EMILY's List that the PAC could not simply sit out the race and was compelled to get involved. In December, EMILY's List commissioned its own poll and met with both the Holtzman and Ferraro campaign teams. Because several members of the steering committee were Ferraro supporters, Ellen Malcolm and Karin Johanson, then the political director of EMILY's List, met with three outside consultants to evaluate the results of the survey and the interviews. It was clear to this group that the stronger candidate was Ferraro, and she received the endorsement and support of EMILY's List.[29] According to Karin Johanson, the decision to support Ferraro against Holtzman was "incredibly important, because EMILY's List made a tough decision, did it in a professional way, and in doing so built up the credibility of the PAC."[30]

WISH List

The third women's PAC that vastly exceeded its expectations for 1992 was WISH List. WISH List is modeled after EMILY's List, but supports pro-choice Republican candidates. The PAC was founded by Glenda Greenwald, a former magazine publisher, early in 1992. Ms. Greenwald made 100 cold calls around the country and raised $120,000 in seed money for the new PAC. "The response to the phone calls told me that a new time had come," stated Ms. Greenwald.[31] When WISH List was officially launched on March 2 and March 5 in New York City and Washington, DC, Greenwald's goal was to have 1,000 members by the time of the Republican convention in August. Instead, WISH List had 1,800 members by the convention, and 2,000 members by the November election, thus doubling the PAC's expectations.[32]

Many of the new supporters of WISH List were Republican women contributors to the Women's Campaign Fund, who were pleased to at last have a Republican counterpart to EMILY's List. As is the case with EMILY's List, WISH List members pledge to contribute to candidates endorsed by the PAC, and the PAC bundles these contributions (Rimmerman 1993). These women felt they did not have as much influence in the Women's Campaign Fund as they wanted, because the WCF, like other bipartisan women's PACs, tends to support primarily Democratic candidates[33] because more Democratic candidates support the progressive agenda of the PACs than Republican candidates.[34]

However, not all of the new contributors to WISH List were seasoned political donors. Many of WISH List's new members were women who had not been asked to contribute before, who had not been paying much attention to politics, or who had not thought politics was relevant to their lives. According to Greenwald, the events of 1991 and 1992 had a snowballing effect on contributions to the PAC. The combination of the Hill-Thomas hearings, the perceived threat to *Roe v. Wade* by the changing composition of the Supreme Court, the existence of experienced women in state and federal offices, and the scandals involving primarily white male officeholders, all led to a sense that women really could be serious competitors in elections. The nominations of Carol Moseley-Braun in Illinois and Lynne Yeakel in Pennsylvania confirmed what women were beginning to think, that women could be successful in their bids to win high political office.[35]

While many political observers felt that the 1992 GOP convention was disastrous for the Republican party, highlighting the party's right wing, for WISH List, the convention was an outstanding success. WISH List hosted an event at the convention which attracted 450 people, all moderate Republican men and women, who told Greenwald that they hoped WISH List could be the voice of moderation within the party.[36]

All three of these women's PACs, the Women's Campaign Fund, EMILY's List, and WISH List, exceeded their expectations for membership, fundraising, and candidate support during the 1992 election cycle. Yet the success of women's PACs was not limited to the federal level; smaller state and local women's PACs also benefited from the Year of the Woman.

Women's PACs at the State and Local Level

Like their counterparts at the national level, most women's PACs active at the state and local level experienced increases in contributions and membership. As Table 10.1 shows, of the four state and local women's PACs active in both the 1990 and 1992 election cycles, three, the Marin Women's PAC, the Minnesota Women's Campaign Fund, and the Missouri Women's Action Fund, experienced increases in both receipts and disbursements in 1992.

While the Hill-Thomas hearings were important to PACs active at the state and local level, other issues were equally important in some states. Both the Eleanor Roosevelt Gay/Lesbian Fund in California and the Missouri Women's Action Fund reported that redistricting played an important role in their fundraising and membership success.[37] In Missouri, the Supreme Court decision in *Webster v. Reproductive Health Services* was far more important to the fundraising efforts of the Missouri Women's Action Fund than either the Hill-Thomas hearings or the more general excitement surrounding the Year of the Woman. While the abortion issue may be less important to women's PACs generally in the immediate future than it has been in the past, Marcia Mellitz, the president of the Missouri Women's Action Fund, feels that the abortion issue will continue to be the major concern of her PAC, because abortion will be an issue at the state level.[38]

Future Role of Women's PACs

Now that the Year of the Woman is past, what role will women's PACs play in elections in the remainder of the 1990s? Generally, the directors of women's PACs seem to think that women have developed the "habit of giving,"[39] and will continue to contribute to these committees and to women candidates. Certainly the continued increase in contributions to women's PACs throughout the 1992 election cycle suggests that contributions to women's PACs were more than just sporadic occurrences.

However, the 1994 election cycle will be different from 1992 in two important ways. First, there will be far fewer opportunities for women candidates in 1994 than in 1992. Women candidates in 1992 benefited from the record number of open seats caused by redistricting and retirements in the House, as well as the general anti-incumbency mood in the country. Redistricting will not be a factor in 1994, and consequently the number of retirements is likely to be far smaller. The anti-incumbency mood will likely be quieted by the change in presidential administrations, coupled with the enactment of term limit legislation in seventeen states. While there are likely to be as many qualified women candidates in 1994 as in 1992, there will be far fewer opportunities for them, apart from challenging incumbents.

A second distinction between 1992 and 1994 is that the pro-choice issue, which so dominated women's PACs for so many years, may become less important. With Justice Byron White's retirement from the Supreme Court, the direction of the Court will shift and the continuation of a woman's right to an abortion guaranteed in *Roe* will be much more certain.

Because the expectation is that 1994 will be a more difficult year for women candidates than 1992, women's PACs will continue, and in the case of WISH List, begin training sessions during 1993 and 1994. WISH List expects its membership to continue to grow, doubling the number of members, the amount of money raised, and the number of candidates supported in the 1994 election cycle.[40]

To help freshmen women better prepare for tough reelection campaigns in 1994, some women's PACs helped newly elected female members of Congress seek committee assignments. As Julie Tippens put it, it is "no coincidence" that there are three freshmen women on the House Energy and Commerce Committee and several first-term women on the House Committee on Public Works and Transportation.[41] Both are committees that have active agendas in the 103rd Congress, and those agendas will lead to opportunities for fundraising. In addition, women's PACs began early in 1993 to help women candidates, both incumbents and non-incumbents, develop fundraising plans for 1994.[42]

Conclusion

In 1992, there was more money available for women candidates, largely due to the successful fundraising efforts of women's PACs, but there were also more women candidates seeking support. With a larger field of qualified candidates, women candidates who might have received support from women's PACs in past election cycles could not assume support in 1992. However, the growth in both the number of women's PACs and their increasingly important role in providing early seed money and other forms of support to women candidates ensures that women's PACs will continue to be players in elections far beyond the Year of the Woman.

Notes

I would like to thank my research assistant, Marni Ezra, for her help with this project.

1.   Interview with Marie Morse, PAC director, American Nurses Association, March 1, 1993.

2.   Interview with Julie Tippens, political director, Women's Campaign Fund, March 1, 1993.

3.   *Thinking of Running for Congress? A Guide for Democratic Women,* EMILY's List, March 1991.

4.   *Notes from Emily,* April 1993, p. 1. For a more extensive discussion of the recruitment efforts of women's PACs, see Susan L. Roberts, "Furthering Feminism and Female Representation? The Role of Women's PACs in Recruitment," presented at the annual meeting of the Midwest Political Science Association, Chicago, 1993.

5.   WISH List is an acronym for "Women in the Senate and House."

6.   *Campaigning in a Different Voice,* prepared for EMILY's List by the Majority Project, Spring 1989, p. 20.

7.   Tippens interview.

8.   *Campaigning in a Different Voice,* p. 17.

9.   Tippens interview.

10. Tippens interview.

11.   Interview with Karin Johanson, communications and research director, EMILY's List, March 4, 1993.

12. Johanson interview.

13. Federal Election Commission data.

14. Tippens interview.

15. Johanson interview.

16. Interview with Andrea Leiderman, chair, Women's Caucus, California Democratic party.

17. Interview with Marcia Mellitz, president, Missouri Women's Action Fund.

18. Federal Election Commission, *Receipts and Disbursements 1991-1992*, (FEC409), January 3, 1993.

19. Tippens interview.

20. Tippens interview.

21. Tippens interview.

22. Tippens interview.

23. Tippens interview.

24. Tippens interview.

25. Johanson interview.

26. Johanson interview.

27. Johanson interview. Ms. Johanson described contributors to EMILY's List as primarily professional women in their thirties and forties. Most contributors give $300 to EMILY's List during an election cycle; some give slightly more money.

28. "Winning with Women," survey conducted by Greenberg-Lake, the Analysis Group, September 1991.

29. Johanson interview.

30. Johanson interview.

31. Interview with Glenda Greenwald, president, WISH List, March 1, 1993.

32. Greenwald interview.

33. In 1992, 74 percent of Women's Campaign Fund contributions went to Democratic candidates. (Calculated from the Federal Election Commission, *Committee Index of Candidates Supported/Opposed (D), 1991-1992.*)

34. Greenwald interview.

35. Greenwald interview.

36. Greenwald interview.

37. Leiderman and Mellitz interviews. The Eleanor Roosevelt Gay/Lesbian Fund, unlike the other PACs discussed above, is not a nonconnected PAC. The PAC is an arm of the Democratic party, and its role in the 1992 election was not raising money but rather influencing which candidates received money from the party. Leiderman reported that the Democratic party gave about $1.2 million to women candidates in 1992, about "100 times" what the party had given in the past.

38. Mellitz interview.

39. Ellen Malcolm's comment, quoted by Karin Johanson, Johanson interview.

40. Greenwald interview.

41. Tippens interview.

42. Tippens interview.

References

EMILY's List. March 1991. *Thinking of Running for Congress? A Guide for Democratic Women.*

Federal Election Commission. 1993a. Committee Index of Candidates Supported/Opposed (D), 1991-1992.

— — —. 1993b. Receipts and Disbursements 1991-1992. FEC 409.

Magleby, David B., and Candice J. Nelson. 1990. *The Money Chase: Congressional Campaign Finance Reform.* Washington, DC: Brookings.

Majority Project. Spring 1989. *Campaigning in a Different Voice.* Prepared for EMILY's List.

Mandel, Ruth B. 1981. *In the Running.* New Haven: Ticknor and Fields.

Notes from Emily. April 1993, p. 1.

Rimmerman, Craig. 1993. "New Kids on the Block: The National Gay and Lesbian Victory Fund and WISH List." In Robert Biersack, Paul Herrnson, and Clyde Wilcox, eds. *Risky Business: PAC Decisionmaking in 1992.* New York: M.E. Sharpe.

Roberts, Susan L. 1992. "Women's PACs: Evolution, Operation, and Outlook." Presented at the annual meeting of the Southern Political Science Association, Atlanta.

Roberts, Susan L. 1993. "Furthering Feminism or Female Representation? The Role of Women's PACs in Recruitment." Presented at the annual meeting of the Midwest Political Science Association, Chicago.

APPENDIX 10.2   FEC Receipts and Disbursements, 1991-1992 (in dollars)

Committee Name	Receipts	Disbursements
American Nurses Association	334,657	335,868
Colorado Democratic Women's PAC	22,733	20,650
Davidson County Democratic Women	1,648	2,435
Democratic Women of Santa Barbara County	1,878	5,077
EMILY's List	4,257,404	3,543,032
Hollywood Women's Political Committee	1,036,580	988,111
Latina PAC	5,846	10,014
Los Angeles Women's Campaign Fund	6,280	6,839
Marin Women's PAC	15,970	20,243
Minnesota Women's Campaign Fund	246,976	243,378
Missouri Women's Action Fund	29,711	34,128
National Federation of Business and Professional Women's Clubs	47,448	44,817
National Organization for Women PAC	707,675	690,885
National Women's Political Caucus Campaign Support Committee	76,079	78,037
National Women's Political Caucus Victory Fund	204,778	198,200
Park Cities Republican Women's Club-PAC Committee	11,471	10,209
Southern California Republican Women	26,027	26,314
WISH List	294,599	259,804
Women for a Change	369,174	368,861
Women for Life	3,728	3,930
Women for:	176,030	181,300
Women in Psychology for Legislative Action	33,729	32,062
Women's Action for New Directions Inc	6,306	7,496
Women's Alliance for Israel	251,683	264,312
Women's Campaign Fund	1,957,561	1,921,567
Women's Political Committee	71,678	70,319
Women's Political Fund	1,400	1,175
Women's Pro-Israel National PAC	345,226	328,741

Source: Federal Election Commission Data

11

Political Advertising in the "Year of the Woman": Did X Mark the Spot?

Leonard Williams

In the 1990 U.S. Senate races, the presence of nine female candidates (mostly Republican) led many to describe it as the "Year of the Woman," but only incumbent Senator Nancy Kassebaum was elected. Military issues like the Iraqi invasion of Kuwait were prominent on the national agenda, so the traditional criticism that female candidates simply were not "tough" enough had prevailed one more time. In 1992, eleven female candidates (nearly all of them Democrats) ran for the Senate, and political observers proclaimed yet another "Year of the Woman." This time, however, five of the women were successful. Why? One answer may lie in the messages broadcast to voters in their 30-second television commercials.

Previous studies of political commercials found significant differences in the ways in which male and female candidates present themselves to the electorate. For example, one study by James Benze and Eugene Declercq (1985, 283) observed that "there appears to be more of a tendency for candidates to stress their strengths rather than counteract their weaknesses." For male candidates, this typically meant emphasizing toughness; for females, it meant stressing qualities such as compassion and warmth. Women running for office often faced a situation where they had to be professional and assertive, yet if they appeared to be too professional or assertive, they would be seen by voters as stiff and aggressive; in short, as unfeminine.

Female candidates thus developed advertising strategies that tried to balance these contradictory demands. A study of campaign commercials by Judith Trent found that female candidates from 1982 to 1986 used just such an approach in their attack ads. As Trent and Robert Friedenberg (1991, 138) report, women running for office projected a "masculine image of strength, competence, and qualifications" by infusing their ads "with male voiceovers, discussion of experience or competence, and the visual picture of a candidate dressed in a highly professional/business manner." To maintain a suitably feminine image of compassion, however, the same candidates would talk about social welfare issues and would appear with children or senior citizens.

Indeed, advertising strategies that blended gender stereotypes were prevalent even in races between two female candidates. Consider the 1986 gubernatorial race in Nebraska between Helen Boosalis and Kay Orr. According to some scholars (Procter, Aden, and Japp 1988, 201), Orr "was more successful in blending traditional female stereotypes with perceptions of leadership." In other words, Orr's advertising effectively portrayed her as both compassionate and tough, as both feminine and masculine—a winning combination of traits.

The Year of the Woman and Political Advertising

If 1992 was indeed the Year of the Woman, it seems likely that traditional approaches to advertising by male and female candidates would have changed significantly. Those women whose candidacies were motivated by the Anita Hill-Clarence Thomas hearings might have highlighted their differences from the male politicians running the show on Capitol Hill. These female candidates might have expressed their anger at a political system that excludes them from full participation.

Similarly, we might have expected female solidarity to have been stressed in a variety of ways. We might expect that campaign ads would have pictured more women, and depicted more of them in non-traditional roles. The campaign spots would have featured voiceovers by women. The ads would have discussed the issues important to women (e.g., abortion rights, family leave, or crimes of violence against women). Moreover, female candidates finally would have been able to develop unique images of their own choosing. No longer would their ads have to balance carefully such traits as compassion and toughness.

Were these expectations realized? To find out, I conducted a content analysis of political spots aired during the 1992 U.S. Senate campaigns. The commercials studied included ads from twelve states: Arizona, California, Colorado, Iowa, Illinois, Kansas, New Hampshire, Ohio, Pennsylvania, South Carolina, Washington, and Wisconsin. Of the fifty-nine spots I obtained, twenty (34 percent) came from the campaigns in California, sixteen of those from the Barbara Boxer-Bruce Herschensohn race.[1] Nearly 56 percent (thirty-three) of the spots were produced for male candidates, and 24 percent (fourteen) of the spots involved races with only male candidates (from five states). Each spot was viewed (first with the sound off, then with the sound on) and then coded for the presence of various kinds of production values, issue mentions, image traits, and emotional appeals.

Like that of Benze and Declercq (1985, 283), this study of political advertising found that there were as many similarities as differences between the ads of male and female candidates. Men and women used similar video and audio techniques, discussed the same issues, and stressed such campaign themes as fairness versus competence, reform versus the status quo, or Washington outsiders versus insiders. In their 1992 Senate advertising, both men and women used positive and negative affective appeals equally often, and both developed candidate images that emphasized empathy and concern for others.

Significant differences between the advertising approaches of male and female candidates also existed, though. While no production technique was privileged, there was a greater tendency for women to appear more formally dressed than men in their campaign commercials. Female candidates rarely used female announcers, but they did portray other women in non-traditional roles and settings more often than those of male candidates did. Perhaps most importantly, female candidates in 1992 emphasized "feminine" image traits associated with values such as compassion and empathy, but they did not necessarily try to balance these traits by appearing "tough" or "competent." Instead, the women running for the Senate more often sought to display a high level of what I will call "connected activity."

Political Advertising: An Overview

Before we take a closer look at the 1992 election, let us briefly examine the nature of political advertising. As Montague Kern (1989, original emphasis) has observed, each political spot includes three components:

> *an* entertainment *device designed to arouse and hold the viewer's attention; a* message, *frequently about character as well as an issue in a process that might be dovetailing; and an* attempt to provoke a reaction, *surprise, excitement, recognition, affect, or an action message.*

The entertainment device is necessary because advertisers have to create and present "a scene that is meaningful, whose meaning can be read in a flash" (Goffman 1976, 27). With 30-second television ads, there is no time for much redundancy, no leisure for telling a story, and no opportunity for dialogue.

Thus, if ads are to have their desired effect, they must create certain images in the minds of the voters. These images are manufactured by transferring meaning from one affect-laden symbol to another, by linking "a particular product, organization or individual with some deep human desire or social value" (Combs 1979, 332). Indeed, as Judith Williamson (1978, 36) noted about product ads, sales are helped greatly if the product cannot merely *mean* happiness, but also *be* (or, at least, *seem* to be) happiness. Advertisements thus involve their viewers in the very process of creating meaning. Yet, as forms of ritualized communication, ads largely tell us what we have heard previously, but they tell it to us in an ideal fashion (Goffman 1976, 84).

Beyond getting our attention and involving us in creating meaning, though, what have been the effects of political commercials on voters? Thomas Patterson and Robert McClure's (1976) work showed that political commercials represented a significant source of information about the candidates. In fact, the spots frequently provided more information about the candidates and campaign issues than did television news. More recently, Christopher Arterton (1992, 97) observed that campaign ads have four possible effects—educative, persuasive, focusing, and cueing. Educative ads provide us with new information about the candidate, while persuasive ones reshape our attitudes toward a candidate. Since ads tend to reinforce voters' attitudes toward candidates, however, their primary impact during campaigns is either to highlight particular issues or concerns (focusing) or to identify a candidate with a voter's own values (cueing).

Political spots are thus many-sided things. They are counters used in the ritual communication processes of an election campaign. They are persuasive devices intended to achieve certain desired effects (Bennett 1992). Plus, they are texts whose content reveals information about our beliefs, our culture, our way of life. Close examination of that content is necessary, for as Erving Goffman (1976, 27) observed: "Behind [advertising's] infinitely varied scenic configurations, one might be able to discern a single ritual idiom; behind a multitude of surface differences, a small number of structural forms." In political advertising, we are most likely to discover these structural forms in such areas as production values, campaign issues, candidate images, and emotional appeals. Let us see how each of these forms appeared in the 1992 Senate campaigns.

TABLE 11.1 Presence of Selected Production Values in 1992 Senate Campaign Advertisements (in percent)

Production Value	Sample	Males	Females
Neutral camera angle	86	94	77
Candidate speaking	69	64	77
Candidate in formal dress	66	48	88
Male announcer	53	45	62
Indoor setting	51	52	50
Candidate direct to camera	41	42	39
N	59	33	26

Production Techniques

In their survey of campaign communication, Trent and Friedenberg (1991, 127-133) noted that today's political commercials display a variety of videostyles but all ads (positive, negative, or response) tend to use a similar set of film or video techniques. Content analysis of the 1992 Senate ads similarly indicated that certain production values were nearly universal. For example, the most typical ad in the 1992 campaigns featured a candidate in formal dress talking directly to the camera in an indoor setting. The data in Table 11.1 also show that the production values used by male and female Senate candidates were remarkably similar. Both males and females used ads in which the candidate speaks directly to the voters from an indoor and usually formal setting, for example.

The expectation that advertising in 1992 would show more women and include more women's narration was not confirmed. However, there were important gender differences. Although only eighteen spots showed women (other than a candidate) at all, and only nine of them portrayed women in anything but such traditional roles as wife and mother. Most of those nine spots showed women mainly as an aide to, or audience for, the candidate. Eight of them were aired by female candidates. This suggests that women who run for office are cognizant of the need to portray other women in a more positive, non-traditional light.

TABLE 11.2 Style of Dress by Sex of Candidate Among Ads Featuring the Candidate

Style of Dress	Male	Female
Formal	70%	92%
Informal	22	4
Both	9	4
N	23	25

Another difference between male and female candidates lies in the voiceovers used in their ads. When the women (or men) running for office last year used an announcer, it was almost always a male one. Ironically for the Year of the Woman, of the thirty-seven commercials that used any off-camera announcer, only six used a woman. Four of those were aired by Bruce Herschensohn, the only male candidate to do so.

Why did the women running for the Senate use male announcers for their ads instead of women? Trent and Friedenberg (1991, 138) saw the use of male voiceovers as enabling women to present a "masculine image of strength, competence, and qualifications." In other words, the male voiceover would signify that, having earned one male's "endorsement," the female candidate could safely receive votes from others. However, the presence of a male announcer could also signify that the female candidate is not simply or exclusively a voice for women. In an age when some people feel alienated from their government, any candidate claiming to be in touch with the concerns of ordinary people would also want to show that she could represent *all* of the people.

The most significant difference comes with the approach to dress taken by male and female candidates. The data in Table 11.1 show that women were far more likely than men to appear in their ads in formal dress. In part, this is because female candidates appeared in almost all of their ads, while male candidates sometimes were not pictured. But as Table 11.2 indicates, among those ads that did show the candidate, women were much more likely to be dressed formally in their commercials than men.

Men apparently felt more at ease and more willing to appear on camera dressed informally. Similar to the attack ads studied by Trent and Friedenberg (1991, 138), female candidates in the 1992 Senate races tended to dress formally in nearly all their ads. This was true even when the candidate was in relatively informal settings, as in a Carol Moseley-Braun spot where she spoke to Illinois voters from what appeared to be her own kitchen.

What accounts for these differences between men and women in the video techniques found in their campaign ads? I would argue that the differences exist because female candidates felt the need to appear business-like, tough, and in-control. In short, women running for office faced the need to exhibit the stereotypically masculine traits we associate with political life. Formal dress shows that a female candidate for office is ready for business. Male candidates, quite simply, can afford the luxury of violating the sartorial conventions of electioneering. After all, their status as "official" candidates is never in question. Indeed, ads featuring a male candidate in an open-necked sports shirt (for example, those run by John Rauh in the New Hampshire Senate race) may express not his slovenliness or his lack of business sense, but rather his degree of empathy for the average person.

Campaign Issues

One recurrent criticism of political commercials is that they do not focus on campaign issues, but instead stress candidate images. A look at the 1992 Senate spots confirms that although issues were discussed, few issues were covered and fewer still were covered well. As a rule, the commercials offered very little analysis of, and very few specific plans for dealing with, the issues of the campaign. More often than not, an ad handled issues by simply reciting a mantra of jobs, deficits, health care, education, Congress, etc. Something of a record may have been set by each of two Moseley-Braun ads in which she managed to mention the environment, jobs, education, health care, and either sales taxes or the right to choose—all in the space of a 30-second spot.

The chief issues mentioned by candidates in their spots were a tripartite set of constituent-oriented needs, namely, congressional reform (mentioned in 22 percent of the ads), jobs (21 percent), and a voice for one's state (10 percent). Congressional reform, for example, was treated cleverly in a Gloria O'Dell spot entitled, "Book Reviews." Rather than attacking Kansas Senator Robert Dole directly, O'Dell showed the covers and discussed the political implications of such books as *The Best Congress Money Can Buy* and *Why Americans Hate Politics*. The public cry for the government to help provide new jobs was met with ads in which candidates toured factories. Senator Ernest Hollings of South Carolina was a master of this kind of spot. Washington's Patty Murray also focused on jobs and the need for retraining, linking the issue with the need for congressional reform. More than one candidate promised to be an authentic voice for her or his state. For example, Claire Sargent's spot summarizing her career in Arizona public life contained the tag line that she was "not another yes man," and Boxer aired more than one spot emphasizing her status as a "fighter" for the state of California. The only other issues identified in five percent or more of the ads were health care (5 percent) and the unsavory characteristics of one's opponent (9 percent).

The two issues that have historically created problems for women candidates—military strength and crime, were not major issues in these campaigns. When the consequences of the end of the Cold War were highlighted, such matters were usually framed in an economic context, e.g., jobs or budget cuts. For example, a spot for John McCain in his race against Sargent focused on his efforts to save the jobs at an Arizona air force base. Crime was mentioned (and briefly so) only in a single spot—a negative ad run by Herschensohn in his race against Boxer.

Among the fifty-nine ads screened for this study, ninety-four specific mentions of issues were coded. As expected, governmental reform and the economy topped the list at 36 percent and 33 percent, respectively. Curiously, despite California's reputation for having one of the worst economic situations of any state, the ads in the two California campaigns focused more on governmental reform than on the economy (43 percent to 26 percent, respectively). In fact, the California spots focused less on the economy than did those in the Senate campaigns in other states (26 percent versus 37 percent).

Perhaps this curious finding can be explained by the fact that California had two Senate races, each with a prominent female candidate. That is, given the traditional exclusion of women from politics in general and from the Senate in particular, female candidates for the Senate might successfully push the reform line. Indeed, with the early primary victories by Lynn Yeakel in Pennsylvania and by Moseley-Braun in Illinois, reform of the Congress quickly became interpreted as a "women's issue" in the mass media, especially in the context of the battle over the Supreme Court nomination of Clarence Thomas.[2]

A look at Table 11.3, however, suggests that male and female Senate candidates did not exhibit any significant differences when it came to the issues mentioned in their ads. Regardless of the candidate's sex, governmental reform and the economy were still the most salient issues, each mentioned more than 30 percent of the time. Moreover, male and female candidates raised these issues in proportions very close to those found in the entire sample.[3]

TABLE 11.3 Frequency of Issue Mentions by Sex of Candidate

Issue	Males	Females
Governmental Reform	36%	36%
Economy	34	32
Opponent	16	14
Social Welfare	12	14
Energy or Environment	2	5
N of codings	50	44

Emotional Appeals

According to Trent and Friedenberg (1991, 124), the style or form taken by political ads frequently reflects the perceived mood of the electorate. This means that candidates and their media consultants prefer harsh, negative spots in some years (e.g., 1986 for Senate campaigns and 1988 for presidential candidates) and fuzzy, feel-good, positive ads in other years (e.g., the 1984 presidential campaign). The spots aired in the 1992 Senate campaigns clearly saw the influence of just such a mood.

Following Kern's (1989, 74, 95) categories, each spot was coded for its primary affect-laden appeal, whether positive or negative. The results presented in Table 11.4 indicate that trust (a feeling of confidence in the candidate) was the prevailing positive appeal made in the fifty-nine ads, while anger (a strong feeling of displeasure or antagonism) was overwhelmingly the most potent negative appeal.

Given the nature of the 1992 election, it is not surprising that the sample as a whole focused on either trust or anger. Kern's (1989, 75ff.) study of spots in 1984 found a greater reliance on the positive appeals of hope and reassurance—themes quite fitting for a time of recovery and prosperity, a time when "It's Morning Again in America" was the refrain on people's lips. However, in 1992, when economic troubles were on everyone's mind, other appeals were clearly more resonant. Hope became channeled into a desire to believe in someone or something again (hence the emergence of trust or confidence), and reassurance gave way to appeals emphasizing the need for action. Interestingly, though, results from this study were similar to Kern's (1989, 96ff.) in that anger and uncertainty remained the most frequently coded negative appeals made by candidates.

To attack or not to attack, that has been the question for female candidates. Since most of the female Senate candidates were Democrats, the conventional interpretation of the lessons from their party's 1988 presidential campaign (i.e., let no opponent's attack go unanswered) made the question all the more poignant. Yet study of the 1992 ads revealed that both men and women struck predominantly positive themes during that year's campaign. Neither women nor men seemed very prone to dwell on the negative.[5]Female candidates in 1992 overcame their traditional reluctance to using negative ads: approximately 31 percent of their spots had a negative affective appeal. This reluctance was seen by Trent and Friedenberg (1991, 137) as an effort to avoid running "the risk of being viewed as too aggressive, shrill, vicious, nagging, and 'bitchy'—in other words, unfeminine; thus losing the advantages of being perceived as nurturant, sensitive, and warm." No matter what reluctance there may have been in the past, nearly 31 percent of the ads for female candidates used negative affective appeals, compared to 30 percent of the ads for male candidates.

TABLE 11.4 Presence of Affect-Laden Appeals

Appeal	Sample	Males	Females
Trust	31%	36%	23%
Ambition	15	18	12
Compassion	12	3	23
Anger	22	18	27
Uncertainty	5	9	4
N	59	33	26

Though women were no less likely than men to use negative appeals, there was (as Table 11.4 shows) a significant difference in the kinds of positive appeals that male and female candidates made in their ads. In line with traditional gender stereotypes, the appeals made by women in 1992 tended to emphasize compassion as well as trust. Women used each of these appeals in 23 percent of their political spots. Men, by contrast, used trust in 36 percent of their ads and compassion in only 3 percent. For male candidates, the second most popular positive appeal was ambition (a sense of urgency to get something done about public problems); an appeal used in 18 percent of their ads.

Candidate Images

One of the chief problems facing any candidate is to design the right image, the most appropriate presentation of self, or the most persuasive political identity (Procter, Aden, and Japp 1988, 191). Typically, this task presents women running for office with a delicate balancing act. In the spots for the 1992 Senate candidates, efforts to handle this balancing act were quite evident.

Richard Joslyn (1986, 162-172) identified six broad categories of personality attributes found in political advertising from 1960 to 1984: compassion, empathy, integrity, activity, strength, and knowledge. The sample of 1992 U.S. Senate ads was coded for the specific personality attributes within each category and for each category as a whole.[6] Two of the most frequent attributes ("Washington outsider" and "In touch, one of us") found in the ads were part of the Empathy group and occurred in 14 percent and 10 percent of the ads, respectively. Other frequently coded attributes were "Forthright" (Integrity group, 12 percent of the sample) and "Dedicated/Committed" (Activity group, 10 percent). Once again, in a year when perceived economic pain motivated large numbers of voters, and when a candidate at the top of a ticket was promising to put "people first," it is not surprising that empathic images were popular among the Senate candidates.

Did male and female candidates differ in their presentations of self? In the 1992 campaigns, as Table 11.5 indicates, candidate images were fairly similar to those sketched by Benze and Declercq (1985, 283), who observed that in the 1980-1983 campaigns male candidates tended to emphasize toughness, while female office-seekers stressed compassion and warmth.

Consistent with previous research, female candidates in 1992 were in fact slightly more likely to present an image of empathy. Males, on the other hand, were much more apt than females to choose an image focusing on integrity. Interestingly, male candidates facing female opponents were more likely to focus on integrity than those facing male opponents. Integrity accounted for 27 percent of the thirty-five image codings for ads aired by male candidates in male-female races versus 18 percent of the twenty-seven codings for ads by those in male-male races.

TABLE 11.5 Frequency of Candidate Images

Image	Sample	Males	Females
Empathy	39	36	42
Activity	20	15	27
Integrity	25	36	12
Compassion	12	6	19
Strength	3	6	0
N	59	33	26

In addition to deciding how feminine to look and sound, how assertive and outspoken to appear, and whether or not to move on the opponent with an attacking stance, women more than men must convince people that they know what public business is all about and that they are equipped to conduct it (Mandel 1981, 51).

However, while male candidates stressed images focusing on their integrity, they also presented images that were at least as likely to highlight empathy. Empathy accounted for 34 percent of the thirty-five image codings for ads aired by male candidates in male-female races versus 37 percent of the twenty-seven codings for ads by those in male-male races. In other words, rather than play to their respective strengths, both male and female candidates in 1992 played to the traditional strengths of women. This paradoxical result, contrary to previous research (Benze and Declercq 1985), suggests that we consider the impact of prevailing stereotypes regarding both "masculine" and "feminine" traits upon the ads in the 1992 Senate campaigns.

For the most part, nearly all of the female candidates presented ads in which stereotypically "feminine" attributes were downplayed. For example, the famous "Mom in Tennis Shoes," Murray of Washington, devoted most of her biographical spot to her indefatigable community work and not to her childrearing skills. The only candidate to picture herself with a family was Jean Lloyd-Jones of Iowa, whose spots also featured a "typical" family imploring her to "ease the squeeze" on the middle class.

Yet, in other ways, stereotypically feminine traits remained evident. This was most apparent in the fact that campaign appeals and candidate images for female candidates stressed such qualities as compassion and empathy. Indeed, more than one such candidate pictured herself in an elementary school classroom (less as a visitor, and more as someone comfortable in teaching) in order to highlight her concern for education.

To explore gender stereotypes further, suppose we conceive of compassion and empathy as "feminine" image traits; activity, strength, and knowledge as "masculine" ones; and integrity as a neutral one (assuming that candidates of either gender want to appear honest). Did the women running for the Senate in 1992 appeal to such stereotypes? The data presented in Table 11.6 give a very mixed answer to that question: nearly 62 percent of the women running for office emphasized more stereotypically "feminine" image traits. But women were just as likely as men to emphasize a more "masculine" image.

TABLE 11.6 Frequency of Stereotypical Image Traits by Sex of Candidate (in Percent)

Gendered Image	Male	Female
Feminine	42	62
Neutral	36	12
Masculine	21	27
N	33	26

This finding confirms the recent observation that:

Female candidates who have run recently for highly visible state or national elected office have waged increasingly combative campaigns in which they have stressed their toughness and aggressiveness, typically masculine qualities. At the same time, their male counterparts have clamored to appear sympathetic, kind, and accessible, typically feminine traits. Apparently, both male and female candidates feel compelled to adopt at least some positions or traits thought typical of the other gender (Huddy and Terkildsen 1993, 120).

In fact, male candidates who faced female opponents were slightly more likely to adopt "masculine" images than were those who faced male opponents. Of the nineteen ads aired by males in male-female races, five (26 percent) presented a "masculine" image. By contrast, of the fourteen ads aired by male candidates in male-male races, only two (14 percent) presented such an image.

Though women and men have developed similar advertising strategies in their campaigns, a closer look at their commercials suggests that male and female candidates took different approaches in 1992. Males tended to use ads that told voters about their compassion or empathy. Either the candidate echoed former President George Bush with something akin to "Message: I care," or the candidate had a surrogate testify to the candidate's good qualities (Senator Arlen

Specter used a number of such ads). Female candidates, on the other hand, showed their compassionate and empathic qualities through film footage (ranging over a substantial part of the candidate's lifetime) of their appearances in a variety of settings with a variety of people.[7]

These different approaches to political advertising are linked in many ways to different approaches to knowledge that have been associated with men and women. For example, men are said to employ an epistemological approach called "separate knowing," an approach rooted in a strict subject/object dichotomy and an analytical frame of mind. Women are posited to prefer to use a "connected knowing" approach that emphasizes the interrelations that link the knower and the known and that characterize phenomena themselves. As a result of these divergent approaches, even in their most empathic ads, male candidates were set apart from others and used rational discourse to make their case. Female candidates instead showed their connectedness with other people. Relying on images of themselves acting with others (images of what may be called connected activity), women running for office in 1992 sent their messages of empathy through visual rather than verbal signs.

Content analysis of the ads in the 1992 campaign thus shows that male and female candidates responded differently to the same national political environment. Economic worries among the electorate apparently led women to highlight their stereotypical and historical advantage—their association with such values as empathy and compassion. In the absence of the Cold War and its focus on military or national security issues, women nonetheless still had to "prove" themselves. They did so by accentuating a more "masculine" image, most often identified as activity. That activity, however, took the form of demonstrating their commitment to, as well as their connectedness with, the lives of other people. Men, on the other hand, responded to new political conditions by first embracing a "feminine" image of empathy (especially when faced with a female opponent) and then adopting a more neutral image highlighting their integrity. For men, both of these characteristics helped to underscore their traditional fitness to rule in a time of crisis. In 1992, it seems, the preferred candidate image was one that stressed both fairness and competence.

Conclusion

As was the case with political advertising in previous elections, this examination of the content of the 1992 Senate campaign commercials found more similarities than differences between the ads of male and female candidates. For example, no one set of video or audio techniques was used exclusively by either male or female candidates. In their ads, both male and female candidates discussed the same issues, similarly used positive and negative affective appeals, and developed images that typically stressed empathy and concern for others.

Nonetheless, significant differences between the advertising approaches used by male and female candidates were also found. Even though no production technique was privileged, there was a greater tendency for women to appear more formally dressed than men were in their commercials. Female candidates generally avoided using female announcers, but their spots were more likely to portray other women in non-traditional roles and settings. While female candidates in the 1992 Senate races emphasized "feminine" image traits associated with values such as compassion and empathy, their efforts to appear "tough" did not include the positions they took on key issues. Rather, they balanced compassion and competence by demonstrating a high level of what I called "connected activity," by recapping their personal histories of working *for* and *with* other people in their life struggles.

Candidates, like generals, typically fight the last war. Political advertising in 1992 made it clear that women candidates were aware of winning strategies in past campaigns, but that they also were aware of the unique opportunities of 1992. Female candidates were careful to offset a feminine image with masculine traits, to balance compassion with competence. Past elections have shown this to be neccessary for women to mount credible campaigns. This time, however, the unique conditions of 1992 made it possible for women to run using a slightly different set of appeals. Female candidates could stress their competence, for example, but do so in a uniquely woman-centered fashion—they could stress a different sort of competence.

Similarities and differences aside, we have to acknowledge that it is not enough to count the number of mentions of a particular issue or the frequency with which a particular video technique is used. As Dan Nimmo and Arthur Felsberg (1986, 251) have stated, the current task for researchers into political advertising must be "to take a series of advertisements, examine the signifiers, explore generative processes, and define what is signified." They also suggested that the signifiers found in political spots could be reduced to exhaustive common denominators (ECDs), hidden themes running throughout individual ads. My suspicion is that, with political commercials, we do not have to dig very deeply to find any ECDs. Indeed, we have already identified several for the 1992 Senate campaign spots, namely, fairness versus competence, reform versus the status quo, or Washington outsiders versus Washington insiders.

Nonetheless, Nimmo and Felsberg's basic point is worth pursuing further, especially since political scientists tend to focus only on the measurable effects of campaign commercials. Generally, we seek answers to such questions as: How many people saw the spots? How many were persuaded to vote for the candidate they promoted? What psychological reactions did people have when they saw the spots? What do people remember from the spots?

One result of this study is to suggest that it is time to begin studying the content of campaign commercials to see what we can learn about the messages that candidates are sending. After all, Converse (1964) and Nie, Verba, and Petrocik (1976) told us long ago that elites transmit political messages in bundles of one sort or another, bundles that the mass public will eventually carry in a more or less recognizable form. We need to take advantage of the advances in cultural theory that have aided our understanding of such cultural products as literature and film. Chief among these advances has been the development of semiology or semiotics, the study of signs.

It seems to me that a semiotic understanding of political spots would yield two basic insights. First, researchers would recognize that viewers are active participants in creating the meaning that political advertisers intend (Williamson 1978). We can therefore study the content of political spots not merely for what they reveal about candidates and issues, but also for what they reveal about the structures, processes, and meanings to be found in political life.

Second, researchers would acknowledge that today's political ads rely upon the "poetry" (experiential rather than didactic presentations) of film more than ever before. Following the lead of product ads, political commercials will be more likely to *show* (using visual or audible cues) that a candidate, for example, has empathy for working people; they will not simply *tell* voters that it is so (Kern 1989). Perhaps with the examples provided by campaign advertising in the 1992 elections, political scientists will finally pay attention to the rapid-fire images regularly presented to the electorate.

Notes

This work benefited from faculty development grants given by Manchester College and by C-SPAN; from videotape supplied by the Public Affairs Video Archives at Purdue University and by *Campaign* magazine; and from research assistance provided by Sara Beery, Christine Glaubitz, and Stacy Stumpf.

1. Because of the difficulty in obtaining ads from the campaigns themselves, I analyzed those commercials that either were aired by C-SPAN (the Cable-Satellite Public Affairs Network) or were compiled by *Campaign* magazine. Because of California's unique situation, more ads from its two races were aired on C-SPAN. However, the overrepresentation of California in the sample made little or no difference in the results of this study.

2. Despite the famous spot Yeakel used in her primary campaign, the Hill-Thomas hearings did not figure prominently at all in the ads of the fall campaign. In the ads screened for this study, only three mentions were made of the hearings: one in a Boxer ad; one in an ad by Patty Murray; and one in an spot for (yes, *for*) Arlen Specter.

3. Whether a male candidate ran against another male or ran against a female made little difference in the issues emphasized. In the former case, governmental reform and the economy were each mentioned 38 percent (N=21) of the time. When male and female candidates opposed each other, 35 percent (N=29) of the issue mentions focused on governmental reform and 31 percent of them highlighted the economy.

4. Italicized appeal categories are those classified by Kern (1989) as negative appeals.

5. The few primary campaign spots that I was able to screen suggest that female candidates appeared more ready to resort to negative ads in their primary battles than in their general election contests. The particularly bitter primary fight among the Democrats in New York was an important example, but we can also highlight particularly effective ads of this sort for both Boxer in California and Yeakel in Pennsylvania. The candidates in those races were not shy about attacking primary opponents, whether out of a need to demonstrate that a woman can be "tough" or out of a desire to stand out in a crowded field (as in product ad "positioning"). However, not enough primary ads were available to analyze the matter further.

6. For a listing of coding categories and specific image traits, see Appendix 11.

7. This difference is reflected in the fact that women candidates appeared in twenty-five of twenty-six ads sampled, while the men appeared in only twenty-three of thirty-three of their ads.

References

Arterton, Christopher. 1992. "The Persuasive Art in Politics: The Role of Paid Advertising in Presidential Campaigns." In Matthew D. McCubbins, ed. *Under the Watchful Eye: Managing Presidential Campaigns in the Television Era.* Washington, DC: CQ Press.

Bennett, W. Lance. 1992. *The Governing Crisis: Media, Money, and Marketing in American Elections.* New York: St. Martin's.

Benze, James G., and Eugene R. Declercq. 1985. "Content of Television Political Spot Ads for Female Candidates." *Journalism Quarterly* 62: 278-283, 288.

Combs, James E. 1979. "Political Advertising as a Popular Mythmaking Form." *Journal of American Culture* 2: 331-340.

Converse, Philip. 1964. "The Nature of Belief Systems in Mass Publics." In David E. Apter, ed. *Ideology and Discontent.* New York: Free Press.

Darcy, Robert, Susan Welch, and Janet Clark. 1987. *Women, Elections, and Representation.* White Plains, NY: Longman, Inc.

Goffman, Erving. 1976. *Gender Advertisements.* New York: Harper & Row.

Huddy, Leonie, and Nayda Terkildsen. 1993. "Gender Stereotypes and the Perception of Male and Female Candidates." *American Journal of Political Science* 37: 119-147.

Joslyn, Richard. 1986. "Political Advertising and the Meaning of Elections." In Lynda Lee Kaid, Dan Nimmo, and Keith R. Sanders, eds. *New Perspectives in Political Advertising.* Carbondale, IL: Southern Illinois University Press.

Kern, Montague. 1989. *30-Second Politics: Political Advertising in the Eighties.* New York: Praeger.

Mandel, Ruth B. 1981. *In the Running.* New Haven: Ticknor and Fields.

Nie, Norman H., Sidney Verba, and John R. Petrocik. 1976. *The Changing American Voter.* Cambridge: Harvard University Press.

Nimmo, Dan, and Arthur J. Felsberg. 1986. "Hidden Myths in Televised Political Advertising: An Illustration." In Lynda Lee Kaid, Dan Nimmo, and Keith R. Sanders, eds. *New Perspectives in Political Advertising.* Carbondale, IL: Southern Illinois University Press.

Patterson, Thomas E., and Robert D. McClure. 1976. *The Unseeing Eye: The Myth of Television Power in National Elections.* New York: Putnam's.

Procter, David E., Roger C. Aden, and Phyllis Japp. 1988. "Gender/Issue Interaction in Political Identity Making: Nebraska's Woman vs. Woman Gubernatorial Campaign." *Central States Speech Journal* 39: 190-203.

Trent, Judith S., and Robert V. Friedenberg. 1991. *Political Campaign Communication: Principles and Practices,* 2nd edition. New York: Praeger.

Williamson, Judith. 1978. *Decoding Advertisements: Ideology and Meaning in Advertising.* London: Marion Boyars.

APPENDIX 11.7 Coding Categories for Candidate Images

Categories	Images
COMPASSION	Compassion Caring Understanding
EMPATHY	Empathy In touch, one of us Dependable Responsive Public-regarding Listens Washington outsider
INTEGRITY	Integrity Honesty Trustworthy Forthright Moral
ACTIVITY	Active Effective Hard-working Dedicated/Committed
STRENGTH	Strong Tough Courageous Fighter
KNOWLEDGE	Knowledgeable Experienced Creative/Innovative Intelligent/Smart Respected

12

Voter Responses to Women
Senate Candidates

Elizabeth Adell Cook

When a candidate wins an election, many explanations are offered
to explain her or his victory. Some candidates have more financial
resources than others, some make better use of the media, and some
are better able to gain interest group support. But ultimately,
candidates win elections because they are able to attract more votes
than their opponents. In 1992 women candidates won an
unprecedented number of Senate seats because voters decided they
were the best candidates.

In this chapter, I will examine voters' reactions to women
candidates for the U.S. Senate in 1990 and especially 1992. The
chapter seeks to answer three questions. First, do women Senate
candidates stimulate potential voters to attend more carefully to the
campaign and to vote at higher rates? Second, are women more likely
than men to vote for women candidates in general elections,
regardless of party, or is the gender gap only operative for Democratic
women candidates? Finally, are women more supportive of women
candidates than male voters in party primaries, when partisan cues
are absent?

It is possible to imagine a number of ways that voters, male and
female, might respond to Senate elections in which one of the
candidates is female. First, the novelty of female Senate candidates
may generate increased media coverage of the campaigns, and thus

increased voter awareness, interest, and turnout. This greater interest and turnout may be highest among women citizens, who may respond enthusiastically to women candidates. The presence of women candidates on the ballot may serve to increase the gender gap in turnout.

Women voters might also respond more positively to women candidates, although gender differences in partisanship complicate this question. As Mary Bendyna and Celinda Lake note in Chapter 13, there has been a gender gap in partisanship and presidential voting since 1972. Women are more likely than men to identify with the Democratic party, and to vote for Democratic presidential candidates (Kenski 1988).

There has been substantially less research on the gender gap in voting for other offices (but see Zipp and Plutzer 1985). Women have been generally more likely than men to vote for Democratic candidates for the Senate, but we know less about the effects of the sex of the candidate on the gender gap. Because there have been both male and female candidates from both parties for the Senate in recent years, an analysis of the gender gap in Senate voting in 1990 and 1992 will allow us to determine whether men and women voters respond differently to men and women candidates.

It may be that women support Democratic candidates, regardless of the candidates' sex. The gender gap in partisanship is at least partly due to party positions on issues of particular concern to women, and women may therefore prefer a male candidate of their party to a female candidate of the other party. In 1986, women voters helped swing the Senate to Democratic control by voting for Democratic candidates in larger numbers than did men. In Alabama, California, Colorado, Georgia, Nevada, North Dakota, and Washington, a majority of men voted for Republican candidates, but a larger majority of women helped elect the Democrat. In Louisiana and North Carolina, men split their votes among the two candidates and women elected the Democrat.

It may also be that the sex of the candidate affects vote choice, and that women will be more likely to support women candidates, regardless of party. It is also possible that women will consider both party and the gender of the candidate, producing larger gender gaps when Democratic women are running and smaller ones when Republican women are on the ballot. Finally, it may be that there is an interaction effect on voters of the gender and party of Senate candidates, with women much more likely to support Democratic women candidates but indifferent to Republican women candidates.

In the concluding chapter of this volume, Susan Mezey distinguishes between two types of representation: "standing for" women and "acting for" women.[1] "Standing for" women occurs whenever women hold elected office, regardless of their policy positions. "Acting for" women occurs when officeholders advocate policies that benefit women. Women may vote for women candidates in greater numbers than men to "stand for" them. Partisanship is irrelevant if women are voting for women candidates to stand for them. However, if women vote for candidates to "act for" them, the ticket on which the candidate runs is relevant. The Democratic party has been consistently more likely to support women's rights than the Republican party. If women are voting for candidates to act for them, we would expect them to vote for the Democratic candidate for Senate in greater numbers than men, regardless of the gender of either nominee. If women value both "standing for" and "acting for" women, then they may be especially likely to vote for Democratic women candidates.

Women candidates won in 1992 in part because they won their parties' nominations in primary elections. These primary elections lack a partisan cue, for all candidates are of the same party. It may be that in party primaries, women are likely to support women candidates to "stand for" them, in part because all candidates share a common partisanship and the range of ideological positions is more circumscribed. For this reason, this chapter will examine not only gender differences in vote choice in Senate general elections, but in primary elections as well.

The Data

The data for this chapter come from three main sources. Data on turnout and voter interest come from the National Election Study Pooled Senate Election Study from 1988 through 1992 (Miller et al. 1993). Random samples of citizens in each of the fifty states were asked questions about their interest in the campaign, about their attitudes toward parties, issues, and candidates, and about their electoral behavior. By pooling the data from three election cycles across all fifty states, we are able to generate reliable estimates of the impact of candidate gender on voter interest and participation.

To examine the impact of gender, partisanship, and issues on Senate voting, I will use data from the 1990 and 1992 Voter Research and Surveys General Election Exit Polls (Voter Research and Surveys

TABLE 12.1 Turnout in Senate Elections With and Without Women Candidates, 1988-1992

	Women	Men
All Senate Races	47%	47%
With 2 Male Candidates	44%	43%
With a Woman Candidate	68%	69%
With Republican Woman	64%	68%
With Democratic Woman	72%	70%

Self-reported voting turnout.
Source: Miller et al., 1993.

1991, 1993). These exit polls include large representative samples of voters from each state, but they include only a limited set of questions on issue positions. The 1992 surveys include all states, but a few states holding Senate elections in 1990 were not included in the study.

Finally, to examine voting in Senate primaries, I will use data from the 1992 Voter Research and Surveys Primary Election Exit Polls (Voter Research and Surveys 1992). This set of surveys is not comprehensive, but includes several key states in which women candidates ran, including California, Illinois, and Pennsylvania. Unfortunately, there are no available data from primary elections from 1990 or from South Dakota, so there is no data to help explore primary election voting for Republican women candidates.[2]

Voter Turnout

It is possible that the relative novelty of women candidates would generate increased media attention, increased voter interest, and higher levels of turnout. However, Kahn and Goldenberg (1991) found that women Senate candidates between 1982 and 1986 received less media attention than their male counterparts, and that the content of media coverage more frequently focused on questions about their viability. But anecdotal evidence suggests that by 1990, women candidates were receiving more positive publicity, and in 1992, "Year of the Woman" stories may have generated additional voter interest. If this is the case, turnout for both sexes in elections involving women candidates for the Senate is likely to be higher than in elections involving only male candidates. Alternatively, we might expect that *women* are especially energized by the presence of a woman candidate on the ballot, and that when women candidates run for office the gender gap in turnout will therefore be greater than in elections involving two men.

The data from the NES Pooled Senate Election Study show that 47 percent of the respondents in this study of Senate elections between 1988 and 1992 reported voting. Although Bendyna and Lake reported a growing gender gap in turnout in presidential elections, the NES data show no gender gap in reported turnout for these Senate elections; 47 percent of men and 47 percent of women reported voting.

In Senate elections featuring women candidates, reported turnout was higher than in elections featuring only male candidates. Nearly two-thirds of respondents reported voting in Senate elections in which a woman was running compared to 44 percent who reported voting in elections in which two men won their parties' nominations. The stimulative effect of women candidates did not create a gender gap in turnout; both men's and women's turnout was higher in elections featuring women candidates. Multivariate analysis shows that the presence of a woman candidate was a significant predictor of turnout after holding constant the respondents' age, education, income, race, strength of partisanship and sex.[3] Further analysis shows that the higher turnout in elections involving women was not due to the year of the election, nor was it an artifact of states with moralistic political cultures nominating more women and having higher rates of voting.

It is unclear whether the sex of the candidate itself serves to bolster turnout, or whether increased media attention on elections involving women is a mediating factor. We do not have information on how much and what kind of media coverage male and female candidates for the U.S. Senate received in these elections. Respondents in states with women Senate candidates did not report more interest in the campaign, but both men and women showed greater knowledge about the Senate candidates. Respondents in states with women candidates for Senate were more likely to know the names and party affiliations of candidates than were respondents in states with only male senatorial candidates.

It appears, therefore, that women candidates stimulate knowledge and participation among both men and women. It seems likely that part of the explanation for this effect lies in greater media attention to races involving women candidates, although this would mark a sharp departure from the findings of Kahn and Goldenberg (1991).

The Gender Gap in Senate Voting

Although it appears that both men and women learn more about Senate campaigns involving women candidates and vote more often when women are on the ballot, it is still possible that women and men will make different choices when they vote. There are at least four possibilities.

First, it is possible that the sex of the candidate will be irrelevant to voters. Men and women may prefer candidates from their party or who share their positions on salient issues. This would suggest that women would be more likely than men to support Democratic Senate candidates, regardless of the candidates' sex. When Republican women run against Democratic men, women would prefer the Democratic man. When Democratic women run against Republican men, then women would prefer the Democratic woman at exactly the same rate as they vote for Democratic male candidates. Second, it is possible that gender overrides partisanship in voting. Women may prefer a Republican woman candidate to a Democratic man because the former can "stand for" them, regardless of the policy positions of the two candidates. Third, it is possible that partisanship and candidate gender are separate, additive effects. This would suggest that there would be moderate-sized gender gaps when two men run against each other, that the gender gap should be larger when Democratic women run against Republican men, and smaller when Republican women run against Democratic men. Finally, gender and partisanship may interact, so that women are not especially interested in voting for Republican women candidates, especially if they take anti-feminist positions, but that women are much more likely to vote for Democratic women candidates who can both "stand for" and "act for" them.

In most Senate elections, both the Democratic and Republican candidates are male, and only once have two women run against each other as major party candidates.[4] In 1990 and 1992, however, there were several instances in which a female candidate from one of the two major parties opposed a male candidate from the other major party. In 1990, the Republicans nominated many more women candidates than did the Democrats, while in 1992, nearly all of the women Senate candidates were Democrats.

We can use the typical election in which there are two male major party nominees as a baseline for analysis. Clearly, when both candidates are men, the sex of the candidate is not a factor in vote choice. We can then compare the gender gap from such elections to the gender gap in elections in which there is a female candidate. Since women are more likely than men to vote for the Democratic candidate, it is important to examine elections in which the female candidate is a Republican separately from elections in which the female candidate is a Democrat. But in 1992, only one Republican woman ran as her party's standard-bearer for the Senate. To make the relevant comparisons, we need to expand the analysis to include 1990 Senate elections.

Nineteen ninety-two was not the first year to be heralded as the "Year of the Woman." Some had called 1990 the "Year of the Woman," for eight women ran for the Senate on a major party ticket, six of them Republicans. Three Republican women gave up House seats to make a try for the U.S. Senate: Patricia Saiki of Hawaii, Lynn Martin of Illinois, and Claudine Schneider of Rhode Island. But despite the predictions of a banner year for women, the only woman elected to the Senate was Nancy Kassebaum of Kansas, who was running for reelection.

If we combine information from races in both 1990 and 1992, there are several elections in which women were candidates—both as Democrats and Republicans, and as incumbents, challengers, and open seat candidates—and we can compare the gender gap in these elections to ones in which two men ran against each other. Table 12.2 shows the percentage of men and women voting for the Democratic U.S. Senate candidates state-by-state[5] in 1990 and in 1992, and the gender gap.

In both 1990 and 1992, there is a "positive" gender gap in most elections, showing that women were more likely than men to vote for Democratic candidates. In elections in which both the Democratic and Republican candidates were male, the gender gap averaged 3.8 in 1990. There were "negative" gender gaps (when women were more likely than men to vote for the Republican) in only three such elections, and two of these are gaps of only one percent.

In elections in which Republican women ran against Democratic men, the average gender gap was very small in 1990 (1 percent). This was primarily due to the large negative gender gap in Kansas, where incumbent Nancy Kassebaum easily won reelection. Kassebaum benefited from a large negative gender gap among older voters, but among the youngest Kansas voters, women were more likely than men to vote for her Democratic male challenger. When Kassebaum is excluded from the analysis, the average gender gap in states in which Republican women ran in 1990 was 3.6 percent. In New Jersey, women's votes reelected Democrat Bill Bradley, for men voted for his Republican woman challenger by a narrow margin. In Illinois, women were even less likely than men to support the fading candidacy of Lynn Martin. In Hawaii and Rhode Island, however, there was no gender gap in Senate voting.

In the two states in which Democratic women ran in 1990, the average gender gap was 3.5 percent. This average represents a wide

TABLE 12.2 Voting for Democratic Candidate in Senate Elections, 1990 and 1992

	1990			1992		
	Women	Men	Gap	Women	Men	Gap
Alabama	61%	54%	7	69%	63%	6
Alaska				36%	35%	1
Arizona				33%	31%	2*
Arkansas				62%	55%	7
California (full)				57%	43%	14*
California (short)				64%	50%	14*
Colorado	46%	38%	8*	58%	53%	5
Connecticut				63%	60%	3
Delaware	66%	58%	8**			
Florida				67%	65%	2
Georgia				52%	46%	6
Hawaii	54%	54%	0**	60%	60%	0
Idaho	38%	37%	1	45%	41%	4
Illinois	67%	63%	4**	58%	51%	7*
Indiana	46%	46%	0	41%	41%	0
Iowa	56%	52%	4	34%	22%	12*
Kansas	21%	31%	-10**#	35%	29%	6*
Kentucky	49%	46%	3	64%	64%	0
Maine	39%	35%	4			
Maryland				76%	66%	10*#
Minnesota	50%	48%	2			
Missouri				49%	40%	9*
Nevada				54%	50%	4
New Hampshire	34%	29%	5	49%	45%	4
New Jersey	54%	47%	7**			
New Mexico	23%	24%	-1			
New York				53%	44%	9
North Carolina	53%	42%	11	51%	44%	7
North Dakota				63%	54%	9
Ohio				57%	53%	4
Oklahoma	86%	82%	4	41%	37%	4
Oregon	48%	44%	4	56%	40%	16
Pennsylvania				54%	44%	10*
Rhode Island	61%	62%	-1**			
South Carolina	34%	33%	1	52%	51%	1
South Dakota	44%	47%	-3	64%	70%	-6**
Tennessee	74%	64%	10			
Texas	39%	34%	5			
Utah				40%	43%	-3
Vermont				61%	51%	10
Washington				58%	51%	7*
West Virginia	74%	61%	13			
Wisconsin				54%	52%	2
Wyoming	35%	36%	1*			

* Democratic candidate is female. ** Republican candidate is female. # Woman is incumbent.

Source: Voter Research and Surveys, 1991, 1993.

divergence between the 8 percent gap in Colorado and a 2 percent negative gap in Wyoming. Josie Heath in Colorado ran on a platform that called for drastic cuts in defense spending, and although this position was ultimately a losing one as America prepared for the Persian Gulf War, women were more likely than men to find her position attractive.

Overall, then, the average gender gap in 1990 in elections in which two men ran was 3.8 percent. When Republican non-incumbent women candidates ran against men the average gap was 3.6 percent, and when Democratic non-incumbent women ran against men the average gap was 3.5 percent. This suggests that in 1990, partisanship was far more important than gender in influencing Senate voting. However, in states where highly qualified Republican women ran (Hawaii, Illinois, Kansas, and Rhode Island), there was an average negative gender gap of 2 percent, and even if we exclude Kansas, the average gender gap was only 1 percent. This suggests that in 1990, highly qualified Republican women candidates were able to attract more women voters than were Republican men.

In 1992, the average gender gap when two men won their parties' nomination was 4.4 percent. When Democratic women ran against Republican men, the average gap was 9.1 percent, more than twice that of the all-male contests. Of the ten women who ran as Democrats in 1992, most ran far better among women than among men. Only in Arizona was the gender gap less than 6 percent. In Kansas, where Republican Nancy Kassebaum had received 10 percent more votes from women than men in 1990, Democrat Gloria O'Dell in 1992 also won more votes from women than from men, effectively reversing the partisan direction of the gender gap. In Illinois, where Paul Simon had won 4 percent more votes from women than men in 1990, Carol Moseley-Braun won 7 percent more votes from women than from men in 1992. In Pennsylvania, Lynn Yeakel won a majority of women's votes, but did poorly enough among men to lose the election. In California, both Senate elections had large gender gaps, and Barbara Boxer won because she carried the women's vote while losing among men. Fully 60 percent of women in California who reported voting in both Senate races voted for both Feinstein and Boxer.

Only one state had a Republican woman candidate in 1992. In South Dakota, Charlene Haar, a conservative schoolteacher who took generally anti-feminist positions, won 6 percent more votes among women than among men. This negative gender gap might suggest that women in South Dakota were more likely to support women candidates, regardless of their party or ideology. Yet there was a negative gender gap in South Dakota in 1990 as well, when two men ran against each other. In this conservative, pro-life state, women may be more likely than men to support Republican candidates. Women in South Dakota are somewhat *less* likely to identify as Democrats than are men, and they were no more likely to vote for Clinton for president than men in 1992.[6]

The data suggest that in 1990, the gender gap was roughly the same in states with no women candidates and when Republican or Democratic women ran as non-incumbents. In 1992, however, the gender gap was far larger when Democratic women were on the ballot, and the gender gap was negative in the one state where a Republican woman ran, with women more likely than men to vote for the Republican woman candidate. This suggests that women may have been especially likely to support women candidates in 1992, perhaps because of a general belief in the need for more women in elected office.

The 1992 exit polls asked voters in California, Illinois, Missouri, Pennsylvania, and Washington how important it was that more women be elected to the U.S. Senate. Table 12.3 shows the percentage of all voters and of male and female voters in these states who indicated it was "very important" to elect more women to the U.S. Senate. More than one-third of all respondents indicated that it was "very important" to elect more women, ranging from a low of 31 percent in Missouri to a high of 44 percent in Washington. Women were *much* more likely than men to believe that it was important to elect more women, with gender gaps ranging from 11 percent in Missouri to 26 percent in Washington. Democrats were far more likely than Independents and especially more likely than Republicans to indicate that electing women was important (not shown), although this may be because in each of these states the Democratic candidate was a woman.[7] College graduates were slightly more likely than those with less education to value the election of more women. In California and to a lesser extent Illinois, voters under 45 years of age were more likely than older voters to believe that it was very important to elect more women. In Missouri, Pennsylvania, and Washington, however, age was unrelated to support for electing more women.

While voters indicated that they wanted more women in the Senate in the abstract, few were willing to indicate that the sex of the candidate influenced their vote. In addition to asking how important it is to elect more women to the Senate, Californians were asked whether the sex of the candidates was very important in making their choices for Senator. Only 14 percent of those who had indicated it was very important to elect more women to the Senate listed the candidate's sex as an important factor in their vote decision. For the entire California electorate, the figure was 6 percent. Differences between men and women on this item were quite small, and were not statistically significant. Of eight possible options, sex of the candidates was chosen as one of the most important factors by the fewest voters. Thus, while many voters may embrace the principle of electing more women to the Senate, when it comes to casting their ballots they focus on more substantive concerns.

TABLE 12.3 Percentage Saying It Is Very Important to Elect More Women to the U.S. Senate

	Total	Men	Women
California	41%	32%	51%
Illinois	38%	30%	46%
Missouri	31%	25%	36%
Pennsylvania	34%	22%	46%
Washington	44%	30%	56%

Source: Voter Research and Surveys, 1993.

Most of the respondents who indicated that sex of the candidates was an important factor in their vote choice voted for Boxer and/or Feinstein.[8] Eleven percent of women who voted for Boxer and 8 percent of men reported that they voted for Boxer in part because she was female. The number of voters motivated by gender was more than enough to account for Boxer's narrow margin of victory.

Tolleson Rinehart and Hansen (1992) have argued that the gender gap in voting is best understood as the sum of separate gender gaps among Republicans and Democrats. Republican men and women, and Democratic men and women all have different reasons for supporting their parties. This suggests the need to examine the gender gap separately among Democrats and Republicans. Zipp and Plutzer (1985) reported that candidate gender matters most to women who are Independents, so it is important to consider Independents as well.

The data show no consistent pattern that fits all states in 1990 and 1992. The gender gap is highest in many states among Independents, as reported by Zipp and Plutzer, but this does not mean that Independent women voters are always more supportive of women candidates. In Illinois, New Jersey, and Wyoming in 1990, the gender gap was largest among Independent voters, but women were more likely than men to support the male candidate. In Arizona, California (both races), Iowa, Maryland, Missouri, and Washington in 1992, in contrast, the gender gap was largest among Independents, and women voters were more likely than men to vote for Democratic women candidates.[9] In Illinois, Kansas, and South Dakota in 1992, the gender gap among Independents was smaller, but again, women were more likely than men to vote for the male candidate.

In 1992, Republican women were more likely than Republican men to cross party lines to vote for Democratic women candidates. In Arizona, Illinois, Iowa, Maryland, and Pennsylvania, the gender gap was largest among Republican voters, suggesting that Republican women were especially attracted to the largely pro-choice Democratic women candidates. In Illinois, Carol Moseley-Braun won a number of cross-party votes from women: the entire gender gap in Illinois was among Republicans.

The gender gap was largest in those states where Democratic women candidates ran in 1992, but it may be that these states were ones in which the gender gap would have been particularly strong regardless of the sex of the candidates. The gender gap in partisanship varies in magnitude from state to state, and perhaps the states that nominated women in 1992 were those in which the partisan gender gap is largest. To test this alternative hypothesis, we need to hold constant the effects of party identification. When partisanship is controlled, there were statistically significant gender gaps in twelve states in 1992, and in eight of those states, women candidates were on the ballot.[10] In most states, controls for partisanship reduced the size of the gender gap, suggesting that part of the reason that women voted more frequently for these Democratic women candidates is that women are more likely to be Democrats. In most of the states in which two men ran, the gender gap in vote choice is explained by the gender gap in partisanship. However, in eight of eleven states with women candidates, the gender gap remains even after controlling for partisanship.

It is worth noting that although voters in 1992 clearly considered the sex of the candidate in deciding their votes, the largest gender gap was in Oregon, where incumbent Robert Packwood defeated challenger Les AuCoin. AuCoin had strong feminist and environmentalist credentials, and Packwood was soon to be accused of a series of incidents of sexual harassment stretching back over a number of years.[11] In 1990, the largest gender gap was in North Carolina, where African-American Democrat Harvey Gantt narrowly lost his bid to unseat pro-life and anti-feminist incumbent Jesse Helms. In both elections, the Democratic candidate clearly "acted for" women far better than the Republican incumbent, and women voters responded.

These data suggest that in 1992, women voters responded more positively to women candidates than did men, in part because of their belief that it was important to elect more women to the Senate. This marked a departure from 1990, when the gender gap was, on average, no greater or less when Democratic or Republican women ran for office. The response of women voters to women Senate candidates in 1992 was indeed special, and the Year of the Woman was possible in part because of the votes of women for women candidates.

TABLE 12.4 Gender Gap in Primary Election Senate Voting, 1992

	Women	Men	Gap
California (Short): Feinstein	62%	58%	4%
California (Long): Boxer	54%	44%	10%
Illinois: Moseley-Braun	42%	34%	8%
Pennsylvania: Yeakel	50%	38%	12%

Percent of women and men voting for woman candidate in party primary.

Long seat=full term; short seat=partial term.

Source: Voter Research and Surveys, 1992.

The Gender Gap in Voting in Primary Elections

As discussed above, one of the reasons that there is a gender gap in Senate voting is the gender gap in partisanship. Women support Democratic candidates more often than men in part because they are more likely than men to identify with the Democratic party. Primary elections provide us with an opportunity to examine whether there are differences in the propensity of male and female voters to vote for female candidates in a situation in which there are no partisan cues. Exit poll data are available for four Senate primary elections in 1992 in which female candidates ultimately won their party's nomination: the two California races and the Illinois and Pennsylvania elections. Table 12.4 shows the percentage of male and female voters in the Democratic primaries in each state who voted for the female candidate. In each election we see a gender gap, with female voters more likely than their male counterparts to vote for the female candidate. For these four elections, the smallest gender gap was 4 percentage points, and the largest was 12 percentage points. In Illinois, Moseley-Braun's opponent, incumbent Al Dixon, received a plurality of the male vote, but Moseley-Braun won by winning an even larger plurality of the votes of women. The gender gap in primary election voting was also especially large in Pennsylvania, where

Yeakel won narrowly among men but won in a landslide among Democratic women.

Why were women more likely than men to vote for women candidates? It may be because women voters want to vote for women to "stand for" them. It may also be that they are voting for these women to "act for" them. If women vote for women candidates solely to "stand for" them, then conservative and liberal women should be equally likely to vote for these candidates. If they are voting for women to "act for" them, then we would expect that women will vote for these women candidates because of their ideology and issues positions.

In each of these contests, the female candidate was arguably the most liberal candidate. It may be the case that women were more likely than men to vote for the female candidates not because of the candidates' sex, but because of their ideology. Controlling for ideological self-identification (whether a voter thinks of her/himself as a liberal, moderate, or conservative) does reduce the gender gap. Among liberal men and women, the gender gaps were much smaller. Thus, in these elections, women were not just voting for women to "stand for" them, but to "act for" them. Note that in California there was a much larger gap for liberal Boxer than for the more moderate Feinstein. Gender and ideology interact to influence vote choice in primary elections.

In addition to ideology, issues may help to explain the gender gap. All of the Democratic women who won nominations to the U.S. Senate were pro-choice. Among voters in the primaries that nominated Boxer, Feinstein, Moseley-Braun and Yeakel, pro-choice voters were more likely to vote for the female candidate, although this association was very weak for Moseley-Braun.[12] Although men and women are about as likely to take a pro-choice position on abortion, some have argued that abortion is a more salient issue for women (Dodson and Burnbauer, 1990). If this is the case, there should be a stronger association between position on abortion and voting for the pro-choice (female) candidate for women than for men.

The data show that this was especially true for the California long seat (Boxer), in which the voter's position on abortion was much more highly correlated with primary election voting among women than among men. This pattern also held for the California short seat (Feinstein) and for Pennsylvania (Yeakel), but the differences were not as great as for Boxer. In Illinois, there was a weak association between position on abortion and voting for Moseley-Braun for women, and none for men. Thus, the abortion issue is also one of the reasons for the gender gap. While men and women take similar positions on abortion, the association between primary election vote and position on abortion is stronger for women than for men.

As discussed in earlier chapters, one of the reasons for elite involvement in the Year of the Woman was the Clarence Thomas confirmation hearings. Both Lynn Yeakel of Pennsylvania and Carol Moseley-Braun of Illinois cited outrage over the treatment of Anita Hill as one of the reasons they decided to run for the Senate. Candice Nelson notes in Chapter 10 that fundraising for women's PACs increased dramatically after the Hill-Thomas hearings.

Issues that matter to elites are not always important to voters. After the hearings, more voters believed Clarence Thomas than believed Anita Hill, and this was true for both men and women. In all four of these primary elections, those who said that Thomas should not have been confirmed were more likely to vote for the female candidate than those who said he should have been confirmed. Although Moseley-Braun emphasized the Thomas hearings in her announcement, it was in Illinois that the association between one's position on Thomas's confirmation and voting for the female candidate was weakest.[13] Although Yeakel focused her campaign on the role her opponent Senator Arlen Specter played in questioning Hill, the association among Pennsylvania Democratic primary voters between opinion on the Thomas confirmation and vote for Yeakel was no stronger than it was in California for Feinstein and Boxer, who did not focus on the issue.

The sex differences in these associations were not large. For Boxer and Yeakel, the issue was only slightly more important in women's votes than in men's. For Feinstein, the issue was slightly more important for men than for women. For Moseley-Braun, there was no association between position on the Thomas confirmation for men, and a very small one for women.[14]

Thus, while the Clarence Thomas confirmation hearings may have spurred female political elites to action, it does not account for the gender gap in primary election voting. Both men and women who believed that Thomas should not have been confirmed were more likely to vote for women in Democratic Senate primaries. Women were only slightly more likely than men to vote on the issue in three of the races and less likely to do so in the fourth. The above analysis is limited by the data available. As Mary Bendyna and Celinda Lake report in Chapter 13, Democratic women were most likely to cite health care as the most important issue that influenced their presidential vote. The primary election exit polls did not ask voters about the health care issue, or about education, family leave, job security, comparable worth, or several other issues stressed by women candidates in their campaigns. Moreover, we have no exit poll information from Republican party primaries in which women candidates ran.

These data do show, however, that women were more likely than men to vote for women in Democratic party primary elections. In part, this is because of ideology: Democratic women are more liberal than Democratic men, and liberals were more likely to vote for these generally liberal women candidates. In part, this was due to issues of particular concern to women, especially abortion. Democratic women and men who cast primary election ballots were equally pro-choice, but women were more likely to vote the issue than men. It was *not* because of attitudes toward the Hill-Thomas hearings, for both men and women who opposed the confirmation of Thomas were more likely to vote for women candidates.

Conclusion

This chapter has sought to answer three questions. First, do women candidates stimulate voter interest and turnout? The data indicate that citizens in states with women candidates are not more interested in the election, but they are better informed, suggesting that they may have been exposed to greater media discussion of the election. Turnout is higher in these elections, among both men and women.

Second, how do gender and party combine to influence vote choice? Four possible relationships were posited: one in which party was dominant and women voted for Democrats, regardless of gender, a second in which gender dominated and women voted for women candidates, regardless of party, a third in which gender and party are additive effects with larger gender gaps for Democratic women and smaller gender gaps for Republican women, and one in which party and gender interacted. In 1990, the data suggest that party was dominant, for the average size of the gender gap was nearly identical for races with two male candidates, and for those with Republican and Democratic non-incumbent women candidates.

In 1992, in contrast, the gender gap was much higher in states with Democratic women candidates than in states with two men running. The real question is what to make of the 1992 Senate election in South Dakota, where an anti-feminist Republican woman received more votes from women than from men. This result is consistent with one in which gender is dominant, and women voters choose women candidates regardless of their party. It is also possible that the result is anomalous.

In Chapter 1, Clyde Wilcox reports that Texas women were less likely than men to support Kay Bailey Hutchison in the 1993 special election, and the data reported in this chapter show that most Republican women who ran in 1990 received fewer votes from women than from men. Perhaps the South Dakota result is part of a generalized Year of the Woman phenomenon, in which women voters sought to expand the number of women in the Senate, regardless of party, but in other years, women's votes are more swayed by party and ideology. It is worth noting, however, that in South Dakota, women are less likely than men to identify as Democrats, the gender gap in voting for senator was negative in 1990 as well when two men ran, and there was no gender gap in voting for Clinton for president in 1992. This suggests that South Dakota may be an unusual case, and that the more general result is that when Republican women run, they receive fewer votes from women than from men.

If the 1992 South Dakota election is anomalous, then the 1992 Senate elections would represent an interaction between gender and party, with a much larger gender gap when Democratic women ran for office. If the 1992 South Dakota election is part of a more generalized pattern unique to the 1992 election in which women voters supported women candidates regardless of party, then 1992 was a year in which candidate gender was more important than party. The available data do not allow us to determine which of these two interpretations is correct, because only one state in 1992 had a Republican woman candidate.

It is worth noting that the gender gap in voting is produced by the voting patterns of both women and men. To say that women were more likely to support women candidates means that men were less likely to vote for them. Although a sizable minority of men indicated that it was very important to elect more women to the U.S. Senate, men were less likely to believe so than women, and less likely to vote for women in 1992 than were women voters. Had men voted for Lynn Yeakel at the same rate as women, Pennsylvania would have elected a woman to the Senate in 1992. In 1992, Democratic women candidates succeeded in energizing and attracting women voters, but they were less successful with men voters.

Finally, this chapter sought to determine whether there were significant gender gaps in Democratic primary elections in 1992. What happens to the gender gap when partisan cues are absent? In the four states for which we have data, women were significantly more likely than men to vote for the woman candidate. In Illinois, women provided the crucial margin to nominate Carol Moseley-Braun. Women voters were much more likely than men to indicate that they thought it was very important to elect more women to the Senate, and to vote the abortion issue in the primary election. Thus, even absent partisan cues, Democratic women voters were more likely than their male counterparts to vote for liberal women candidates.

Notes

1. These concepts parallel what Tolleson Rinehart calls descriptive and substantive representation in Chapter 2.

2. The data were made available by the Inter-University Consortium for Political and Social Research. Special thanks to Peter Granda for his help in obtaining clean copies of the 1992 exit poll data.

3. Raymond Wolfinger and Steven Rosenstone have found that these are among the most important factors in predicting voter turnout (Wolfinger and Rosenstone 1980).

4. In 1986, Barbara Mikulski was opposed by Linda Chavez in Maryland.

5. Exit poll data were not available for all states in which Senate elections were held in 1990. Those states for which data are unavailable were excluded from the table and the analysis presented here.

6. In highly conservative states, women may be more Republican than men in part because of their religious values. Tolleson Rinehart and Hansen (1992) argue that Republican women are more likely than Republican men to be highly religious, and Wilcox, Brown, and Powell (1993) report that among Republican political contributors, women were far more religious and more likely to contribute money to ultra-conservative candidate Pat Robertson than men.

7. An important caveat to keep in mind when examining responses to this question is that this question was only asked in states with a Democratic female candidate for Senate. Some voters may be responding to the question as a general principle, which is the way it is phrased. Others may be responding as to whether it is very important to elect the woman Senate candidate in their state. Further analysis (not shown) reveals that in each state except California, partisanship is associated with attitude toward the importance of electing more women to the U.S. Senate even after controlling for Senate vote. Democrats in these states were more committed to electing more women to the U.S. Senate.

8. Of course, even in a "Year of the Woman" some voters will vote *against* a candidate because she is a woman. One in five of the voters who indicated that sex of the candidate was one of the most important reasons in

deciding how to vote for senator voted for male Republicans Bruce Herschensohn and John Seymour.

9. In Arizona, the gender gap was actually negative among Democrats and there was no gender gap among Republicans. Thus the large gender gap among Independents entirely accounted for Claire Sargent's stronger showing among women voters. In California, the gender gap for Feinstein was 7 percent among Democrats, 8 percent among Republicans, and 23 percent among Independents.

10. The list included South Dakota, where Haar drew disproportionately from women voters, even after holding constant the fact that women are slightly more likely to identify as Republicans in that state.

11. The harassment charges were not publicly leveled until after the election, however. Although AuCoin had better feminist credentials, Packwood had consistently taken a pro-choice position in the Senate.

12. Controlling for race did not increase the association for Moseley-Braun.

13. This was true even after controls for race.

14. When the analysis was conducted separately for black and white voters, there was no statistically significant relationship for black men or women. Among whites, there was a stronger association for women than for men.

References

Dodson, Debra, and Lauren Burnbauer. 1990. *Election 1989: the Abortion Issue in New Jersey and Virginia.* New Brunswick NJ: Eagleton Institute of Politics, Rutgers University.

Kahn, Kim Fridkin and Edie N. Goldenberg. 1991. "Women Candidates in the News." *Public Opinion Quarterly* 55:180-199.

Kenski, Henry C. 1988. "The Gender Factor in a Changing Electorate." In Carol Mueller, ed. *The Politics of the Gender Gap.* Newbury Park, CA: Sage.

Miller, Warren E., Donald R. Kinder, Steven Rosenstone, and the National Election Studies. 1993. *American National Election Study: Pooled Senate Election Study, 1988, 1990, 1992.* Computer file, second release. Ann Arbor MI: Inter University Consortium for Political and Social Research (distributor).

Tolleson Rinehart, Sue, and Kenneth Hansen. 1992. "Gendered Parties, Partisan Gender Roles: The Four Groups Who Cause the Gender Gap, 1980-1988." Presented at the annual meeting of the Midwest Political Science Association, Chicago.

Voter Research and Surveys. 1991. *Voter Research and Surveys General Election Exit Polls, 1990.* Computer file. Ann Arbor MI: Inter University Consortium for Political and Social Research (distributor).

— —-. 1992. *Voter Research and Surveys Primary Election Exit Polls, 1992.* Computer file. Ann Arbor MI: Inter University Consortium for Political and Social Research (distributor).

— — —. 1993. *Voter Research and Surveys General Election Exit Polls, 1992.* Computer file. Ann Arbor MI: Inter University Consortium for Political and Social Research (distributor).

Wilcox, Clyde, Clifford Brown, Jr., and Lynda Powell. 1993. "Sex and the Political Contributor: The Gender Gap Among Presidential Contributors in 1988." *Political Research Quarterly* 46: 355-376.

Wolfinger, Raymond and Steven Rosenstone. 1980. *Who Votes?* New Haven, CT: Yale University Press.

Zipp, John F., and Eric Plutzer. 1985. "Gender Differences in Voting for Female Candidates: Evidence from the 1982 Election." *Public Opinion Quarterly* 49:179-197.

13

Gender and Voting in the 1992 Presidential Election

Mary E. Bendyna
and Celinda C. Lake

Although other chapters in this volume are about women candidates and the election of women to political office, this chapter focuses on the election of Bill Clinton and the role of gender in the 1992 presidential election. The presidential election obviously did not result in the election of a woman, but it was an important part of the "Year of the Woman" nonetheless. Clinton's election has important consequences for women both in terms of policy and in terms of representation.

If what matters for women is having people in public office who "act for" women as well as "stand for" women as Susan Mezey argues in Chapter 14, then the Clinton administration clearly matters for women. Almost immediately after taking office, President Clinton issued executive orders lifting restrictions on abortion rights and signed the Family and Medical Leave Act into law. If acting for women means promoting policies such as these, then having Clinton in the White House furthers the interests of women. Indeed, as the opening chapter of this volume suggests, Bill Clinton probably accomplished more in a few weeks on these issues than additional

Democratic women in the House or Senate could have achieved had George Bush won reelection.

In addition to being a president who "acts for" women through his policy positions and actions, Clinton also indirectly "stands for" women through the relatively large number of women he has appointed to important positions in government. By appointing women to serve in such prominent positions as attorney general, secretary of Health and Human Services, chair of the Council of Economic Advisors, ambassador to the United Nations, and associate justice of the Supreme Court, Clinton has furthered the representation of women who can "stand for" — and presumably also "act for" — women.

In this chapter, we will show that the presidential election of 1992 was characterized by significant gender differences in attitudes and voting behavior. These differences were apparent in patterns of party identification, in issue perspectives and priorities, and, finally, in perceptions of and preferences for candidates. Although the final gender gap in voting was relatively small, the 1992 presidential election reaffirmed that the gender gap has become one of the enduring features of American politics.

The Emergence of the Gender Gap

The voting patterns of women and men that were evident in 1992 were a continuation of trends that first emerged in 1964 and were solidified in the 1980 election (Miller 1988). In the 1952, 1956, and 1960 presidential elections, women were more likely than men to vote for the Republican candidate. In 1964, however, Goldwater's militaristic rhetoric and his attacks on the welfare state led to a gender gap in which women were more likely than men to vote for the Democratic candidate. This pattern has been repeated in every presidential election since 1964. In 1964 and 1972 the gender gap was substantial, but in 1968 and 1976 women were only slightly more likely than men to vote for Hubert Humphrey and Jimmy Carter. In most elections, a variety of polls show slightly different results. The exit poll data presented later in this chapter does not show any gender gap in the 1976 election. Yet from 1964 until 1980, women appear to have at least marginally preferred Democratic candidates.

The 1980 presidential election marked a significant turning point in the voting behavior of women and men in presidential elections in the United States. The gender gap in the presidential vote in 1980 was larger than in any presidential election before or after, and the 1980 election also marked a widening of differences in the partisanship of women and men (Kenski 1988). This partisan gender gap was not produced by women moving into the Democratic party, but by men shifting to the Republican party at higher rates than women. This growing partisan gender gap solidified the gender gap in presidential voting. Although the gender gap in presidential voting had waxed and waned between 1964 and 1976, women remained a fairly steady source of Democratic votes during the 1980s and into 1992.

In addition to signifying a shift in patterns of party identification and partisan vote choice, the 1980 election also witnessed the culmination of a trend in changing participation rates of women and men in presidential elections. In the elections before 1980, women consistently turned out to vote at lower rates than men. This male participation advantage eroded with each passing election, and since 1980, women have turned out to vote at higher rates than men in each presidential election. This is true for the population as a whole, and for many social groups (Mueller 1988).

The confluence of changing patterns of turnout, partisanship, and vote choice in 1980—and all subsequent presidential elections—produced what has come to be known as the "gender gap." Until the emergence of this gap in the 1980s, political scientists paid little attention to the relationship between gender and political attitudes and behaviors. According to Kathleen Frankovic, "[t]here has been little evidence from the 1940s to the 1970s that gender plays a role in determining issue positions, candidate evaluations, or candidate preference, as a quick perusal of some well-read political science works would confirm" (Frankovic 1982, 439). The little research that did address gender differences in political attitudes and behavior found that women participated less than men and were slightly more Republican than men (see, for example, Campbell et al. 1960). Once it became clear that women were significantly different from men in turnout, partisanship, and vote choice, political scientists began to examine the role of gender in political behavior more carefully.

Before turning to our analysis of the 1992 presidential election and the role women played in sending Bill Clinton to the White House, we first examine recent trends in each of the three key components of the gender gap: turnout, partisanship, and vote choice.

Turnout

In one of the earliest comprehensive studies of American voters, Campbell et al. (1960) estimated that the voter participation rate of women was consistently 10 percent below that of men. Campbell and his colleagues assumed that gender differences in political participation were due in large part to differences in sex roles. Although many students of the gender gap cite the major findings and assumptions of Campbell et al., they largely ignore other relevant results from this landmark study.

Campbell et al. found that there was a great deal of variation in participation rates among social groupings and suggested that changing role definitions might lead to increased participation among women. Among other things, they found that gender differences in voter turnout were greater in the South and in non-metropolitan areas than in other sections of the country. They also found that older women and women with young children were less likely to vote than their male counterparts. Perhaps their most interesting finding was that while gender differences were large among those with lower levels of education, there was little difference in turnout between college-educated women and college- educated men. Moreover, among younger people who were single or married without children, women with a college education were actually more likely to vote than their male counterparts. Campbell et al. presciently predicted that "sex differentials" in voter turnout might diminish as women became more highly educated and as "new sex role definitions" became more widely diffused in rural areas and among those with lower levels of education.

Studies of gender differences in political participation in the 1970s found that the participation rates of women had indeed begun to change as the role of women began to change. Andersen (1975) found that gender differences in political participation had narrowed in the period from 1952 to 1972 and that this change was due to the growth in the number of women working outside the home. Andersen found that these women participated at rates equal to those of men. Wolfinger and Rosenstone (1980) also found a narrowing of the gender gap in voter turnout rates in the 1970s. They found that by 1972, men were only 2 percent more likely to vote than women. Moreover, they found that women and men under the age of 40 voted at virtually the same rate, but that among those over 40, men enjoyed an advantage in participation over women that increased with age. However, Wolfinger and Rosenstone also found that nearly all of the differences in turnout between older women and men could be accounted for by differences in other demographic variables such as education, income, and marital status.

Figure 13.1 shows the percentages of women and men who reported voting in presidential elections from 1964 through 1992, according to Census Bureau surveys. These data indicate that turnout rates for both women and men have generally declined since the 1960s. However, turnout rates for women have not declined as sharply as those for men.

FIGURE 13.1 Gender Differences in Presidential Election Turnout, 1964-1992

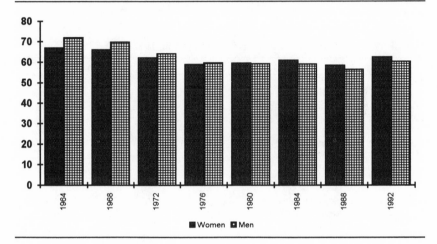

Source: U.S Bureau of the Census

As a result, women have voted at higher rates than men since 1980. The table also indicates that while voter turnout rates increased for both women and men in 1992, the percentage increase was slightly higher for women than for men. Because women comprise a larger proportion of the population than men, the increasingly higher turnout rates for women relative to men take on even greater significance.[1] The combination of more women in the potential electorate and a higher rate of voting among women meant that in 1992, 53 percent of the electorate were women, and 47 percent were men. These figures indicate that there were 6.3 million more women than men in the electorate in 1992.

Partisanship

Table 13.1 shows the changes in partisan identification for women and men from 1952 through 1992, according to data from the American National Election Studies. As some of the early studies of voting behavior suggested, women were slightly more likely to identify as Republicans than were men in the 1950s and 1960s (see, for example, Campbell et al. 1960), and this trend continued through 1980. However, these data also show that women have consistently been more likely than men to identify as Democrats since 1960, and that the gap between women and men has generally widened. This seeming inconsistency—that women in the 1970s were both more Republican

TABLE 13.1 Gender Differences in Party Identification, 1952-1992

		Women	Men
1952	Democrats	49	48
	Independents	20	26
	Republicans	30	26
1956	Democrats	45	46
	Independents	21	28
	Republicans	34	26
1960	Democrats	51	46
	Independents	18	26
	Republicans	31	28
1964	Democrats	54	51
	Independents	21	25
	Republicans	26	24
1968	Democrats	48	43
	Independents	28	31
	Republicans	24	26
1972	Democrats	44	38
	Independents	32	39
	Republicans	24	23
1976	Democrats	43	37
	Independents	31	42
	Republicans	26	21
1980	Democrats	45	38
	Independents	32	40
	Republicans	23	22
1984	Democrats	41	33
	Independents	32	39
	Republicans	27	28
1988	Democrats	40	30
	Independents	32	41
	Republicans	28	29
1992	Democrats	40	32
	Independents	37	40
	Republicans	23	28

Source: Center for Political Studies, American National Election Studies, 1952-1992. Independents who lean toward parties are coded as Independents.

and more Democratic than men—is possible because women were less likely than men to consider themselves to be Independents.

The net partisanship gender gap became much wider during the 1980s, as women became slightly less likely than men to identify as Republicans and much more likely than men to identify as Democrats. Both women and men became more Republican (and less Democratic) in the 1980s, but men defected from the Democratic to the Republican party at higher rates than women (see Bolce 1985; Wirls 1986; Miller 1991).

These aggregate patterns mask some of the interesting differences among women, who were and are far from monolithic. There were important shifts in partisanship among certain groups of women in the 1970s and 1980s. During this period, older women, homemakers, and the large number of evangelical women who supported the Christian Right became increasingly Republican. At the same time, however, younger women, women working outside the home, and college-educated women maintained and strengthened their Democratic preferences.

Vote Choice

Table 13.2 shows the voting patterns of selected groups of women and men in the presidential elections from 1976 through 1992 as reported in CBS News and CBS/*New York Times* exit polls. The data in this table indicate that in 1976 there were no significant differences between women and men in vote choice. Beginning in 1980, however, women consistently have been more supportive of the Democratic candidate than their male counterparts across a range of demographic categories. Women voters had far more reservations about Reagan's policy priorities and personality than men, and these different reactions to Reagan were the catalyst for the formation of the gender gap that persisted through the next twelve years (Gilens 1988).

The figures in Table 13.2 indicate that the gender gap in the vote for the Democratic candidate was largest in 1980, when women were 9 percent more likely than men to favor incumbent Democrat Jimmy Carter over Republican challenger Ronald Reagan. The Democratic gender gap was only slightly smaller in 1984 and 1988. In these two elections, women were more supportive of Democratic challengers

TABLE 13.2 Gender Differences in Vote Choice, 1976-1992

	1976		1980			1984		1988		1992		
	JC	GF	JC	RR	JA	WM	RR	MD	GB	BC	GB	RP
Total Vote	50	48	41	51	7	40	59	45	53	43	38	19
Gender												
Men	50	48	36	55	7	37	62	41	57	41	38	21
Women	50	48	45	47	7	44	56	49	50	46	37	17
Race												
White Men	47	51	32	59	7	32	67	36	63	37	41	22
White Women	46	52	39	52	8	38	62	43	56	41	41	18
Black Men	80	19	82	14	3	85	12	81	15	77	15	9
Black Women	86	14	88	9	3	93	7	91	9	86	9	5
Age												
Men, 18-29	50	47	39	47	11	36	63	43	55	38	36	26
Women, 18-29	51	47	49	39	10	44	55	50	49	48	33	19
Men, 30-44	49	49	31	59	8	38	61	40	58	39	38	22
Women, 30-44	49	49	41	50	8	45	54	49	50	44	38	18
Men, 45-59	48	51	34	60	5	36	62	36	62	40	40	20
Women, 45-59	46	53	44	50	5	42	57	48	52	43	40	17
Men, 60 and over	44	55	40	56	3	37	62	46	53	49	37	14
Women, 60 and over	49	50	43	52	4	42	58	52	48	51	39	10
Education												
Men, < High School			47	51	2	47	52	50	49	49	30	21
Women, < High School			56	41	2	52	46	62	38	58	27	15
Men, High School			42	53	3	37	62	49	50	43	34	23
Women, High School			44	50	5	41	58	50	50	43	38	19
Men, Some College			31	59	8	33	65	38	60	39	37	24
Women, Some College			39	52	8	41	58	45	54	43	38	18
Men, College Grad			28	59	11	36	63	36	63	40	41	19
Women, College Grad			44	42	12	47	52	51	49	49	35	16

Sources: 1976 CBS News Exit Poll; 1980, 1984, 1988 CBS News/New York Times Exit Polls; 1992 Voter Research and Surveys Exit Poll.

Walter Mondale and Michael Dukakis by margins of 7 percent and 8 percent, respectively.

It is important to note that although women were more likely than men to support the Democratic candidate, the CBS News/*New York Times* exit polls in Table 13.2 show at least a plurality of women voting for Republican candidates throughout the 1980s. Some other exit polls in 1988 showed that Dukakis won a narrow plurality of women's votes, and the National Election Study showed women splitting their votes evenly between Bush and Dukakis (Abramson, Aldrich, and Rohde, 1991). The existence of a gender gap in the 1980s did not mean that a sizable majority of women voted for Democratic candidates, but rather that women were more likely than men to cast Democratic ballots.

Nonetheless, the gender differences in the Republican margins of victory in the 1980s are striking. In the presidential elections of the 1980s, the Republican candidate defeated the Democratic candidate among men by large margins of 19, 25, and 16 percent, respectively. Although women preferred Reagan to Mondale by a fairly large margin of 12 percent in 1984, women were only 2 percent more likely to favor Reagan over Carter in 1980 and less than 1 percent more likely to favor Bush over Dukakis in 1988. This means that any imputed electoral mandate from the 1980 and 1988 elections came almost entirely from male voters. The preferences of women working outside the home and women under 50 contributed most to the pro-Democratic edge among women during this period.

The data in Table 13.2 also show that the gender gap after 1980 was consistently higher among blacks than among whites, and also higher among men and women with college degrees, or with less than a high school education. It is interesting that the gender gap was greatest among the most and least educated Americans. This suggests that references to a single gender gap may sometimes be misleading, for there are several gender gaps with different sources among various social groups (e.g., Tolleson Rinehart and Hansen 1993).

Although the changes in turnout, partisanship, and vote choices examined thus far did not affect the ultimate results of any of the presidential elections in the 1980s, it is important to note that they did determine the outcome of a number of House and Senate races. As Elizabeth Adell Cook notes in Chapter 12 of this volume, women's votes were critical in some of the Senate elections in 1986, when the Democrats regained control of the U.S. Senate. More importantly for present purposes, these changes also contributed to Bill Clinton's margin of victory in the presidential election of 1992.

The 1992 Presidential Election

The 1992 presidential election was characterized by significant gender differences in attitudes and voting behavior. These differences were apparent in a variety of ways at different times throughout the campaign. At different points in the campaign, younger and older women had reservations about Bill Clinton. For example, during the early primaries, after allegations surfaced of Clinton's marital infidelity and his efforts to avoid the military draft during the Vietnam War, liberal and college-educated women reported they did not completely trust him. After the primaries, however, these women were among Bill—and Hillary—Clinton's strongest supporters. Women also faced a real dilemma as they looked at the Bush candidacy. Although they generally trusted George Bush as a person, they were more troubled than men early on about the economy and its impact on middle-class families. Throughout the campaign, however, women consistently had more reservations about Ross Perot and supported him in lower numbers than men.

Although there was some volatility in the attitudes of certain groups of women during the campaign, an analysis of the polls conducted by Greenberg-Lake between the end of the primaries in June and the general election in November reveals that, in general, women favored Clinton at higher rates than men throughout most of this period. In the period preceding the Democratic National Convention in mid-July, the gender gap in support for Clinton averaged around 5 percent. Following the Democratic National Convention and the temporary withdrawal from the campaign of erstwhile candidate Ross Perot, support for Clinton increased significantly among both women and men. However, levels of support for Clinton continued to be higher among women and an average gender gap of 6 points persisted until the Republican National Convention in mid-August. Following the Republican convention, support for Bush increased slightly more among women than among men which resulted in the temporary disappearance of a gender gap in late August and early September. This pattern was due in part to born-again and Southern religious women who found the values and message of the Republican convention appealing. On the other hand, Democratic women and college-educated women consolidated behind Bill Clinton and called upon Hillary Clinton to defend herself.

The gender gap reemerged following Perot's reentrance into the campaign in October and grew to an average of over 8 percentage points during and immediately after the debates. During this period, levels of support for Perot among men increased steadily. Support for

Perot remained significantly lower among women, who had greater reservations about his style of politics and less concern about the deficit than men. In the final weeks of the campaign, levels of support for all three candidates remained fairly constant among women, but shifted somewhat among men. During this period, men became more supportive of Perot and Bush and less supportive of Clinton. The gender gap narrowed in the final days of the campaign, however, and on election day, only 5 percent more women than men voted for Clinton.

Closer analysis of these polls reveals more interesting patterns among certain groups of women and men. For example, throughout most of the campaign, the gender gap was particularly large between college-educated women and men, with women generally being 10 to 12 percentage points more supportive of Clinton than men. Although the magnitude of this gap fluctuated slightly over the course of the campaign, college-educated women were consistently among the demographic groups that were most supportive of Clinton.

Candidate preference was much more volatile among women and men with less than a college education. During much of the campaign, when a gap existed between these two groups, it was generally fairly small. It was not until the last month of the campaign that this gap became larger. This gap appears to be due in large part to the high levels of support for Ross Perot among non-college men, particularly in the last weeks of the campaign. Similar dynamics also produced a particularly large gender gap between women and men in the 18 to 29 age category. Men in this group were particularly supportive of Perot, while women favored Clinton.

Election Results

According to exit poll data collected by Voter Research and Surveys and reported in the *New York Times* and elsewhere, Bill Clinton won 43 percent of the vote, George Bush won 38 percent of the vote, and Ross Perot won 19 percent of the vote. There was a 5-point gender gap in the Clinton vote, with Clinton winning 46 percent of the votes cast by women and 41 percent of the votes cast by men. There was a gender gap in the vote for Perot as well, with 4 percent more men than women voting for the independent candidate. There was virtually no gender gap in the vote for Bush, with the incumbent president winning 38 percent of men and 37 percent of women. Viewed in terms of the two-party vote, however, the gender differences in candidate choice are more striking: Clinton defeated Bush by 9 percent among women but by only 3 percent among men. These figures, along with other relevant data from the exit polls, are presented in Table 13.2.

The 1992 election was characterized by a collapse of the Republican coalition that had put Ronald Reagan and George Bush into power. George Bush dropped from 53 percent of the vote in 1988 to only 38 percent in 1992. In the face of this dissolution, Bill Clinton was able to maintain support among traditional Democratic constituencies and improve on Dukakis's performance in many key areas. Although Clinton actually won a lower percentage of the vote than Dukakis in 1988, his 43 percent of the vote was enough for a winning plurality given the collapse of the Reagan-Bush coalition and the relatively successful independent candidacy of Ross Perot.

Although a wide range of variables contributed to Clinton's margin of victory, his success among certain groups of women may have been a decisive factor in winning the 1992 presidential election. Clinton ran particularly well among both college- educated women and women with less than a high school education, among women from the youngest and oldest age groups, and among working women, African-American women, and women with Democratic or Independent party identification.

As the data in Table 13.2 indicate, the differences between women and men with a college education and between women and men with less than a high school education were particularly large. In both cases, the gender gap was 9 percent. Perhaps even more notable is the fact that Clinton's margin of victory over Bush among women with less than a high school education was 21 points. These women came into the election least impressed by and interested in Bush's foreign policy victories and most worried about the U.S. economy. These women felt themselves to be marginal elements of the nation's economy, and they were greatly concerned with their children's future and their own families' economic futures. They wanted a president who represented change and someone who would get the economy moving again.

Among women with a college education, the margin was 14 points. Although this margin was smaller than that among voters with less than a high school degree, the gap is more significant because these women made up one-fifth of the electorate and are especially likely to be ticket-splitting voters. As noted earlier, Clinton ran particularly well among college-educated women throughout the general election campaign. These voters liked Clinton's economic plan, pro-choice stance, and general values.

Clinton also ran very well among women from both the youngest and the oldest age cohorts. Women aged 18 to 29 were 10 percent more likely to vote for Clinton than their male counterparts. Although a majority of women aged 60 and over voted for Clinton, the gender gap was not large because men in this age cohort also favored Clinton by a significant margin. Interestingly, women in the 30 to 44 and 45 to 59 age categories were only 3 to 5 percent more likely to favor Clinton than their male counterparts. Clinton and Bush ran even among men in each of these age categories.

Another group among whom Clinton ran well was working women, who favored Clinton over Bush by a 10-point margin. The support of working women was particularly important to the Clinton campaign since these women comprised almost a third of the electorate. One of the few groups of women among whom Clinton did not fare well was homemakers. According to the exit polls, 45 percent of homemakers supported Bush, while only 36 percent supported Clinton. Although Clinton lost this group, the 9-point Republican edge was much smaller than the margin in favor of the Republican candidate in either 1984 or 1988, when homemakers favored Reagan over Mondale and Bush over Dukakis by 24 percent and 17 percent, respectively (see Table 13.2).

Although Clinton did relatively well among most groups of women, it is important to note than he did not win a plurality of white women. White women split their votes evenly between Clinton and Bush, giving each of the candidates 41 percent of their vote. Nonetheless, white women gave a higher percentage of their vote to Clinton than did white men: Clinton lost the votes of white men by 4 percent. Moreover, because white women made up a larger proportion of the electorate than did white men, they accounted for a substantial share of the Clinton vote. According to the exit polls, women accounted for 55 percent of all votes for Clinton. Finally, it should be noted that although the gender gap among African-American voters was larger than the gap among white voters, overwhelming majorities of black women and black men favored Clinton.

Although the national gender gap was relatively small, it was much more substantial within certain states. In the 1992 elections, women backed Clinton by double-digit margins in twenty states;[2] men backed Clinton by such large margins in only six states.[3] Moreover, women provided the winning margin for Clinton in six states. In three of these states—Nevada, New Hampshire, and Tennessee—Clinton and Bush ran even among men, but Clinton won among women. In three other states—Georgia, Iowa, and Oregon— Clinton lost among men but won among women voters. In Georgia, Clinton lost to Bush by 6 points among men, but won among women by 5 points. Because women comprise a larger proportion of the electorate, Clinton was able to narrowly win the state. In Iowa and Oregon, Clinton lost to Bush among men by 10 points and 3 points, respectively, but ran ahead among women by large margins of 16 points in Iowa and an astounding 24 points in Oregon. These 6 states accounted for 46 electoral votes.

The data reported thus far reveal interesting differences in the voting patterns of women and men in the 1992 presidential election. Data from a post-election survey of voters conducted by Greenberg-Lake from November 4 to 8, 1992 suggest that there were also differences in the enthusiasm with which women and men voted for Clinton. In response to a question on whether the respondent cast his or her vote "for Clinton" or "against Bush," women were more likely than men to report a positive vote for Clinton while men were more likely than women to report a negative vote against Bush. Positive voting for Clinton was particularly strong among working women, four-fifths of whom reported voting "for Clinton" rather than "against Bush."

Data from the Voter Research and Surveys exit polls suggest that women voters were also motivated by somewhat different issues and other research shows that women often view the same issues through different experiences.. Voters were asked what one or two issues most influenced their votes, and what one or two candidate qualities were important in helping them decide which candidate to support. Although men and women who voted for Clinton shared a common set of concerns, women were relatively more interested issues such as education, health care, and abortion, and male Clinton voters were relatively more interested in the budget deficit and the general state of the economy. During the campaign, Clinton emphasized both additional spending programs to deal with the "social deficit," and cuts in spending on other programs, along with increased taxes on the wealthy to help deal with the fiscal deficit. Women were more concerned with the former, men with the latter.

Women who voted for Clinton were more than twice as likely as men to indicate that the abortion issue was most central to their vote. Indeed, women who voted for either Clinton or Perot were more likely than their male counterparts to mention abortion as important to their vote choice, suggesting that the abortion issue was more salient to pro-choice women than to pro-choice men.

Yet abortion was even more salient for women who voted for Bush, and female Bush supporters were also more likely than men who cast Republican ballots to focus on "family values." These morally conservative women who voted for Bush were mostly older, less educated women who attended church regularly and who identified themselves as born-again Christians. In contrast, men who voted for Bush were relatively more concerned with foreign policy and the budget deficit. Men who voted for Bush were far more concerned than women with Clinton's draft record and Bush's achievements in the Persian Gulf War.

Women and men who supported each candidate focused on a common set of candidate characteristics that influenced their vote, but again there were differences in emphasis. Women voters showed more interest in the candidate's character than did men. Women who voted for Clinton were more likely to indicate that they supported him because he represented change and because he cared, while men were somewhat more likely to stress his experience as governor. Women who voted for Bush were far more likely than men to say that they valued his experience, while men were more likely to indicate that Bush had the best plan for the economy. Interestingly, very few women who voted for Bush indicated that they supported him because he cared, but men were much more likely to perceive Bush as concerned about average Americans.

Data from a series of polls by Greenberg-Lake suggest that the 1992 election reflected a broad set of changes in the roles of women. the sharp increase in the numbers of women working outside the home over the past two decades has had a major impact on how women feel about their lives and the changes they want for themselves and their daughters. It is the increase in women working outside the home more than anything else that has led to women's advantage in political participation. It has also led many women to focus on different political issues than in past elections.

Women who work outside the home were most concerned with two issues in 1992: how to combine work and family, and how to make enough money to help their families make ends meet. Women who were more economically secure—higher income, better educated, middle and upper class—tended to be most concerned with combining work and family, and with having enough time for their families. Women who were less economically secure were more worried about the immediate concern of having enough money to pay bills.

Women in 1992 had an agenda, and to a surprising extent they agreed—whatever their class or race—about what the agenda should be. By far, the three policies women most wanted were health care (86 percent wanted guaranteed health insurance for everyone, 49 percent indicated that it was a top priority), flextime (58 percent of women preferred flextime to a traditional schedule), and equal pay; all items reflecting women's basic economic concerns.

These issues directly affect the daily lives of women and their families, and they are the issues of a broad-based women's movement. Women view the economy in very personal terms, and in 1992, the economy was the most important issue to women. Although some younger, college-educated women voted the abortion issue, women were less worried on a personal level about policies such as day care and abortion rights—policies that are often the focal point of activity for the women's movement. These issues mattered less in their votes. Women were primarily concerned in 1992 about he economic well-being of their families.

Conclusion

The gender differences in voting that were evident in the 1992 election were generally similar to those that have existed in presidential elections since 1980. Of course, the obvious difference between the 1992 presidential election and the three presidential elections that preceded it is that the Democratic candidate won. Although the gender differences in 1992 were not very large, the votes of women were certainly significant in building the coalition that gave Clinton his margin of victory. As shown in the data presented above, women have not only continued to be more supportive of the Democratic candidate than men, they have also continued to turn out to vote at higher rates than men and thus to comprise a larger share of the electorate than men.

The 1992 presidential election thus confirmed a number of important trends in American politics. In addition to continuing trends in turnout, partisanship, and vote choice, the 1992 election also showed that even when women and men arrive at the same conclusions, they may have different perspectives and experiences that influence their judgment of candidates and their priorities on policies. The 1992 presidential election also suggests that at the margin, women and men continue to make different choices in politics that can affect the fortunes of candidates and the outcome of elections. For example, if women's support for Clinton had never exceeded that of men, Clinton would have won a far more narrow victory, which might have made governing more difficult. If women had fewer doubts about Perot, he might have surged earlier and more forcefully.

Although the 1992 election confirmed important gender differences, it also suggested that differences among groups of women can be greater than those between women and men. Large differences in preferences continue to appear between homemakers and women who work outside the home and between religious right women and more secular college-educated women. However, while women may have disagreed about the final results, the presidential elections of 1980 and through 1992 show that women bring a different perspective to politics than men. In 1992, women gave greater weight to style and character issues and had greater reservations about both Clinton and Perot than did men. Women also had economic issue perspectives and priorities that were different from those of men. This was reflected in their greater concern for the personal economics of their families than about macro-accounting issues like the deficit. Candidates who ignore these important differences risk generating even greater gender gaps in the future.

Notes

1. According to 1990 Census Bureau statistics, there is a 2.6 percent difference in the population levels of women and men in the United States, with women comprising approximately 51.3 percent of the population and men comprising approximately 48.7 percent of the population.

2. Arkansas, California, Colorado, Connecticut, Delaware, Hawaii, Illinois, Iowa, Maryland, Massachusetts, Michigan, Minnesota, Missouri, New Mexico, New York, Oregon, Pennsylvania, Rhode Island, Vermont, and Washington.

3. Arkansas, Illinois, Massachusetts, Rhode Island, Washington, and West Virginia.

References

Abramson, Paul R., John H. Aldrich, and David W. Rohde. 1991. *Change and Continuity in the 1988 Elections.* Washington, DC: CQ Press.

Andersen, Kristi. 1975. "Working Women and Political Participation, 1952-1972." *American Journal of Political Science* 29: 439-453.

Bolce, Louis. 1985. "The Role of Gender in Recent Presidential Elections: Reagan and the Reverse Gender Gap." *Presidential Studies Quarterly* 15: 372-386.

Campbell, Angus, Philip E. Converse, Warren E. Miller, and Donald Stokes. 1960. *The American Voter.* New York: John Wiley & Sons, Inc.

Frankovic, Kathleen A. 1982. "Sex and Politics: New Alignments, Old Issues." *PS* 15: 439-48.

Gilens, Martin. 1988. "Gender and Support for Reagan: A Comprehensive Model of Presidential Approval." *American Journal of Political Science.* 32: 19-49.

Kenski, Henry C. 1988. "The Gender Factor in a Changing Electorate." In Carol M. Mueller, ed. *The Politics of the Gender Gap: The Social Construction of Political Influence.* Newbury Park, CA: Sage.

Miller, Arthur. 1988. "Gender and the Vote: 1984." In Carol M. Mueller, ed. *The Politics of the Gender Gap: The Social Construction of Political Influence.* Newbury Park, CA: Sage.

Miller, Warren E. 1991. "Party Identification, Realignment, and Party Voting: Back to the Basics." *American Political Science Review* 85: 557-568.

Mueller, Carol M. 1988. "The Empowerment of Women: Polling and the Women's Voting Bloc." In Carol M. Mueller, ed. *The Politics of the Gender Gap: The Social Construction of Political Influence.* Newbury Park, CA: Sage.

New York Times. 1992. November, p. B9.

Tolleson Rinehart, Sue, and Kenneth N. Hansen. 1993. "Gendered Parties, Partisan Gender Role: The Four Groups who Cause the Gender Gap, 1980-1988." Presented at the annual meeting of the Midwest Political Science Association, Chicago.

Wirls, Daniel. 1986. "Reinterpreting the Gender Gap." *Public Opinion Quarterly* 50: 316-30.

Wolfinger, Raymond E. and Steven J. Rosenstone. 1980. *Who Votes?* New Haven: Yale University Press.

14

Increasing the Number
of Women in Office:
Does It Matter?

Susan Gluck Mezey

During the Senate debate in early 1993 over the Family and Medical Leave bill, Washington Senator Patty Murray told her Senate colleagues that she was forced to quit her job as an executive secretary when she became pregnant because there were no options for maternity leave. California Senator Dianne Feinstein echoed Senator Murray's words by relaying her experiences of the difficult choices she faced being pregnant and working for the state government.[1] These were words that senators were not accustomed to hearing from one of their own. Senate debate will often include letters from constituents and newspaper accounts of hardships suffered by people "out there." But for the "Men's Club" to hear personal accounts about the problems of women who try to combine work and family is rare. "They just don't get it."

In October 1991, the Senate Judiciary Committee held hearings to confirm the nomination of District of Columbia Circuit Court Judge Clarence Thomas to fill the seat vacated by retiring Justice Thurgood Marshall on the Supreme Court. During those hearings, the all-male committee was forced to investigate accusations of sexual harassment against Judge Thomas by University of Oklahoma Law Professor Anita Hill.

In a highly publicized demonstration of support for Hill, seven female House members marched up the stairs of the Capitol and knocked on the door where their Democratic colleagues had their regular Tuesday caucus. Their purpose was, as one of them put it, to give their colleagues "the woman's point of view."[2]

The hearings revealed that even senators who claimed to be sympathetic to Anita Hill demonstrated insensitivity to the issue of sexual harassment and its effect on its victims. Although Thomas was ultimately confirmed, the image of those fourteen men grilling Anita Hill was fated to haunt a number of male candidates in the 1992 election, especially perhaps the senior senator from Illinois, Alan Dixon. The cry throughout the nation following the Thomas hearings and into 1992 was that women should be elected because they "get it" and men don't.

Stories like Patty Murray's and Anita Hill's are testimony to the fact that women may serve a special role in public office: research evidence over the last ten years supports the belief that many women politicians are different because they see things differently, because they understand the needs of women in society in a way that men cannot, and because many, if not most of them, will try to make the nation a better place for women and their families.

The 1992 Elections

What do the states of Illinois, California, Washington, Maryland, and Kansas have in common? The answer is, of course, that these states are now represented by women senators. After the 1992 election, the total number of women in the U.S. Senate rose to six, up from only two. Although half of the major Senate committees still have no female members, in the 103rd Congress, women sit on the Appropriations Committee; the Banking, Housing, and Urban Affairs Committee; the Environment and Public Works Committee; the Judiciary Committee; the Foreign Relations Committee; the Labor and Human Resources Committee; and the Ethics Committee.[3] Fearful of the reputation of certain panels for insensitivity to women's concerns, Senate leaders especially sought women to fill seats on the Judiciary and Ethics Committees.[4]

The 1992 elections also resulted in forty-seven women sitting in the U.S. House of Representatives, almost doubling the twenty-nine congresswomen in the 102nd Congress. Today, women representatives sit on such diverse committees as Energy and Commerce, Judiciary, and Merchant Marine and Fisheries, as well as the Appropriations, Rules, and Ways and Means Committees.[5]

With the election of Bill Clinton as President, more women than ever before were appointed to high cabinet and executive branch positions: the Departments of Energy, Health and Human Services, and Justice are headed by women, and women hold posts as U.N. ambassador, head of the Environmental Protection Agency, and chair of the Council of Economic Advisors.

Was 1992 a special year? The 1992 elections were especially notable for the marked increase of women elected at the federal level. The number of women elected to state and local office increased as well, but the results there were less dramatic as women had been making steady strides in filling state, county, and municipal offices over the years (Hartman 1989; Reingold 1992).

Despite the achievements of women candidates at the federal level and the continual increase in the number of women officeholders at local and state levels, women nevertheless remain underrepresented in American political office. With women comprising more than half the population, with equitable representation, they would occupy at least 50 percent of the public offices in the nation.

Why so few women in public office? Studies of local political activists and state and local officeholders have shown that factors associated with sex roles, including primary obligations for childcare, may be largely responsible for the limited participation of women in public office (Lee 1976). Similarly, women's role in the household has made it more difficult for them to seek political office, and, to a great extent, they were unable to do so unless their husbands acquiesced in their decisions; husbands were less constrained by their wives' lack of support (Mezey 1978a).

While conditions at home may account for women being unable to make the decision to seek public office, research (Ambrosius and Welch 1984; Darcy and Schramm 1977; Darcy, Welch, and Clark 1987) has shown that once women decide to enter the political arena, neither voter bias against women candidates nor structural bias against women by party organizations explain the underrepresentation of women in office. These studies point to the power of incumbency and the relative paucity of women in the candidate pool as the primary explanations for the disproportionately low number of women in office.

Thus, the numbers of women in office does not appear to be a reflection of purposeful discrimination against women, but rather a function of the normal business of politics. For a number of reasons, 1992 appeared to deviate from the normal business of politics. But beyond feeling pride and joining in celebrating the victories of the individuals who succeeded in gaining political office, we must ask ourselves "Why does it matter if women hold public office?" The answer is that it might matter if electing women officeholders has public policy consequences.

Representation of Women

Is "the increasing presence of women in public office... changing legislative agendas", as Mandel and Dodson (1992, 162) assert? The excitement over the growing numbers of women in public policymaking positions is based on assumptions about the effect of their presence on the representation of women's interests. A key assumption is that women who enter public life will have different goals and priorities; will behave differently from men; will demonstrate more concern about issues important to women; and will be more amenable to demands from women and women's groups. In other words, there is a widely-held belief that electing or appointing women to office will produce public policy beneficial to women.

As Sapiro (1981, 703) points out, "in order to discuss representation of women, we must consider whether women as a group have unique politically relevant characteristics, whether they have special interests to which a representative could or should respond." Thus, a prior question to the one asking whether women in office make a difference is to ask "make a difference in what"? Most studies of women officeholders begin with the assumption that women in society have common interests, that is, that there are identifiable women's public policy issues; we will adopt that assumption here.

Women's issues can be designated "as those issues where policy consequences are likely to have a more immediate and direct impact on significantly larger numbers of women than of men" (Carroll 1985, 15). Thus, we assume that in representing women, female officeholders will support issues of concern to women, that is, they will endorse the policy positions of the major feminist organizations such as the National Organization for Women (NOW) and the National Women's Political Caucus (NWPC), reflecting as well the goals adopted as far back as the 1977 Women's Conference in Houston (Mandel and Dodson 1992, 156).

Although there might be some dispute over what constitutes feminist issues, most would agree that feminism stands for a belief in expanding women's roles and opportunities (Mezey 1992). Specifically, such issues would include advocacy of federally funded childcare, concern about rape and domestic violence, a desire to improve women's employment opportunities through pay equity and affirmative action policies and enforcement of sex discrimination and sexual harassment laws, and support for reproductive rights. Moreover, because of their identification with domestic and nurturing activities, women have been linked to issues concerning family, education, and health and welfare policy as well (Sapiro 1981). The extent to which women still perceive *these* issues as *their* main concerns is perhaps subject to debate.

Several answers have been proposed for the "why does it matter" question. Darcy, Welch, and Clark (1987, 11-14) argue that it matters if women play a role in political decisionmaking for several reasons. First, they say, women in public office would further a feminist agenda. Second, women lend a special expertise to legislating in certain public policy areas such as education or social services. Third, the quality of public officials would improve because of the larger pool of qualified individuals from which to select. Last, representative bodies would more accurately mirror the society from which they come, thus providing legitimacy for the system. Mandel (1988, 83) adds that women in politics would serve as role models, encouraging other women "to follow their example."

Mandel and Dodson (1992) further suggest that the underrepresentation of women in office indicts U.S. society by revealing the denial of equal opportunity to a significant segment of society, by demonstrating the waste of talent, and by depriving policymaking institutions of the perspectives and priorities that women, with their unique experiences, can bring and that men, because of their different experiences, are unable or unwilling to bring.

These reasons essentially fall into two broad categories: first, women's participation in public life benefits society; second, women's participation in public life benefits women. Although both are important, we are primarily concerned with the latter category. Before accepting the validity of the assertion that women are better at representing women's interests, we must ask whether simply counting the number of women in office is a sufficient measure of the degree to which women's public policy goals will be realized. Would proportional representation, that is, women occupying 50 percent of all public offices, accomplish the desired results in public policy outputs (Mezey 1978b; Mezey 1978c)?

To judge the degree to which women in office seek to translate women's issues into public policy, a more precise definition of representation is required. Women in office perform two essential representative tasks: "descriptive" and "substantive" representation (Pitkin 1967). The former, also known as "standing for", is accomplished simply by occupying seats of power, without necessarily advocating women's policy positions.[6] The latter type of representation, "acting for", occurs when women in office accomplish goals advocated by women's groups. The two types of representation are not mutually exclusive. Indeed, they are quite the contrary. The assumption is generally made that women in office will not simply "stand for" women but that they will "act for" them as well.

An example of the difference between these two concepts of representation is demonstrated by Republican Senator Nancy Kassebaum's vote against the 1993 Family and Medical Leave bill, a measure that women's groups had championed for a long time. The bill allowed family members to take an unpaid leave of up to twelve weeks following the birth or adoption of a child or an illness in the family. By her presence in office, Kassebaum "stands for" women, but as seen from a feminist perspective, in her vote on this bill, she did not "act for" women.[7]

"Descriptive" representation, which is accomplished merely by electing women to public office, offers a number of benefits: it confers greater legitimacy on the political system; it employs more of the available political talent in society; and it allows women to serve as role models. However, it does not necessarily achieve women's policy goals. While "one might speculate that being a member of a group arouses one to act for that group," this is not always the case, and we must pursue the question further to determine whether women in office "act for women or simply stand for women" (Mezey 1978c, 373).

Women's Organizations and Representation

The debate over representation is reflected in the activities of organizations such as the Woman's Campaign Fund (WCF), the National Women's Political Caucus, and the National Woman's Education Fund, formed on behalf of women candidates during the 1970s, whose work has been directed toward increasing the number of women in office (Carroll 1985). More recently, EMILY's (Early Money Is Like Yeast) List has been active in raising money for women candidates and deserves credit for swelling the numbers of women in public office.

These organizations do not always agree on the primacy of the goal of electing or appointing more women to office. While they generally adhere to the view that the number of women in public life should be increased, disagreement arises over whether they should support only women who will "act for" women or whether their support should be extended to women who will simply "stand for" women. Acting on the belief that "whatever symbolic value women politicians might have would be outweighed... by [their] failure to support particular policies" (Leader 1977, 267), some groups have endorsed feminist men candidates rather than lend their support to those they perceive as nonfeminist women (Carroll 1985; Hartman 1989; Morris 1992).

Leader (1977) reports that the WCF used its funds only to aid in the election of "qualified progressive" women candidates, as defined at that time by support for the Equal Rights Amendment (ERA) and Title IX of the 1972 Education Amendments. Because the Fund was satisfied with the policy positions of Senator Charles Mathias of Maryland, it did not endorse Barbara Mikulski (now Senator) for the Senate in 1974.[8] When Nancy Kassebaum ran for the U.S. Senate in 1978 and opposed the extension for ratification of the ERA, the NWPC and NOW joined in supporting her male opponent.

More recently, in 1982, the New Jersey NOW backed Senate candidate Frank Lautenberg over Millicent Fenwick, a Republican member of the House of Representatives. Although she had strong feminist credentials, Fenwick had voted for Reagan economic policies and her election would have increased Republican domination of the Senate. NOW reasoned that Lautenberg merited their support because he not only supported women's rights but also opposed the Reagan economic plan. Similarly, in the same year, some women's organizations endorsed a Democratic male over Massachusetts Congresswoman Margaret Heckler, a Republican who opposed abortion and voted for Reagan economic policies as well. Also in 1982, Representative Nancy Johnson of Connecticut, a feminist Republican, failed to receive NOW's endorsement which went to feminist Democrat William Curry for the same reasons.

The actions of these groups show that the debate over representation is not simply one over abstract doctrine but a debate that has practical consequences in the political arena.

Do Women Make a Difference?

Examining the extent to which women in office make a difference in support for women's public policy issues has occupied scholars for almost two decades. Most of the research has been designed to test the assumption that, compared to men, women in office will be more inclined to initiate and support women's policy goals. The results of this research have been mixed: most studies show that sex differences in political behavior exist and consequently, the presence of women in office has public policy implications. Studies also show that support for feminist concerns does not present a neat dichotomy along male and female lines.

Some studies have focused on sex differences in support for women's issues; others have examined sex differences in support for liberal ideology as a surrogate of support for feminist issues.[9] These studies have been based on attitudinal surveys or statistical analyses of the voting behavior of women and men officeholders.

Carroll's (1985) analysis of women running for state and national office in 1976 found that most women candidates did not belong to feminist organizations, nor did they emphasize women's issues in their campaigns. In the privacy of their survey responses, however, they identified with women's movement positions on a variety of issues such as sex-role stereotyping, reproductive rights, equal credit opportunity, and the ERA.

Based on surveys of state legislators conducted by the Center for the American Woman and Politics (CAWP), Mandel and Dodson (1992) found that women bring different concerns to public office and, when compared to their male colleagues in the same party and same ideological category, are more likely to express feminist and liberal views. The responses to CAWP's 1988 survey of women and men lawmakers showed that women were more supportive than men on such feminist issues as the ERA, abortion rights, and more likely to identify themselves with liberal attitudes on such issues as the death penalty and construction of nuclear power plants. Conversely, they found that party rather than sex determined endorsement for government-sponsored childcare and raising taxes for social services. They concluded that views on these latter issues are "driven more by party (and party-oriented views about the appropriate role of government and government spending) than by gender, with Democrats generally more supportive of both policies than their Republican colleagues" (Mandel and Dodson 1992, 157).

Examining the attitudes of men and women local politicians, Mezey (1978b) sought to determine whether sex plays a role in support for such feminist policy issues as abortion, affirmative action in federal and state appointments, and rape crisis centers. Slight differences between the sexes were found but when the public officials were asked to rank these issues in priority with competing issues such as roads and transportation, pollution, and public recreation, the differences between the sexes dissipated.[10] Furthermore, the analysis revealed that party and political ideology (that is, liberalism) were better predictors of support for feminist policy issues than sex.[11]

Looking at the actual votes of men and women state legislators on approval of the ERA, Leader (1977) found that, on the whole, sex played a role in determining levels of support for the proposed amendment but that party was also an important variable.

Seeking to determine whether women members of Congress were more liberal and more feminist than men members, Leader examined voting behavior in the 92nd to 94th Congresses, using Americans for Democratic Action (ADA) scores and feminist ratings established by the *Woman Activist* and the Women's Lobby. She found that congresswomen were more liberal and feminist than the House as a whole but that party was an important factor in voting on these issues. She concluded that "women are, on the whole, more supportive of feminist goals and policies than men. But party, rather than sex, is a stronger predictor of voting behavior" (Leader 1977, 282).

Similarly, in another study of voting behavior, Welch (1985) used *Congressional Quarterly's* conservative coalition support scores to examine liberalism in congressional voting over an eight-year period — from 1972 to 1980. She, too, found sex differences, especially among Southern Democrats and Republicans. She attributed much of the sex difference to the characteristics of the constituencies women were likely to represent, that is, more urban, more Northern, and more culturally diverse. She also found that differences between male and female liberalism diminished over time, with women becoming less liberal. However, after noting these qualifications, she nevertheless concluded that "it appears that while the gender gap in congressional voting is not as large as it was, women members still vote in a slightly more liberal direction than do men" (Welch 1985, 132).

How Women Make a Difference

Taken together, these studies indicate that the attitudes and voting behavior of politicians are partially attributable to sex, but that sex *alone* does not account for differences in support for feminist issues. They suggest that although sex plays a role in determining the direction of legislative behavior in support for women's issues, other factors, that is, ideology and party, are determinative as well.

Perhaps there are other indicators of support for women's issues that are not tapped by these studies of voting behavior. After all, a yes or no vote does not manifest the degree to which the legislator worked for the bill — to the exclusion of others. As Leader (1977, 284) pointed out, voting records do not indicate the strength of support for issues. Women play an important role in legislative office, she believed, because "the initiators [of women's issues] are invariably women." Eleanor Smeal (1984, 19-20), former President of the National Organization for Women, similarly argued that:

> Women support these [feminist issues] with more intensity and have a better understanding of what is at stake.... Furthermore, women are more likely to act on the basis of this commitment than are men.[12]

Thus, a complete picture of the importance of sex in legislative behavior requires investigation of whether sex plays a role in establishing priorities and levels of support for issues of concern to women.

Early studies (e.g., Gehlen 1977; Johnson and Carroll 1978; Kirkpatrick 1974; Mezey 1978b; Mezey 1978c; Mueller 1982) reported that women were not anxious to identify themselves as women's candidates and did not confer a higher priority on women's issues than men once in office. Perhaps their reluctance stemmed from their apprehension that they would be penalized by the voters and their male colleagues for showing greater interest in women's issues. Their unwillingness to describe themselves as feminists likely stemmed from their fear of being labeled radical and perceived as only responsive to the needs of the women in the constituency.

More recent studies of state and local officeholders have suggested that today's political women are less concerned with the possibility of being stigmatized by an interest in, and identification with, women's interests. These studies show that, compared to men, women express more concern for women's issues and accord a higher priority to them; they are also more likely than men to translate their concern into legislative action.[13]

Although relatively little research has concentrated on women at the local level, Boles' (1991) analysis of men and women holding county and city offices in the Milwaukee County area is an exception. Boles found that the women in office were more "active" on a range of women's issues such as day care, sexual assault, and sexual violence and, moreover, accorded a higher priority to these issues than men did.

Because of the continuing increase of women in state legislatures and because members of state legislatures are more accessible than members of the national legislature, the bulk of the research on sex differences in office have been conducted at the state level (Thomas 1991).

The 1988 national CAWP survey of state legislators (Mandel and Dodson 1992), discussed above, also examined the degree to which women differed from men in working on women's rights bills and the importance they accorded to bills reflecting women's distinctive concerns. Their definition of women's rights legislation included bills related to rape, teen pregnancy, women's health concerns, pay equity, maternity leave, and spousal retirement benefits. They found that a higher percentage of women than men spent time promoting passage of a woman's rights bill. In an open-ended question they also asked legislators to identify the bill to which they gave their highest priority. In addition to women's rights policy, they broadly characterized bills in such policy areas as health care, welfare, and education as "women's distinctive concerns." They found that a greater percentage of women than men "gave top priority" to a matter related to women's distinctive concerns.[14]

After surveying their findings, Mandel and Dodson (1992, 176) concluded that, even with the relatively small proportion of women officeholders, they "can go so far as to say that having more women in public office is bringing new perspectives to issues, new issues onto the docket, and different priorities, values, or emphases—perhaps even different styles of leadership—into the public policy arena."

The results of surveys of more localized samples agree that women have begun to make a difference, that their presence has given a new meaning to representation of women's interests. Focusing on successive Arizona state legislatures from 1969 to 1986, Saint-Germain (1989) found that women legislators showed a greater propensity than men to introduce feminist legislation (bills explicitly seeking greater equality for women or seeking to improve the status of women) as well as legislation dealing with women's traditional interests, such as children, education, and family health. Moreover, she reported that as the number of women in the state legislature increased, the degree to which women gave attention to women's issues also increased. Based on her research, she concluded that "women do make a difference in state legislatures" (Saint-Germain 1989, 965).

In a twelve-state survey of state legislators ranging from Mississippi to Vermont, Thomas and Welch (1991) questioned whether sex made a difference in determining the priorities of state legislators. Their main concern was whether women legislators were more attentive to women's issues, which they defined as issues related to women, family, and children.[15] Although their findings did not reflect large sex differences, they showed that women introduced more bills relating to children and welfare and were more likely than men to cite such bills as accomplishments in which they took pride (Thomas and

Welch 1991). Later research also focused on the degree to which women in office believed that they had a special responsibility as women to represent the interests of their women constituents. In her study of the survey responses of state legislators in California and Arizona, Reingold (1992, 531) found that on the whole women legislators were more predisposed to represent women's concerns, were more likely to perceive themselves as receiving support from women constituents and to consider such support important, and last, felt themselves "uniquely qualified to handle the concerns of their women constituents."

Studies also showed that the proportion of women in office affected the degree to which women took a lead on women's issues in their state houses. In her longitudinal study of the Arizona legislature, Saint-Germain (1989) found that women's activities on behalf of women increased as the ratio of women to men rose (see also Flammang 1985). Similarly, Thomas' (1991) twelve-state study found that the number of women in office is associated with the degree to which women introduce and support legislation related to women, family, and children. In sum, these studies show that women representatives are more willing to "act for" women when they are in the presence of other women. The existence of a formal legislative caucus dedicated to women's concerns also proved to be an impetus to passage of legislation related to women's public policy issues.

This research shows that "the times they are a-changing." Many women politicians now apparently believe in a representation in which they "act for" their women constituents as evidenced by the fact that women in office are more willing to adopt policy positions that are overtly and expressly related to women's concerns. The evidence also shows that women are no longer afraid to pursue different agendas from men and to be noted for their interest in "women's issues."

The activities of a women's caucus in the U.S. Congress also provides evidence of women's greater willingness to be associated with women's issues. This body was established by congressional women in 1977, with fifteen of the eighteen women in the House becoming members (Hartman 1989). In 1981, the name of the organization was changed to the Congressional Caucus for Women's Issues and men were allowed as members, although males were not permitted to serve on the executive committee. Over the years, the bipartisan caucus has promoted such issues as childcare, family and medical leave, domestic violence, and maternal and child health (Mandel and Dodson 1992). With the marked increase in the number of women in Congress as a result of the 1992 elections, we can expect an even more active caucus to emerge in the future (Saint-Germain 1989; Thomas 1991).

Conclusion

Our review of the importance of sex differences in politics brings us back to the original question of whether it matters if women hold public office. The answer is a qualified yes, that women make a difference in a number of ways. Sex, along with party affiliation and political ideology, plays an important role in determining legislative support for women's issues. More significantly, as recent research shows, women officeholders "act for" women in society because women's issues matter more to them. Women representatives are more likely to accord bills related to women's issues a higher priority and to expend political capital in securing their passage. Moreover, they are more likely to do so when their numbers are greater. While still underrepresented in both state and federal office, for the first time it appears possible that women officeholders will jointly be able to make their voices heard well enough to make a difference.

Although many men champion women's issues as well, the research shows that women are better champions. Support for childcare, parental leave, welfare reform, and reproductive rights at the federal level, funding for battered women's shelters, and increased sensitivity for victims of rape and child abuse are all issues to which women accord higher priority and to which they commit themselves with greater intensity than men.

These problems urgently require solutions, and by placing these issues on the public policy agenda and working to find solutions for them, women in public life may benefit not only the nation's women but the nation as a whole. Because of the presence of more women in office, the 1992 elections may be a milestone in focusing national attention on such issues.

Notes

1. *New York Times*, February 11, 1993.

2. *New York Times*, October 9, 1993.

3. *Congressional Quarterly Weekly Report*, January 16, 1993, Supplement to No. 3, 150-151.

4. At the start of the 103rd Congress, the Senate Ethics Committee indicated it will conduct hearings on the accusations of sexual misconduct

against Senator Robert Packwood of Oregon. It would be expected that the presence of women on the committee will affect the nature of the questioning, if not the actual outcome.

5. *Congressional Quarterly Weekly Report*, January 16, 1993, Supplement to No. 3, 152-159.

6. Reingold (1992, 509-510) describes this as "passive" representation.

7. While Senator Kassebaum would dispute the assertion that women officeholders must adopt feminist positions in order to "act for" women in society, most feminists (including myself) would argue that women in office "act for" women to the extent that they support feminist positions on questions such as family leave, child care, or reproductive rights.

8. This was, perhaps, an unfortunate decision since Senator Mikulski is an articulate voice for feminist issues in the Senate today.

9. Conservatism is generally associated with opposition to feminism for at least two reasons: feminism seeks to alter traditional lifestyle arrangements within the family and advocates an active role for governmental funding and regulation in dealing with the problems feminists wish to solve (Hartman 1989).

10. An earlier study comparing women and men politicians in Hawaii (Mezey 1978c) also found a positive but weak relationship between sex and feminist policy positions. But when men and women were asked to rank the status of women along with issues such as consumer protection, education, and open government, there was almost perfect agreement (r= .95) that the status of women was the least important concern. Similarly, they were asked to rank their concern for specific feminist issues such as childcare, equal pay, and reform of rape laws with nonfeminist issues such as unemployment, the environment, and prison reform. Except for prison reform, the three women's issues were ranked at the bottom by both men and women; agreement between the sexes was again nearly perfect (r= .95).

11. Sex played a greater role in determining attitudes toward the existence of sex discrimination against women in office and appreciation of the difficulties of women with family responsibilities in deciding whether to commit themselves to a political career.

12. Smeal's reference to the word "act" suggests Pitkin's notion of "acting for."

13. That these studies found more support among women legislators for women's issues than earlier studies may also be attributable to the fact that, as a rule, they cast a wider net over the definition of "women's issues." Moreover, many of these later studies do not control for the effects of political party or ideology, two factors that are related to support for feminist issues.

14. The study also showed that feminism and political ideology (liberalism) played a role in determining whether legislators worked on women's issues and accorded top priority to women's distinctive concerns.

Among feminists and liberals, more women than men evidenced concern about women's issues in the legislatures.

15. These include a wide range of issues beyond those we have designated as "feminist" issues.

References

Ambrosius, Margery and Susan Welch. 1984. "Women and Politics at the Grassroots: Women Candidates for State Office in Three States, 1950-1978." *Social Science Journal* 21:29-42.

Boles, Janet. 1991. "Local Elected Women and Policymaking: Movement Delegates or Feminist Trustees?" Paper prepared for delivery at the Annual Meeting of the American Political Science Association.

Carroll, Susan. 1985. *Women as Candidates in American Politics*. Bloomington, IN: Indiana University Press.

Congressional Quarterly Weekly Report. January 16, 1993. Supplement to No. 3. 150-159.

Darcy, Robert and Sarah Slavin Schramm. 1977. "When Women Run Against Men." *Public Opinion Quarterly* 41:1-12.

Darcy, Robert, Susan Welch, and Janet Clark. 1987. *Women, Elections, and Representation*. White Plains, NY: Longman, Inc.

Flammang, Janet. 1985. "Female Officials in the Feminist Capital: The Case of Santa Clara County." *Western Political Quarterly* 38:94-118.

Gehlen, Frieda. 1977. "Women Members of Congress." In Marianne Githens and Jewell Prestage, eds. *A Portrait of Marginality*. New York: McKay.

Hartman, Susan. 1989. *From Margin to Mainstream*. Philadelphia: Temple University Press.

Johnson, Marilyn and Susan Carroll. 1978. *Profile of Women Holding Office II*. New Brunswick, NJ: Center for the American Woman and Politics.

Kirkpatrick, Jeane. 1974. *Political Woman*. New York: Basic Books.

Leader, Gilbert Shelah. 1977. "The Policy Impact of Elected Women Officials." In Joseph Cooper and Louis Maisel, eds. *The Impact of the Electoral Process*. Beverly Hills: Sage.

Lee, Marcia Manning. 1976. "Why Few Women Hold Public Office: Democracy and Sexual Roles." *Political Science Quarterly* 91:297-314.

Mandel, Ruth. 1988. "The Political Woman." In Sara E. Rix, ed. *The American Woman*. New York: W.W. Norton.

— — — and Debra Dodson. 1992. "Do Women Officeholders Make a Difference?" In Sara E. Rix, ed. *The American Woman*. New York: W.W. Norton.

Mezey, Susan Gluck. 1978a. "Does Sex Make A Difference? A Case Study of Women in Politics." *Western Political Quarterly* 31:492-501.

— — —. 1978b. "Support for Women's Rights Policy: An Analysis of Local Politicians." *American Politics Quarterly* 6:485-497.

— — —. 1978c. "Women and Representation: The Case of Hawaii." *Journal of Politics* 40:369-385.

— — —. 1992. *In Pursuit of Equality: Women, Public Policy and the Federal Courts.* New York: St. Martin's Press.

Morris, Celia. 1992. "Changing the Rules and the Roles: Five Women in Public Office." In Sara E. Rix, ed. *The American Woman.* New York: W.W. Norton.

Mueller, Carol. 1982. "Feminism and the New Women in Public Office." *Women and Politics* 2:7-21.

New York Times. October 9, 1991.

— — —. February 11, 1993.

Pitkin, Hannah. 1967. *The Concept of Representation.* Berkeley: University of California Press.

Reingold, Beth. 1992. "Concepts of Representation Among Female & Male State Legislators." *Legislative Studies Quarterrly* 17:509-537.

Sapiro, Virginia. 1981. "When Are Interests Interesting? The Problem of Political Representation of Women." *American Political Science Review* 75:701-716.

Smeal, Eleanor. 1984. *Why and How Women Will Elect the Next President.* New York: Harper.

Thomas, Sue. 1991. "The Impact of Women on State Legislative Policies." *Journal of Politics* 53:958-976.

— — — and Susan Welch. 1991. "The Impact of Gender on Activities and Priorities of State Legislators." *Western Political Quarterly* 44:445-456.

Welch, Susan. 1985. "Are Women More Liberal Than Men In the U.S. Congress?" *Legislative Studies Quarterly* 10:125-134.

About the Book and Editors

It was a long time in coming, but the elections of 1992 finally gave us "the Year of the Woman" in American national politics. Not only did more women run or consider running for office than ever before, but the number of women elected to the House of Representatives nearly doubled and to the Senate tripled. This book tells the story of those key races, revealing the underlying tales of voter and institutional reaction to the women candidates and highlighting the unprecedented levels of support garnered from individuals and PACs on their behalf.

The diverse contributors to this volume place the elections in context and draw out themes and trends beyond the salient impact of the Clinton-Gore campaign and the Hill-Thomas hearings. Perspective and balance combined with original data and interviews ensure provocative discussion of both the successes and failures of women candidates, showing how "the Year of the Woman" was at once "politics as usual" and yet "politics with a difference."

Elizabeth Adell Cook is visiting assistant professor of political science at The American University. **Sue Thomas** is assistant professor of government at Georgetown University. **Clyde Wilcox** is associate professor of government at Georgetown University.

About the Contributors

Mary E. Bendyna, R.S.M. is a Ph.D. candidate and University Fellow in the Department of Government at Georgetown University. Her areas of interest include public opinion, political behavior, and judicial politics.

Robert Biersack is Supervisory Statistician at the Federal Election Commission. He has written extensively on congressional elections and campaign finance.

Carole Chaney is a graduate student in political science at the University of California, Riverside. She is the recipient of the graduate Dean's Fellowship and her areas of interest include congressional decision-making and the impact of gender on the political process.

Elizabeth Adell Cook teaches political science at The American University. She is the author of articles on feminism, abortion politics, and co-author of *Between Two Absolutes: Public Opinion and the Politics of Abortion* (Westview Press, 1992). She is currently working on a book on feminist consciousness.

Susan B. Hansen (Ph.D. Stanford, 1972) is associate professor of political science and director of the Women's Studies Program at the University of Pittsburgh, where she has taught since 1980. She taught previously at the universities of Michigan, Illinois-Urbana, and Washington State. She is the author of *The Politics of Taxation: Revenue Without Representation* (Praeger, 1983), *The Political Economy of State Industrial Policy* (forthcoming, University of Pittsburgh Press), the chapter on public policy in Ada Finifter, ed., *The State of the Discipline* (APSA, 1983), and a chapter on state taxation in Virginia Gray et al., eds., *Politics in the American States*, 5th edition (Little, Brown, 1992).

Professor Hansen's main teaching and research interests are in American state politics, women in politics, public policy, and religion and politics. She has published numerous articles and book chapters on political participation, tax issues, economic development, and the abortion issue in the states. She and a co-author (Professor Sharon Sykora, Slippery Rock State University) have recently completed a study of women in the Pennsylvania legislature.

Paul S. Herrnson (Ph.D., University of Wisconsin-Madison, 1986) is an Associate Professor of Government and Politics at the University of Maryland at College Park. He is the author of *Party Campaigning in the 1980s* (Harvard, 1988) and *Campaigning for Congress: Candidates, Parties, and PACs* (CQ Press, forthcoming 1994). He is also co-editor (with Robert Biersack and Clyde Wilcox) of *PAC Decision Making and Strategy in the 1992 Congressional Elections* (M.E. Sharpe, forthcoming 1994) and has written numerous articles on political parties, campaign finance, and congressional elections. He has consulted for the Democratic Caucus of the U.S. House of Representatives and served as an American Political Science Association Congressional Fellow.

Ted G. Jelen is Professor of Political Science at Illinois Benedictine College in Lisle, Illinois. His main research interests are in public opinion, religion and politics, feminism, and the politics of abortion. He has contributed many articles to scholarly journals and books. He is the author of *The Political Mobilization of Religious Beliefs* (Praeger, 1991), *The Political World of the Clergy* (Praeger, 1993), and is co-author (with Elizabeth Cook and Clyde Wilcox) of *Between Two Absolutes: Public Opinion and the Politics of Abortion* (Westview Press, 1992).

Celinda C. Lake is a principle in Mellman Lazarus Lake, Inc. Lake is one of the Democratic Party's leading political strategists, serving as a tactician and senior advisor to the national party committees, dozens of Democratic incumbents and challengers at all levels of the electoral process, and democratic parties in several Eastern European countries. Lake is the author of *Public Opinion Polling: A Manual for Public Interest Groups*, published in 1986. Lake is one of the nation's foremost experts on electing women candidates and on framing issues to women voters. *American Politics* called Lake a "super-strategist or, better yet, the Godmother" and *Working Woman* says she is "arguably the most influential woman in her field."

Susan Gluck Mezey, Ph.D., J.D., is a Professor of Political Science at Loyola University Chicago. Her articles on women and politics, abortion policy, social security disability policy, gender equality in education, and inter spousal immunity in civil litigation have appeared in political science journals and law reviews, including the *Journal of Politics*, *American Politics Quarterly*, *International and Comparative Law Quarterly*, *Rutgers Law Review*, *Women and Politics*, and the *Policy Studies Journal*. Her first book, *No Longer Disabled: The Federal Courts and the Politics of Social Security Disability*, was published by Greenwood Press in 1988. Her second book, *In Pursuit of Equality: Women, Public Policy, and the Federal Courts*, was published by St. Martin's Press in 1991. She is currently working on a book about children's policy and the federal courts.

Candice J. Nelson is an Assistant Professor of Government at The American University and Director of the University's Campaign Management Institute. Prior to coming to The American University she was a Visiting Fellow at The Brookings Institution, where she wrote, with David B. Magleby, *The Money Chase*. She has also been an American Political Science Association Congressional Fellow and a Special Assistant to Senator Alan Cranston. She is the co-author of *The Myth of the Independent Voter*, as well as numerous articles on congressional elections and campaign finance. Her expertise includes the U.S. Congress, electoral behavior, interest groups, and campaign finance.

Craig A. Rimmerman, Associate Professor and Chair of the Department of Political Science at Hobart and William Smith Colleges, is the author of *Presidency by Plebiscite: The Reagan-Bush Era in Institutional Perspective* (Westview Press, 1993) as well as articles in American politics, public policy and democratic theory. Rimmerman was awarded the American Political Science Association's William Steiger Congressional Fellowship during the 1992-93 academic year. He is currently working on a book examining issues of participation, democracy, and citizenship.

Jean R. Schroedel (Ph.D. Massachusetts Institute of Technology 1990) is an assistant professor in the Center for Politics, Economics and Policy at the Claremont Graduate School. Her primary research and teaching interests are gender politics and congressional politics. Schroedel has written two books, *Alone in a Crowd: Women in the Trades Tell Their Stories* (Temple University Press, 1985) and *Congress, the President and Policy-making: A Historical Analysis* (M.E. Sharpe, Inc., forthcoming 1994) and numerous articles.

Barbara Sinclair is professor of Political Science at the University of California, Riverside. Her publications include *The Women's Movement: Political, Socio-Economic and Psychological Issues* (Harper and Row 1975, 1979, 1983), *Congressional Realignment 1925-1978* (University of Texas Press 1982), *Majority Leadership in the U.S. House* (Johns Hopkins University Press 1983), and *Transformation of the U.S. Senate* (Johns Hopkins University Press 1989).

Bruce Snyder is a doctoral candidate in Political Science at the Center for Politics and Policy at the Clarmont Graduate School and has written on Congress and on civil rights legislation. He also holds a J.D. (Loyola at Los Angeles, 1979) and is a member of the California Bar.

Sue Thomas is Assistant Professor of Government at Georgetown University. Her primary research interest is legislative behavior with an emphasis on women officeholders. In addition to several articles on this subject which have appeared in *Journal of Politics, Western Political Quarterly*, and *Women & Politics*, she has written *How Women Legislate*, which is forthcoming in January, 1994 from Oxford University Press.

Sue Tolleson Rinehart is Associate Professor of Political Science at Texas Tech University. She is author of *Gender Consciousness and Politics* (Routledge, 1992) and, with Jeanie R. Stanley, *Claytie and the Lady: Ann Richards, Gender, and Politics in Texas* (University of Texas Press, 1994), and Articles in the *American Politics Science Review, Comparative Politics, Political Behavior*, and *Women & Politics*, as well as other articles and book chapters. She edits Women/Politics, the newsletter of the American Political Science Association organized section for Women and Politics Research. Her current projects include longitudinal analyses of gender and voting behavior, and the influence of gender role ideologies on political leadership.

Clyde Wilcox is Associate Professor of Government at Georgetown University. His research interests are gender politics, religion and politics, public opinion on foreign policy, and campaign finance. He is the author of *God's Warriors: The Christian Right in 20th Century America.* He is co-author of *Between Two Absolutes: Public Opinion and the Politics of Abortion* (Westview Press, 1992), co-editor of *The Quest for National Office* and *Risky Business: PAC Decision making in the 1992 Elections.*

Leonard Williams is Associate Professor of Political Science at Manchester College, where he also chairs the Department of History and Political Science. He is the author of several essays focusing on such topics as political ideology and the philosophy of social science. He also co-edited the textbook, *Political Theory, Classic Writings, Contemporary Views.*

Index